IMAGES
of Modern America

MONTGOMERY

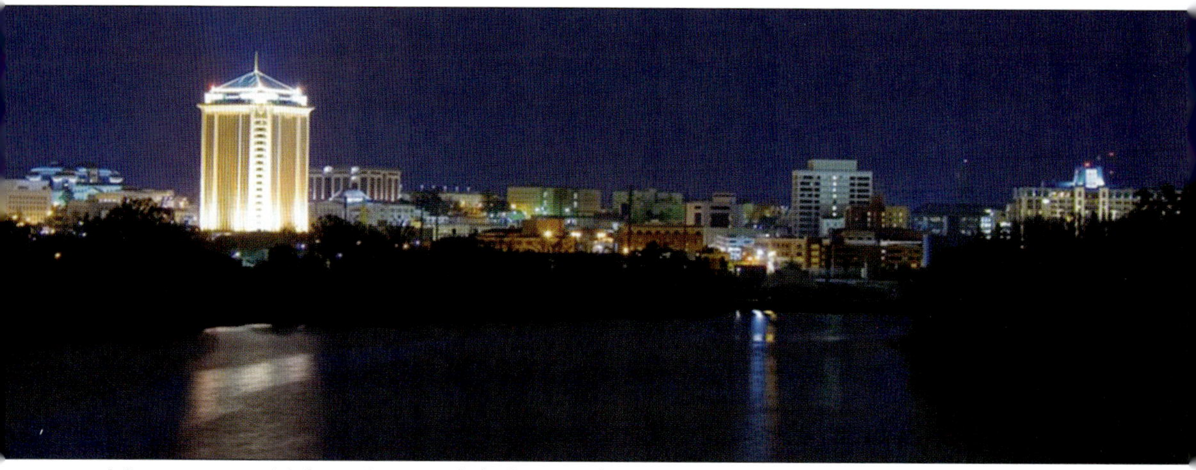

Montgomery, Alabama's capital, lights up the night as seen from across the rolling waters of the Alabama River. (Courtesy Montgomery Area Chamber of Commerce Convention & Visitor Bureau.)

ON THE FRONT COVER: Clockwise from top left: Traffic passes in front of the Alabama State Capitol on Dexter Avenue around 1960 (Courtesy Landmarks Foundation of Montgomery, see page 42); the Joy to Life Walk of Life is a yearly event to raise funds to fight breast cancer (Courtesy Dreemz Production and Joy to Life Foundation, see page 40); Hebe, cupbearer to the gods, stands atop the fountain at Court Street Square (Courtesy Landmarks Foundation of Montgomery); downtown Dexter Avenue was quiet in the late 1960s (Courtesy Landmarks Foundation of Montgomery, see page 15); Rosa Parks and Morris Dees stand at the Civil Rights Memorial (Courtesy Alabama Department of Archives and History, see page 36).

ON THE BACK COVER: From left to right: The Montgomery Symphony Orchestra presents its annual Jubilee Pops Concert on the steps of the Alabama Department of Archives and History (Courtesy *Montgomery Advertiser*, see page 34); Greta Lambert thrilled audiences as Titania in *A Midsummer Night's Dream* at the Alabama Shakespeare Festival in 1985 (Courtesy Greta Lambert and Alabama Shakespeare Festival, see page 38); marching band members from the Alabama State University lead the Turkey Day Classic Parade (Courtesy Landmarks Foundation of Montgomery).

IMAGES of Modern America

MONTGOMERY

Karren Pell and Carole King

ARCADIA PUBLISHING

ISBN 978-1-4671-1363-2

Published by Arcadia Publishing
Charleston, South Carolina

Printed in the United States of America

Library of Congress Control Number: 2015936755

For all general information, please contact Arcadia Publishing:
Telephone 843-853-2070
Fax 843-853-0044
E-mail sales@arcadiapublishing.com
For customer service and orders:
Toll-Free 1-888-313-2665

Visit us on the Internet at www.arcadiapublishing.com

Montgomery is dedicated to the Landmarks Foundation of Montgomery. Since 1967, the Landmarks Foundation has worked "to foster, encourage, and lead the historic preservation movement in Montgomery, Alabama."

Contents

ACKNOWLEDGMENTS

This book is the result of many people contributing photographs, information, and support. We appreciate the Landmarks Foundation of Montgomery (Landmarks Foundation) for making the archives available and Mary Ann Neeley for sharing her endless wealth of knowledge. Credit is due to Jeff Benton, as we continue to pull information from his important work *A Sense of Place*. Patricia Crowley, Debbie George, Randy Shoults, and Foster Dickson went above and beyond any call of duty to find the family photographs used here. We are in debt to Allison Griffin and the *Montgomery Advertiser* for use of the photographs from its archives. The Alabama Department of Archives and History also deserves credit for its assistance. We much appreciate Chip DeShields of Sherlock, Smith & Adams, who spent an afternoon with us and shared the drawings published in this book. Cindy Clark and the Southern Poverty Law Center have our gratitude for the use of its photographs. We also enjoyed our tour of the center. Thanks go to Craig Gates for sharing his fun family photographs. Franklin Collier and Joe Holloway, noted midcentury professional photographers, continue to have our admiration and appreciation. We are grateful to Carolyn Voshell for the slides and to Bernard and Ann Carmichael for the real estate appraisal photographs. Truly, we would not have been able to include the Martin Luther King family portrait if not for the expertise of Auburn University at Montgomery librarians Barbara Hightower and Ricky Best—thank you so much. Much thanks to Jina Clark and Meg Lewis with the Montgomery Area Chamber of Commerce Convention & Visitor Bureau for all the photographs. We especially thank Meg for the spectacular last one.

We appreciate the patience of our editor, Maggie Bullwinkel, as we bumped, clunked, and finally ran to the finish line.

INTRODUCTION

Perhaps it is the Alabama River, with its constant current, constant movement, that makes Montgomery, Alabama's capital, a place of change. Often, these changes are not limited to Montgomery but are shared across the spectrum of American society and are part of the nation's history.

This book begins with a look at Montgomery's role in World War II as the home of Maxwell Field, then designated as the Southeast Air Corps Training Center, where pilots from all the Allied forces trained. Living accommodations on the base were limited, and the people of Montgomery opened their homes, churches, and hearts to the servicemen and servicewomen. Maxwell and Gunter Air Force Bases continue to be an important part of Montgomery.

The era of prosperity following the war created a busy downtown. Shoppers enjoyed a variety of retail establishments housed in buildings dating from the antebellum period to the first part of the 20th century. Since Montgomery is Alabama's capital, lawyers and state agencies maintained offices downtown, adding to the bustle on the streets. In the late 1950s, residential and shopping areas developed beyond downtown. Normandale Shopping Center was popular and successful, and many companies maintained stores both downtown and in Normandale. Eastbrook Shopping Center was developed to serve the new neighborhoods on the east side of town. Construction began on Garrett Coliseum, then called the State Coliseum, in 1949. It served to showcase and help support Alabama's agricultural sector. The venue continues to host the Alabama National Fair, as well as national and local events.

However, not all of Montgomery's citizens fully partook of postwar prosperity. In his book on Montgomery and World War II, *Montgomery in the Good War*, Wesley Phillips Newton quotes Montgomery resident John Sawyer, who described the way African Americans were treated when returning to their homes in Montgomery after serving overseas: "There was very little effort to show any respect for the Negroes who had served their country." Change was needed, and change did come. The Reverend Martin Luther King Jr. moved to Montgomery as pastor of the Dexter Avenue Baptist Church in 1954. Reverend King lived with his family in Montgomery until 1960. As president of the Montgomery Improvement Association, Reverend King was a leader in the 1955–1956 Montgomery Bus Boycott. On December 1, 1955, Rosa Parks refused to give up her seat on a downtown Montgomery bus to a white man. Her action has become an iconic moment in American history. The result of which, the Montgomery Bus Boycott, is considered one of the first events of the civil rights movement. The boycott certainly also initiated Reverend King's role as the civil rights movement's foremost leader. In 1959, Federal Court Judge Frank Johnson ruled that Montgomery's segregation of recreational facilities was unconstitutional. Rather than comply, city officials closed all city parks on December 31, 1959; the city commission reopened the parks on February 24, 1965. Dr. King was no longer a resident of Montgomery when he led the 1965 Selma-to-Montgomery Voting Rights March up Dexter Avenue to the Alabama State Capitol.

While society worked on changing laws, habits, hearts, and minds, the physical and architectural landscape was also changing. Urban renewal and the construction of interstate highways resulted in the loss of significant amounts of historic buildings and areas. Hailed as a step toward becoming a modern city, these changes drastically altered residential and downtown areas. An entire block of historic buildings behind the Court Square Fountain was lost to the bulldozer of "urban renewal" in the 1960s. The interstates were constructed through three historic neighborhoods, dividing areas, rerouting streets, and causing antebellum homes—both mansions and cottages—to fall prey to the wrecking ball. Beyond downtown, the 250-acre Blount Cultural Park was initiated with the construction of the Alabama Shakespeare Festival in 1985 and the Montgomery Museum of Fine Arts in 1988. The beautiful park features large wide-open spaces enjoyed by Montgomery residents and visitors alike. The Shakespeare Festival and the Montgomery Museum of Fine Arts attract national and international visitors, making Montgomery an artistic and cultural destination in addition to its historical roots.

While the river rolled and change swept Montgomery and the country, the city's residents, like most Americans, lived a day-to-day life with families and friends. Downtown, shoppers and workers dined on two hot dogs in a bun and fries at Chris' Hot Dogs. In suburbia, the Sahara Restaurant served elegant Southern food, Country's Barbecue offered classic fare plus the ever-popular "meat and three," and the Ranch Restaurant pleased guests with a fun Western theme. Sports teams won and lost, churches held services, schools held classes, and the annual Turkey Day Classic Parade was the highlight of the year.

The Alabama River continues to roll at the foot of downtown Montgomery. Currently, the downtown area is undergoing a renaissance. As Alabama's capital, the home of the Alabama Shakespeare Festival, a National Civic League All-America City, and the winner of *USA Today*'s contest for Best Historic City, Montgomery graciously hosts a variety of visitors. Residents also enjoy the downtown restaurants, Biscuits baseball, and concerts. Sightseers, diners, and revelers board the riverboat *Harriott II* and sail away—and back—several times a day. Music lovers attend concerts in the Riverfront Amphitheater perched beside the river. Friends stroll and lovers sneak a kiss along a scenic river walk. Montgomery, the Capital of Dreams, is ready for whatever changes the Alabama River might bring.

One

The War Effort

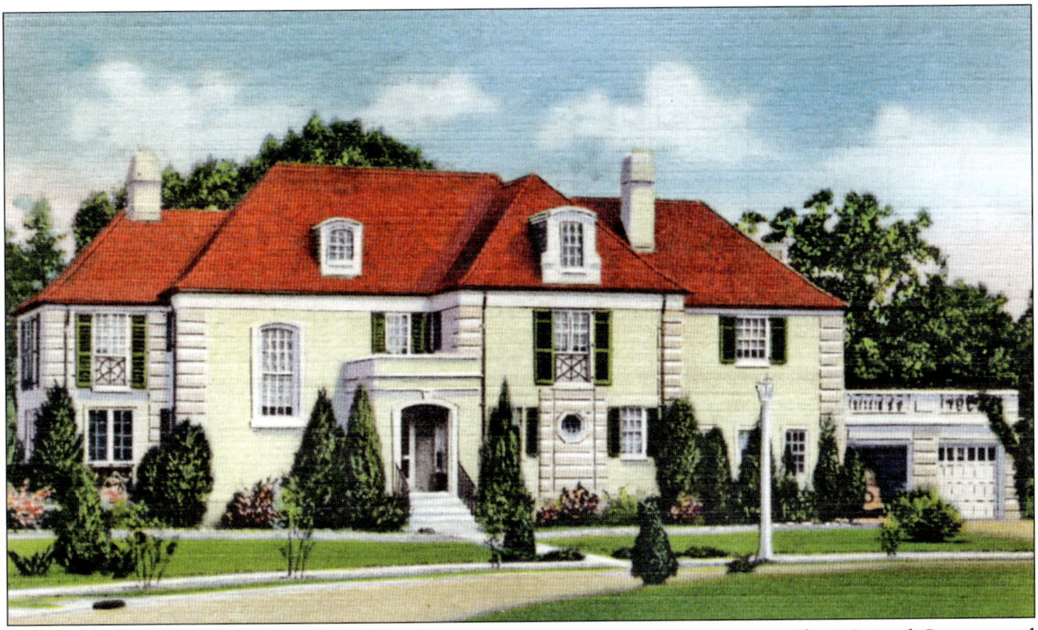

During World War II, servicemen and servicewomen came from across the United States and from England, France, and Canada to train at Maxwell Air Force Base. The influx of people from outside the South and the sense of unity for the war effort contributed to Montgomery becoming a modern city. This vintage postcard shows the Senior Officers' Quarters at Maxwell Air Force Base, built in the 1930s and still occupied today. (Courtesy Landmarks Foundation.)

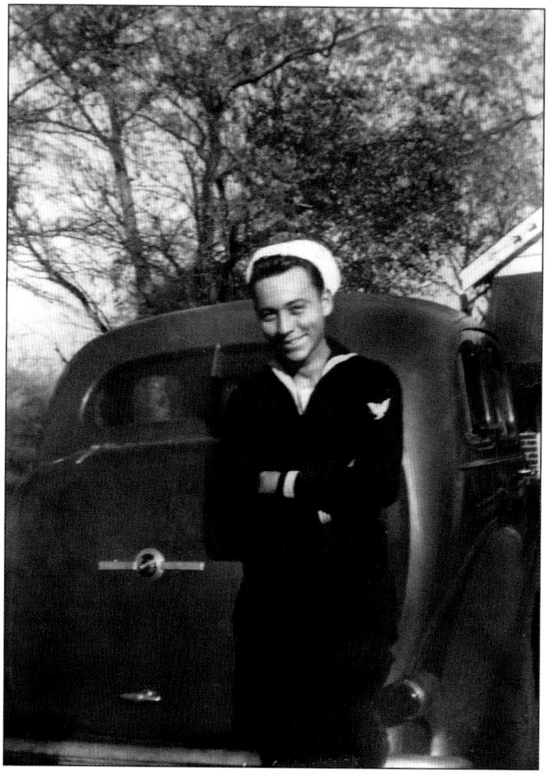

James Hudson leans against his car while on leave from the Navy during World War II. (Courtesy Debbie George.)

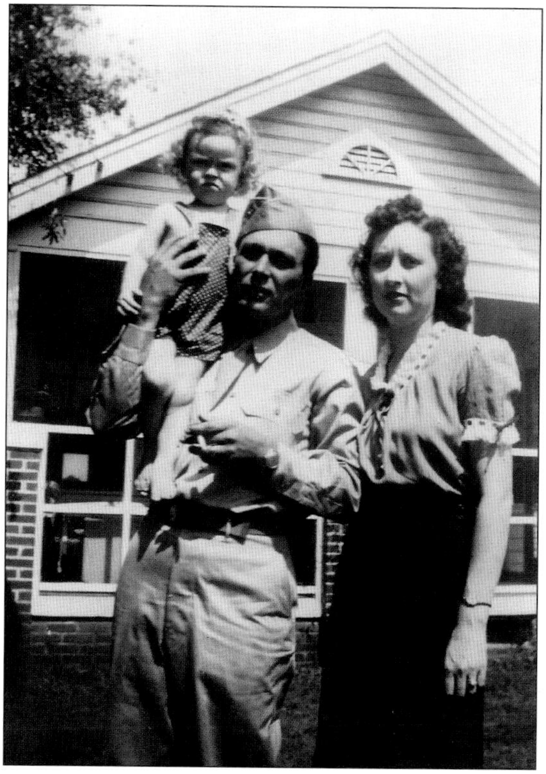

Arthur Lee Thompson (holding Brenda) and Annie Thompson stand in front of their home on Ann Street. At the time, Arthur Lee was home on leave from the Army during World War II. (Courtesy Debbie George.)

During World War II, Capitol Heights Baptist Church created a Sunday school class for soldiers stationed in Montgomery. Shown here on September 24, 1944, are, from left to right, (first row) David Bryant (Alabama), Louis Dobson (Florida), C.H. Ward (teacher), Glynn Hill (Tennessee), and Joe Hoover (Kentucky); (second row) Marvin Burley (South Carolina), Jack Blue (Alabama), Paul Hamrick (North Carolina), Bill Lankford (South Carolina), and Maury Perry (Mississippi). (Courtesy Capitol Heights Baptist Church.)

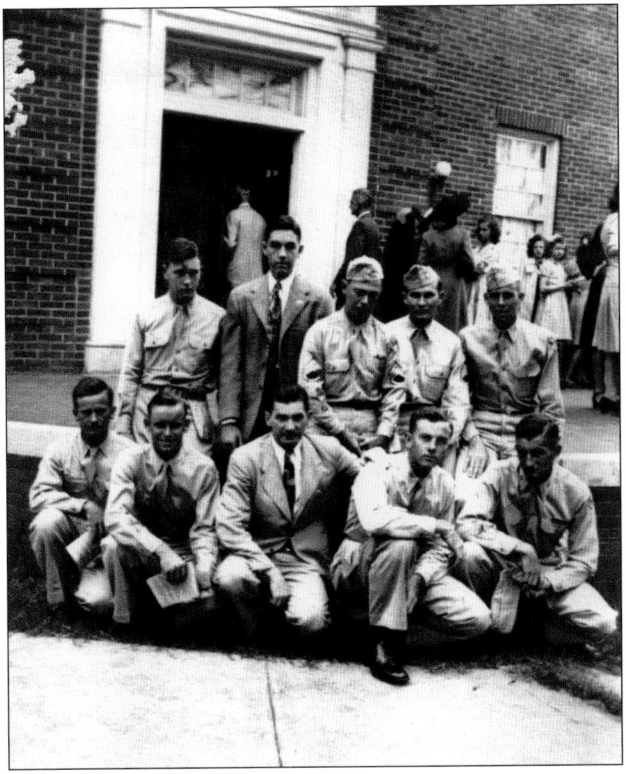

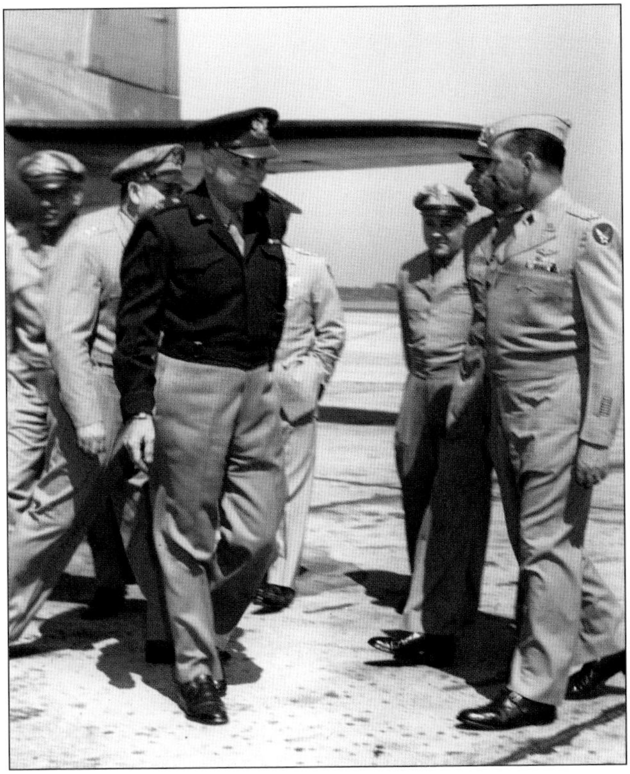

Here, Gen. Dwight D. Eisenhower visits Maxwell Air Force Base in April 1947 on a military facilities inspection tour. (Photograph by Franklin Collier; courtesy Landmarks Foundation.)

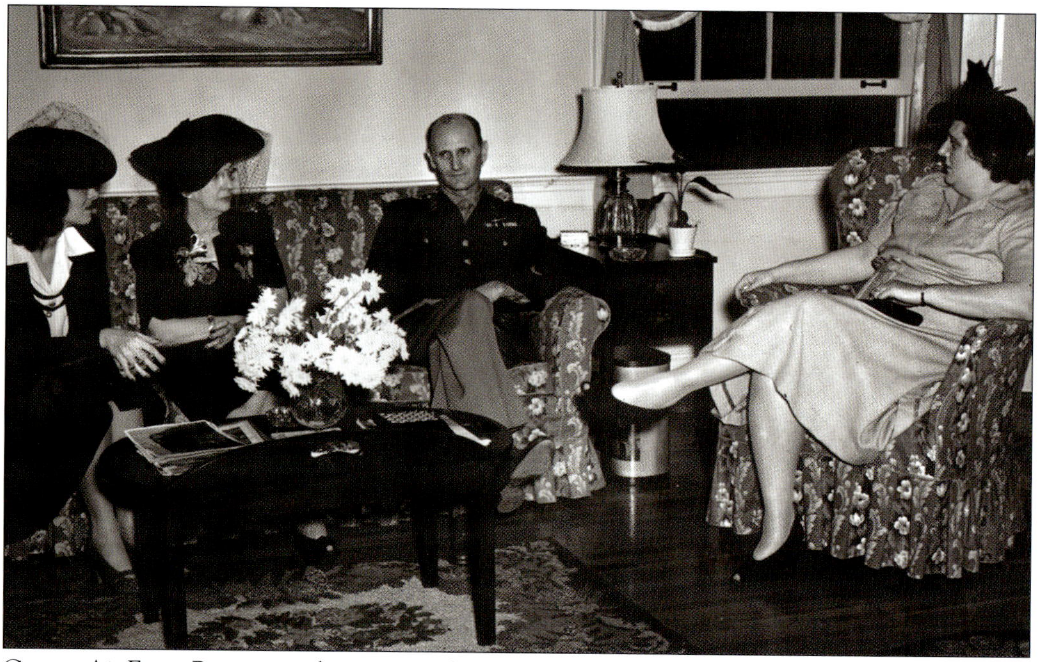

Gunter Air Force Base opened in 1940 under the command of Maxwell Air Force Base as a flying school for American, British, French, and Canadian pilots. Named for former Montgomery mayor William Adams Gunter, it is currently known as Gunter Annex. In November 1942, the Hornsby Room was dedicated. It was named for Alabama native Brig. Gen. Aubrey Thomas Hornsby, who was Gunter's first base commander. (Courtesy Air Force Historical Research Agency.)

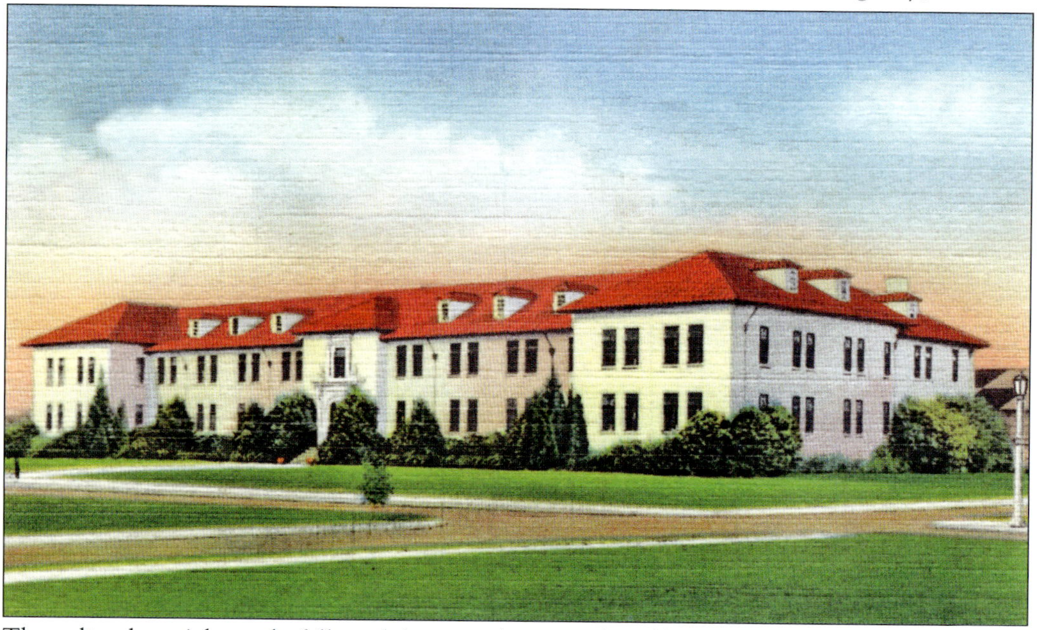

The enlisted men's barracks followed the same design as the officers' quarters. However, there was not enough lodging for the amount of pilots training for World War II. Montgomery residents rented out rooms, created garage apartments, and welcomed the servicemen and servicewomen into the community. (Courtesy Landmarks Foundation.)

Two

Growth and Expansion

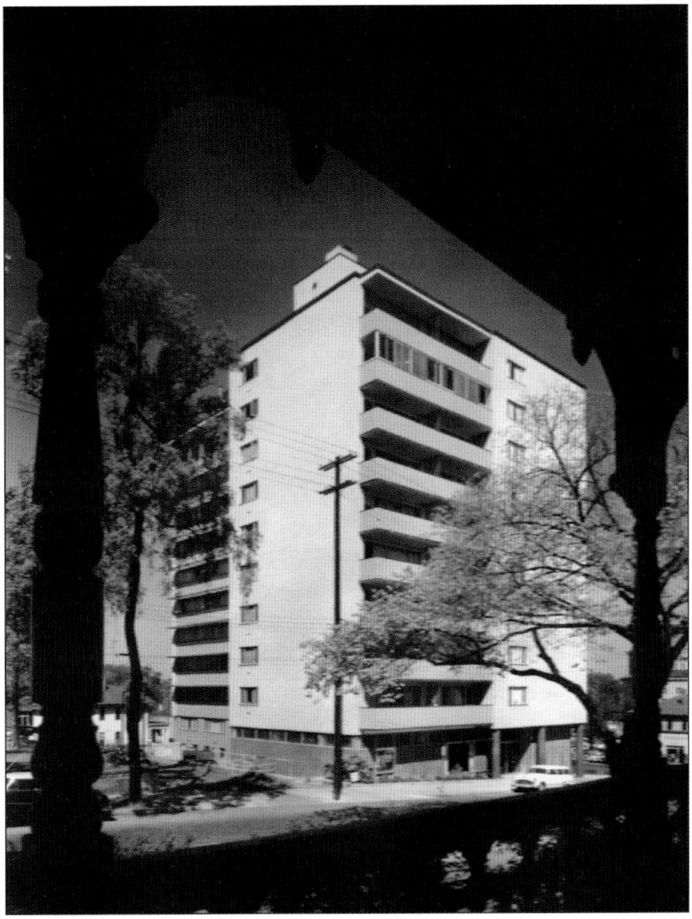

The Capitol Towers, designed by architectural firm Sherlock, Smith & Adams in the late 1950s, was one of Montgomery's first high-rise apartments. A newspaper noted, "In the land of white columns, the long struggle by architects . . . on behalf of a new and honest approach to architecture . . . is beginning to pay off." In 1967, a horrendous fire killed 26 people at Dale's Penthouse restaurant on the top floor. In the wake of the tragedy, the city enacted new fire codes. (Courtesy Sherlock, Smith & Adams.)

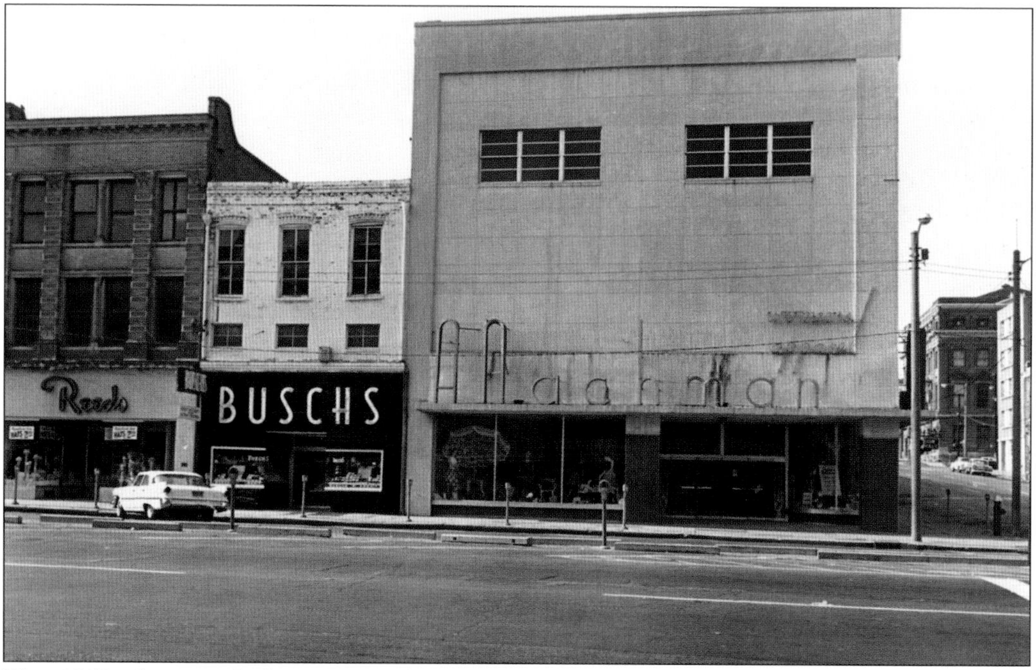

This 1950s photograph shows A. Nachman department store on the southeast corner of Dexter Avenue and Perry Street. Shoppers could also visit Buschs jewelry and Reeds hat shop. (Photograph by Franklin Collier; courtesy Landmarks Foundation.)

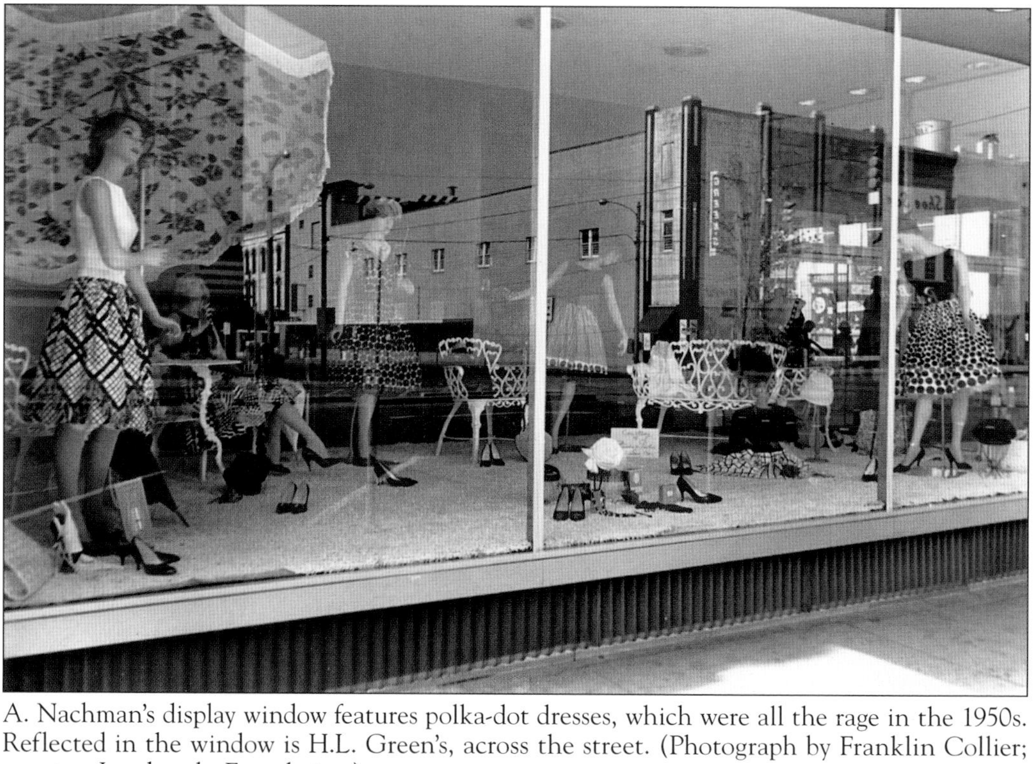

A. Nachman's display window features polka-dot dresses, which were all the rage in the 1950s. Reflected in the window is H.L. Green's, across the street. (Photograph by Franklin Collier; courtesy Landmarks Foundation.)

In the 1950s, before the streets were designated for one-way traffic, cars moved along in both directions at the intersection of Dexter Avenue and North Perry Street. (Photograph by Franklin Collier; courtesy Landmarks Foundation.)

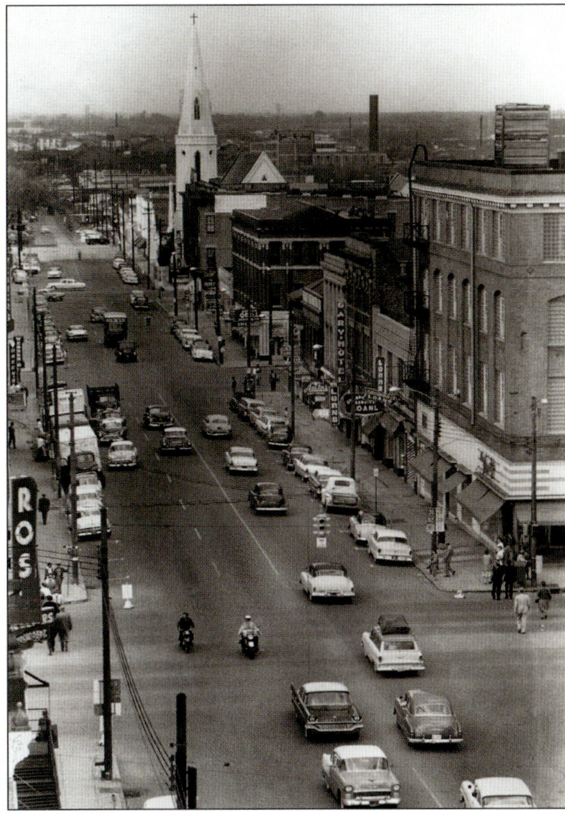

Parker-Sledge Hardware Store and the 21 Supplies camera shop on South Court Street still do a brisk business in this late-1960s photograph. Note the rooftop advertisement for Bamboo Lounge and Embers Restaurant. (Courtesy Landmarks Foundation.)

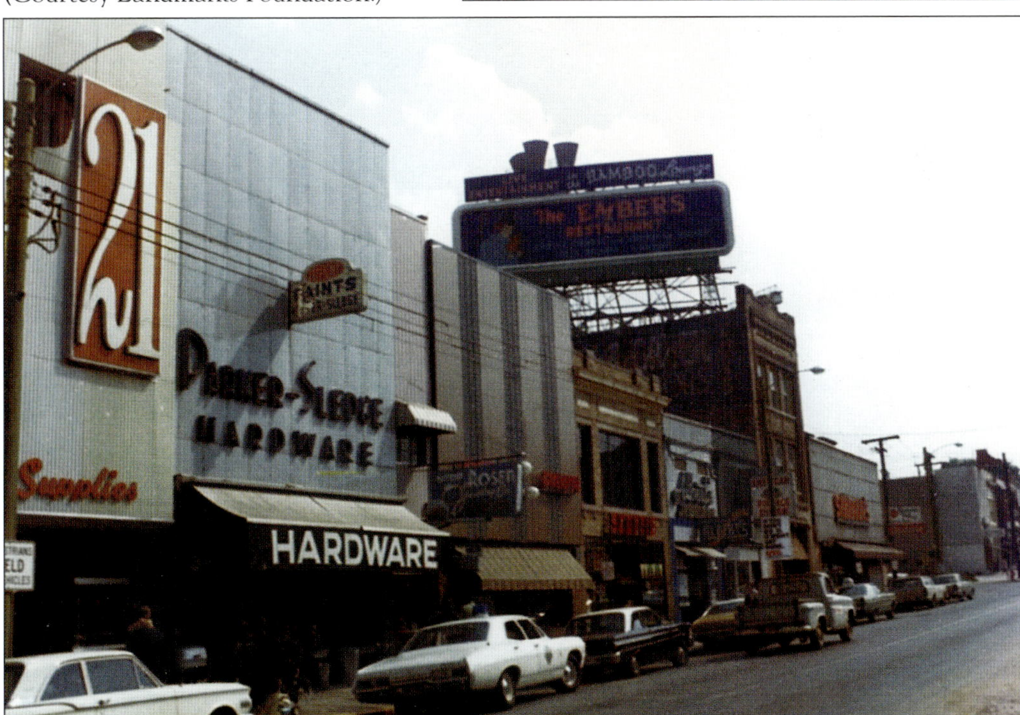

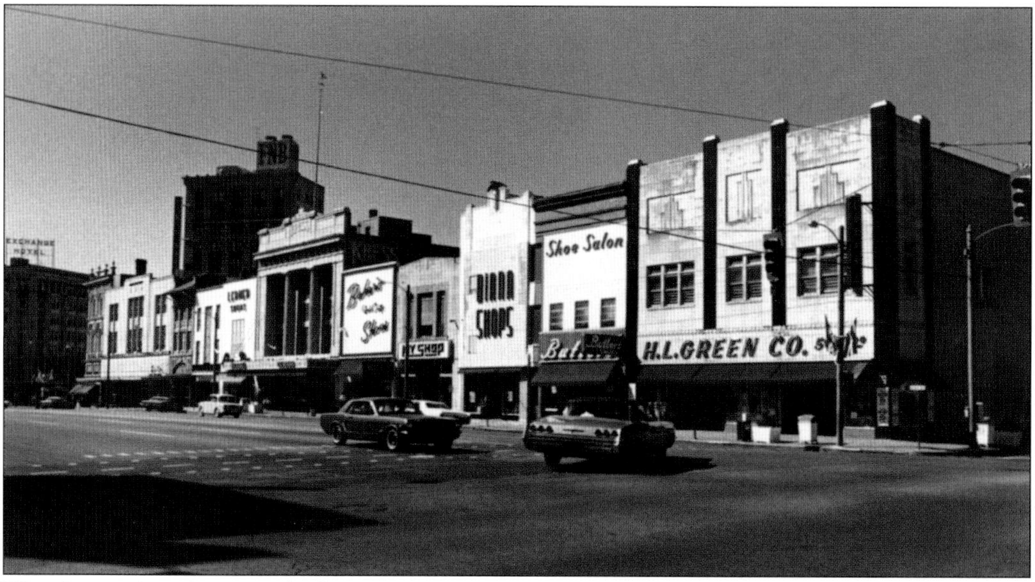

This late-1960s photograph shows many of the shopping options on the north side of Dexter Avenue, including Baker's Shoes, Lerner Shops, and Kress. A few of these buildings date to the antebellum era and remain standing today. Note the 1967 Mustang at left. (Photograph by Franklin Collier; courtesy Landmarks Foundation.)

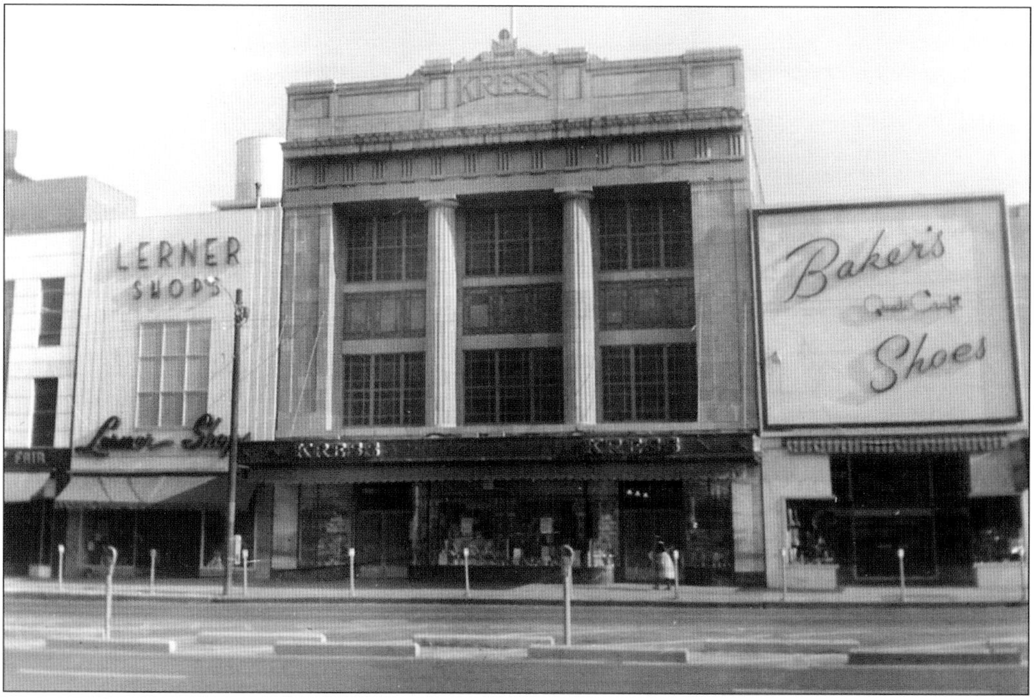

In 1927, the Kress store burned down. In 1929, the building that had replaced it collapsed. The design of the third, and current, building borrows elements from the Temple of Hera, as seen here. Samuel Kress got the inspiration for this design when the king of Italy knighted him for helping to preserve ancient monuments. Kress closed in 1981; the location stayed open as a variety store until 1997. (Courtesy Landmarks Foundation.)

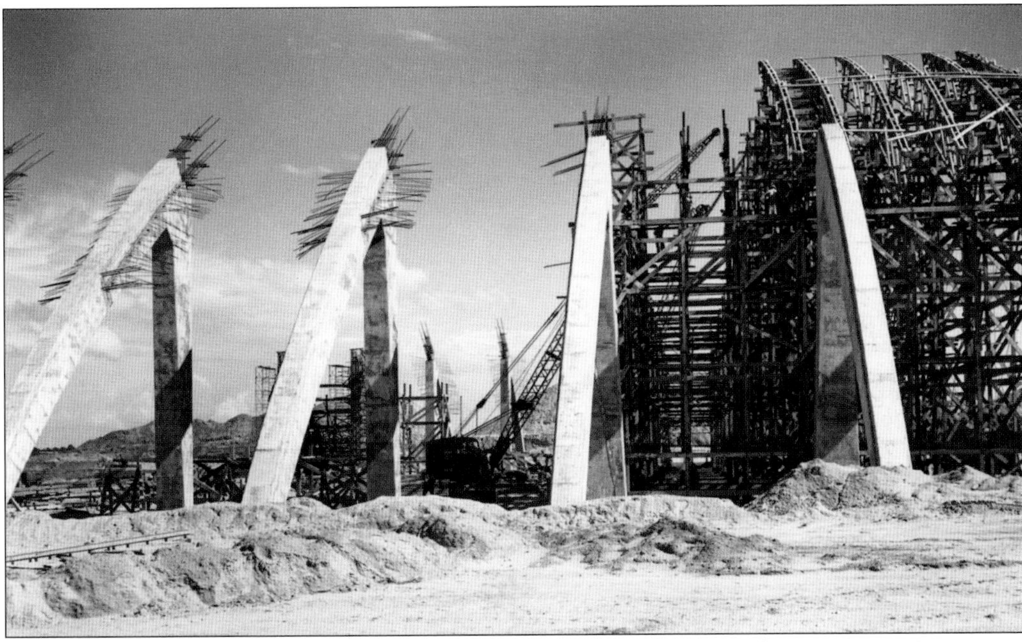

The Garrett Coliseum was first called the State Coliseum. Construction began in 1949. Renovation and improvements have kept it a popular host for the Alabama National Fair, rodeos, and musical events. (Courtesy Landmarks Foundation.)

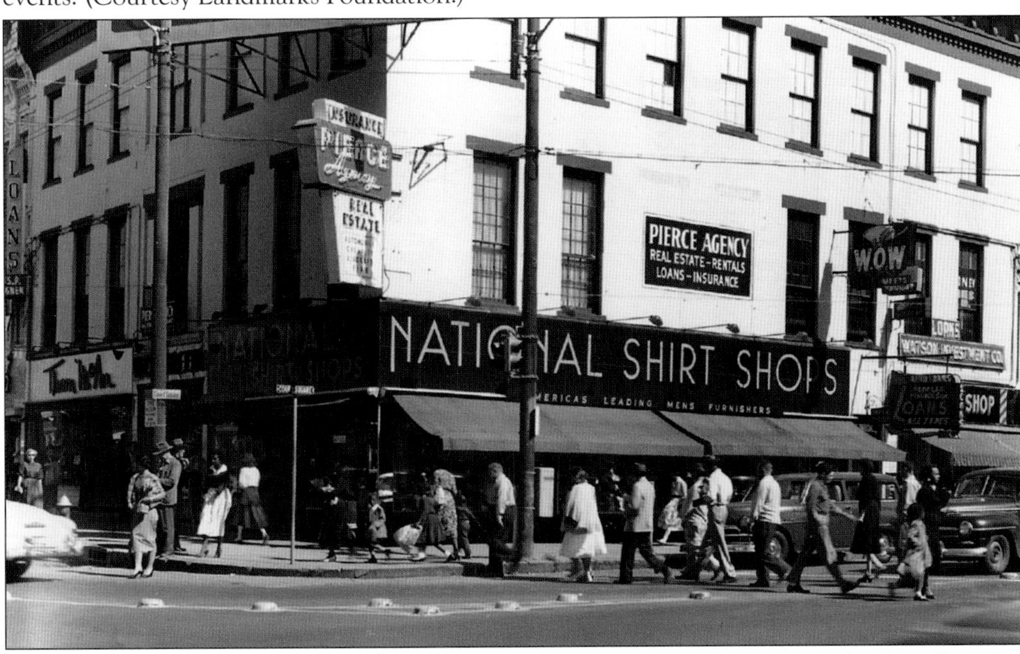

Seen here in the 1950s, the antebellum Winter Building housed retail on the first floor and a variety of business offices in the upper stories. Built in 1841 to house St. Mary's Bank and retail firms, the building is famous as the origination of the telegram with orders to fire on Fort Sumter—the first act of the Civil War. The Winter Building continues to anchor Court Square, where it is currently undergoing renovations for its new role in the downtown Market District. (Photograph by Franklin Collier; courtesy Landmarks Foundation.)

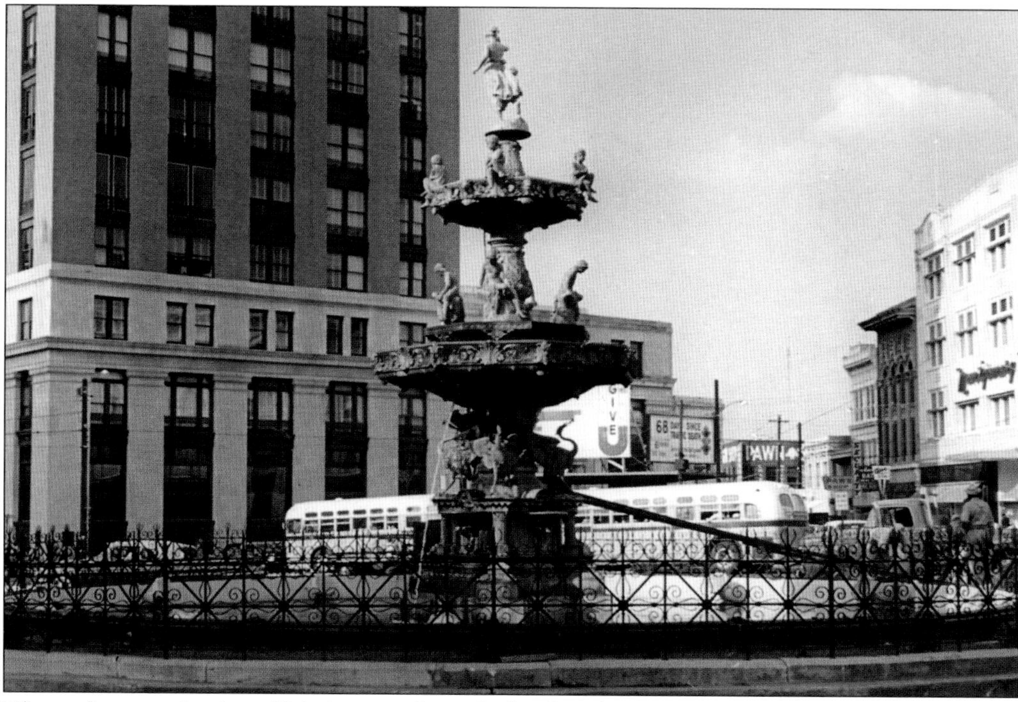

These photographs show Hebe's reign through the decades. Court Square is the heart of the city, and Court Square Fountain is its romantic center. The figure at the top of the fountain, Hebe, cupbearer to the gods, has reigned over Court Square since 1885. In the above photograph, buses roll by in the late 1950s. It was at this stop in Court Square that Rosa Parks boarded the bus where she would make history. The below photograph shows Hebe in 1960 in a different street configuration; the Winter Building retained its post on the corner of Dexter Avenue and Court Street. (Both, courtesy *Montgomery Advertiser.*)

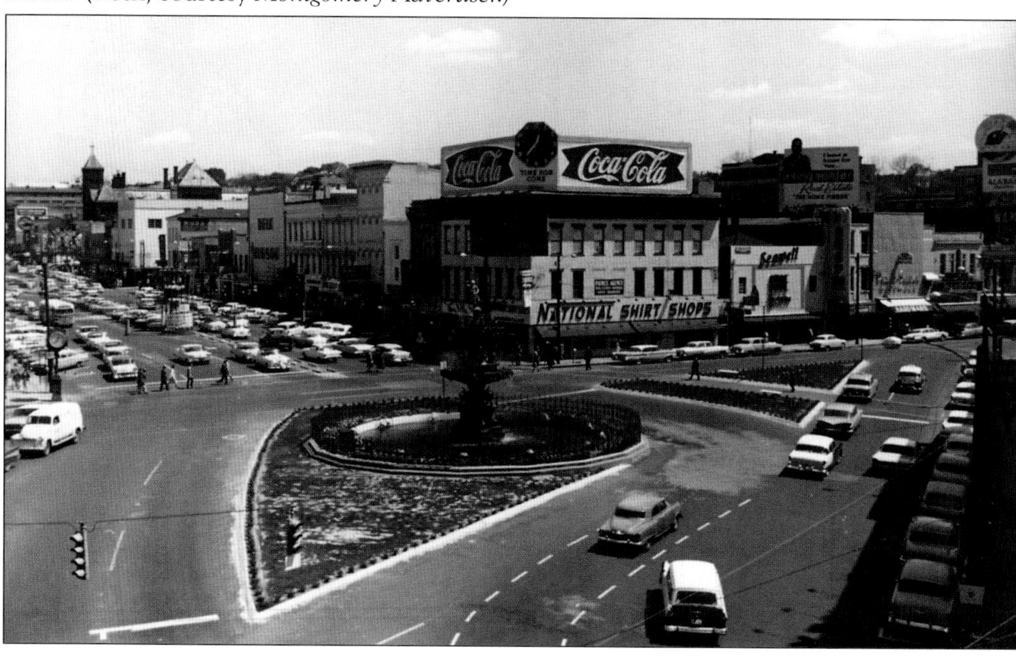

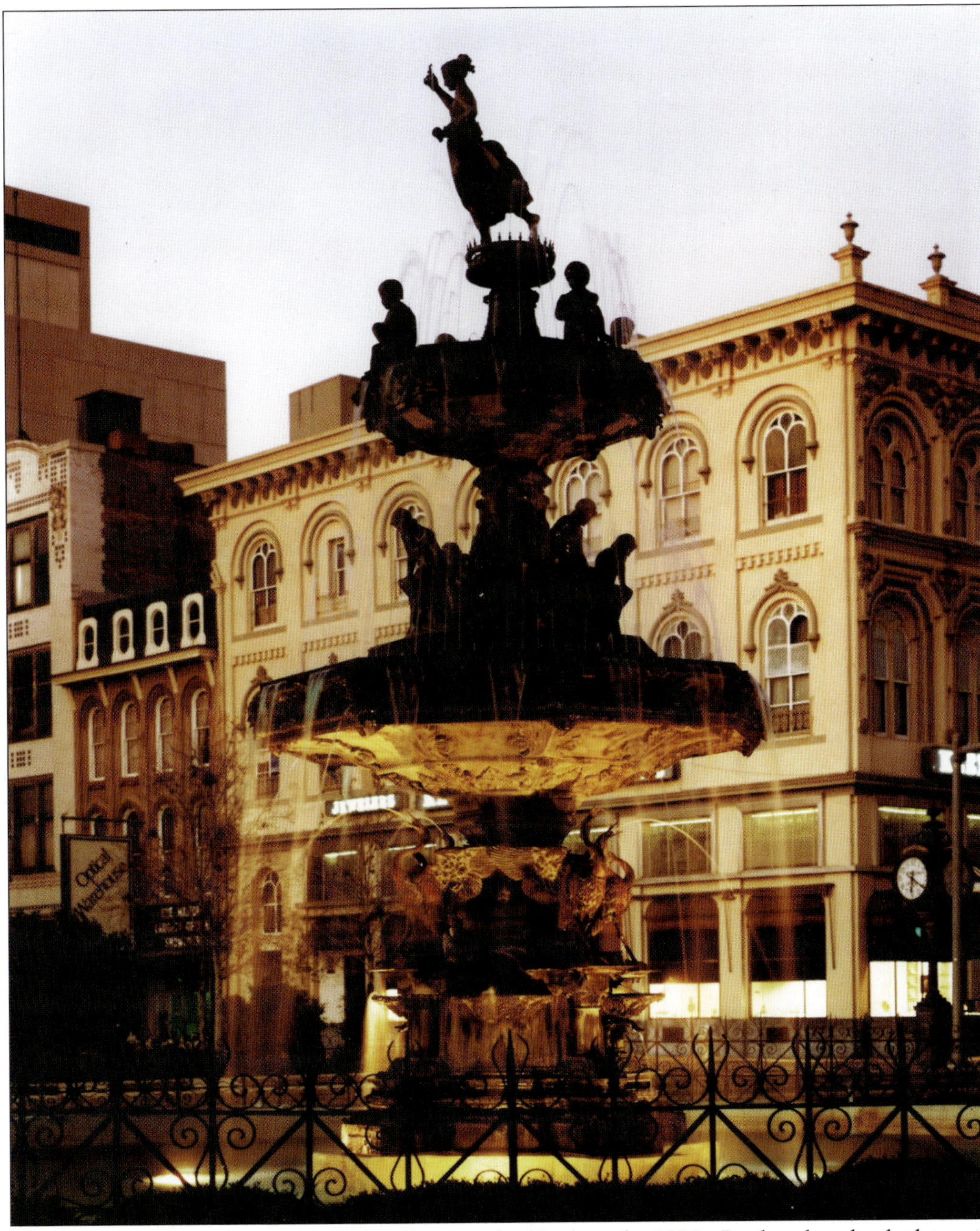

The Court Square Fountain is artfully photographed here in the 1980s. By that decade, the historic buildings behind Hebe had fallen to progress, but she still held her place in Court Square and in the hearts of lovers of beauty and history in Montgomery. (Courtesy Landmarks Foundation.)

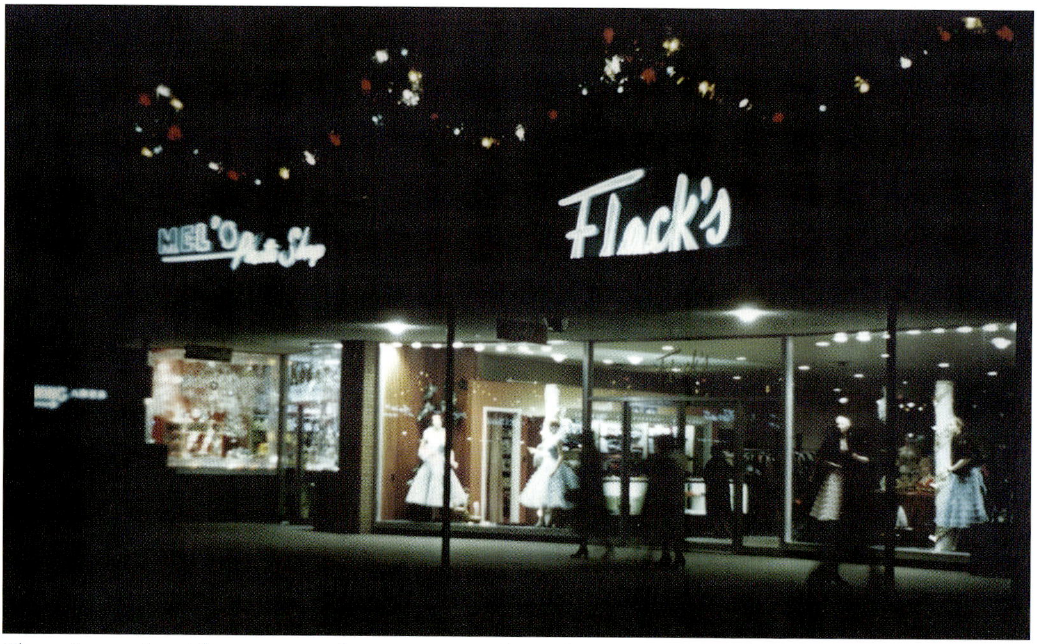

Shopping and residences started moving away from downtown as early as the 1950s. One of the first and most popular of the new areas was Normandale. In the shopping center, Flack's was an upscale ladies' shop. Mel's Photo Shop was a counterpart to the 21 Supplies camera store downtown (see page 15). (Courtesy Sherlock, Smith & Adams.)

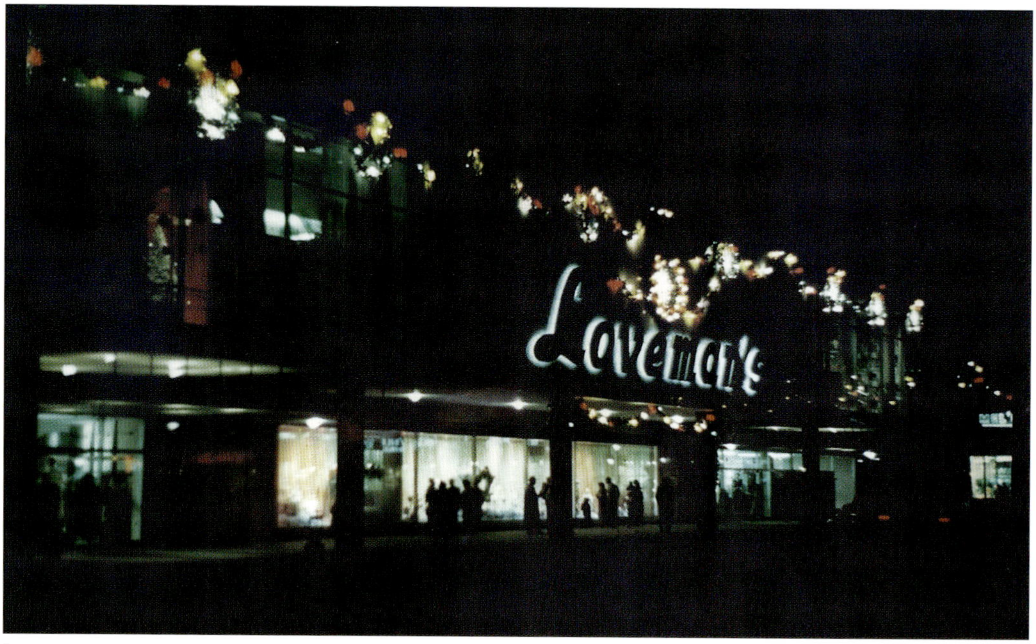

Loveman's was Normandale Shopping Center's anchor store. Family owned and operated, it originated out of Birmingham. It is seen here decorated for Christmas. Shoppers are enjoying the animated figures in the windows. Although not visible in this photograph, Santa and his visitors sat in front of a second-story window and could be seen from the pavement. (Courtesy Sherlock, Smith & Adams.)

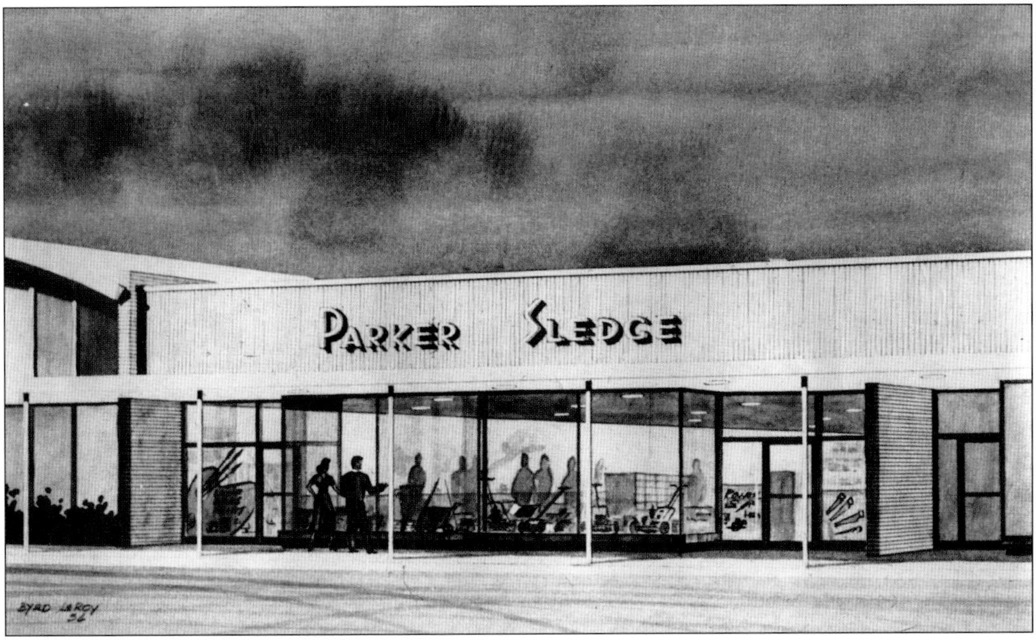

This 1956 architectural rendering by Byrd LaRoy shows the plans for Parker Sledge, a popular hardware store, in the new shopping area of Normandale. Parker Sledge had a downtown counterpart as well (see page 15). (Courtesy Sherlock, Smith & Adams.)

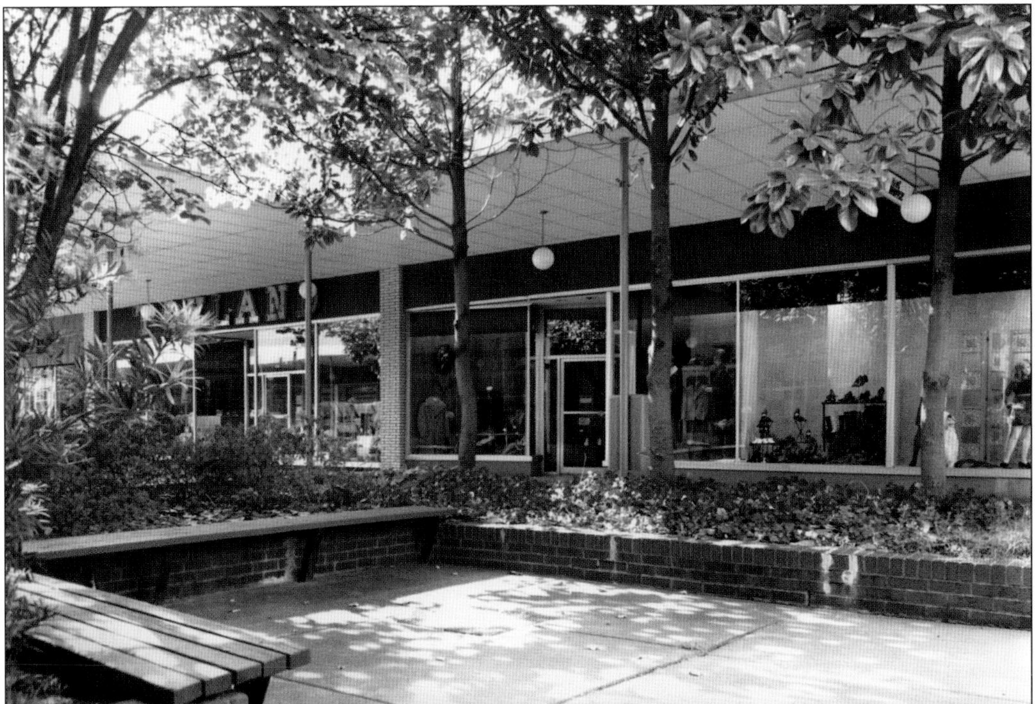

Development continued at Normandale Shopping Center. A later addition, known as the Arcade, included facilities for socializing and resting from the arduous task of shopping. (Courtesy Sherlock, Smith & Adams.)

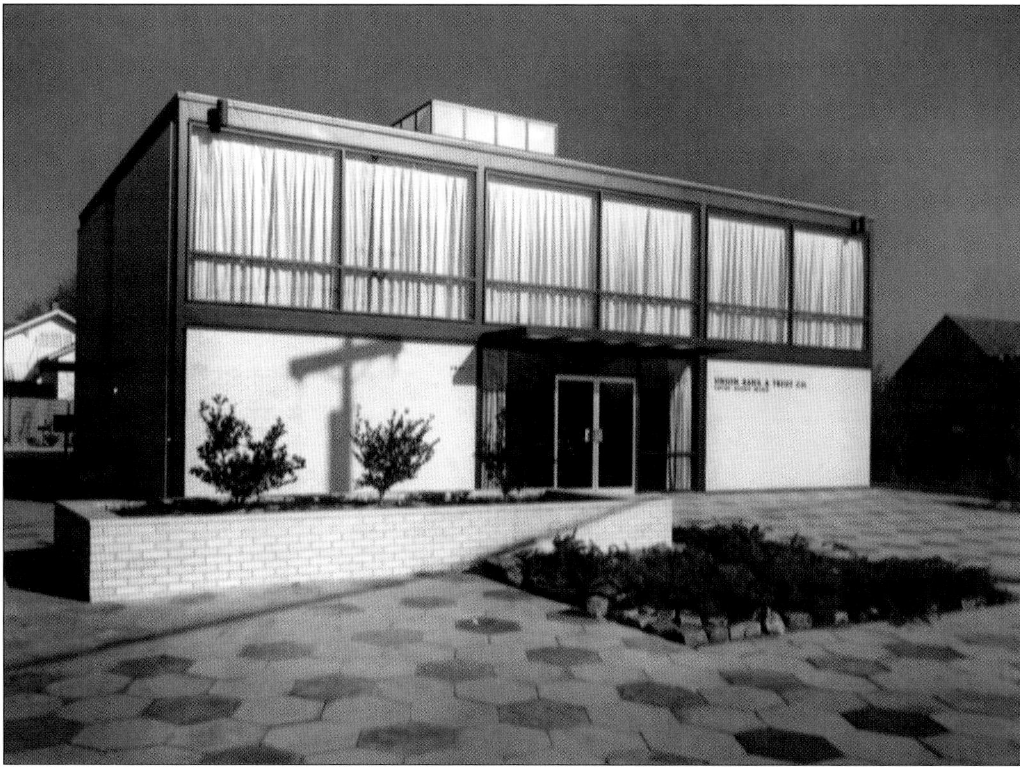

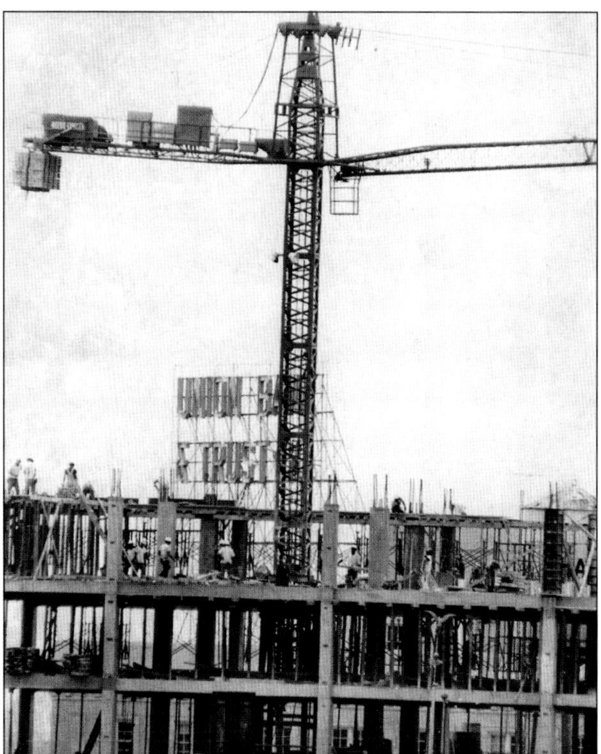

This late-1950s architectural photograph shows the plans for expanding Union Bank services to Mount Meigs Road in the suburbs, near the Capitol Heights neighborhood. (Courtesy Sherlock, Smith & Adams.)

In 1969, Union Bank, feeling good about its prospects, built a home office on Commerce Street in downtown Montgomery. (Courtesy *Montgomery Advertiser*.)

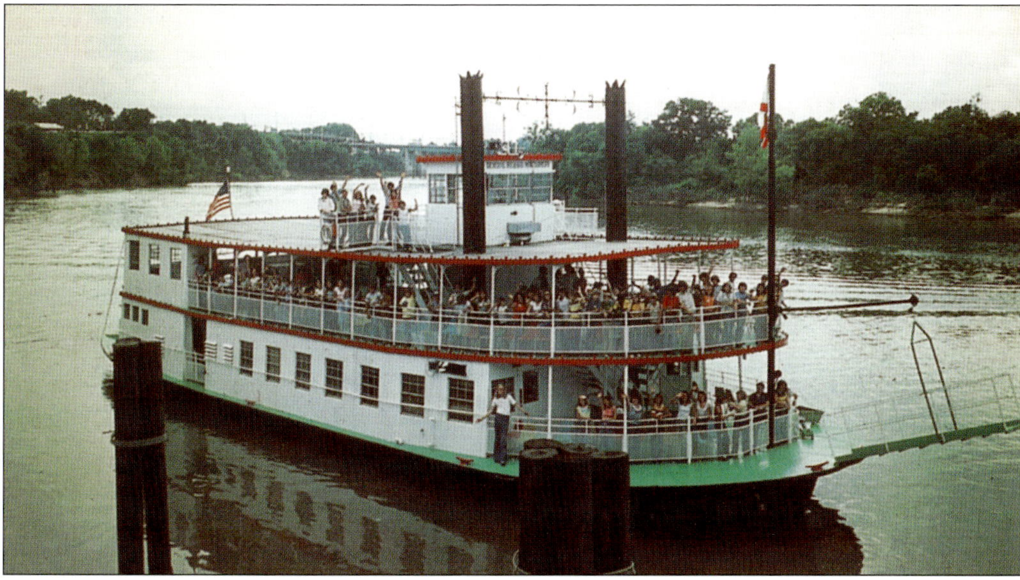

The *General Montgomery* riverboat was purchased in 1964 with funds raised by schoolchildren. Here, the youngsters enjoy their purchase as they roll down the Alabama River. (Courtesy Landmarks Foundation.)

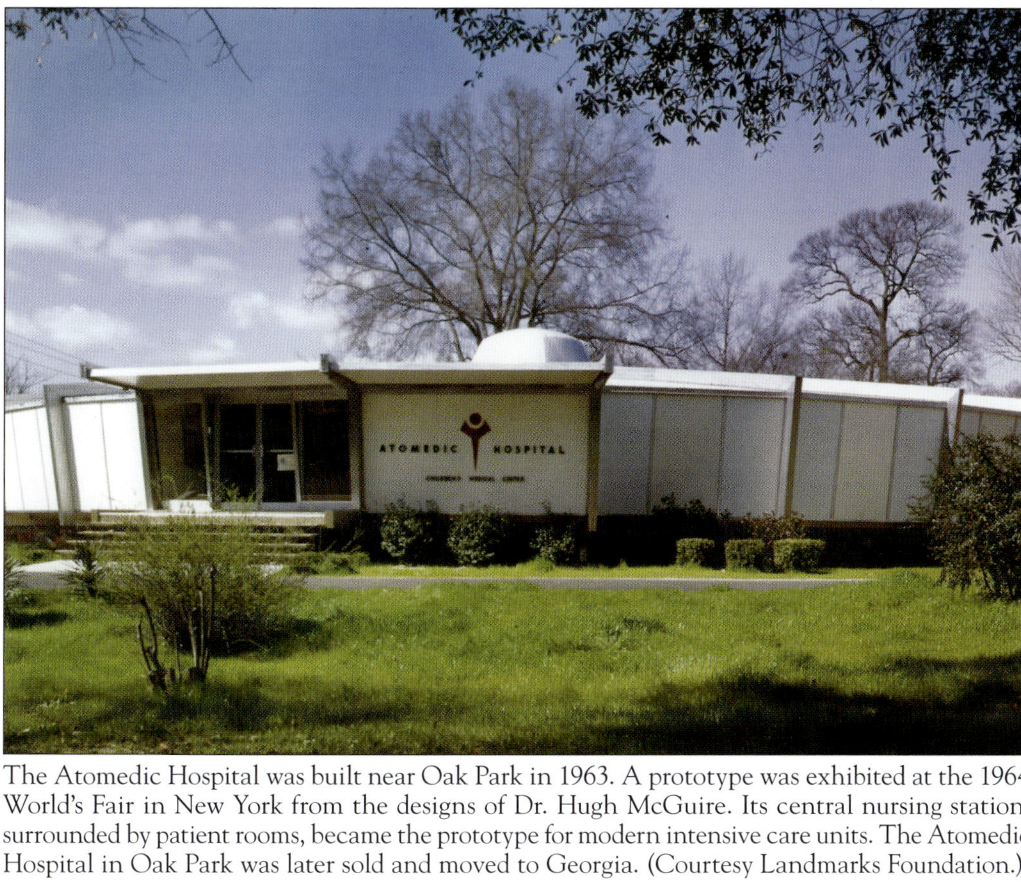

The Atomedic Hospital was built near Oak Park in 1963. A prototype was exhibited at the 1964 World's Fair in New York from the designs of Dr. Hugh McGuire. Its central nursing station, surrounded by patient rooms, became the prototype for modern intensive care units. The Atomedic Hospital in Oak Park was later sold and moved to Georgia. (Courtesy Landmarks Foundation.)

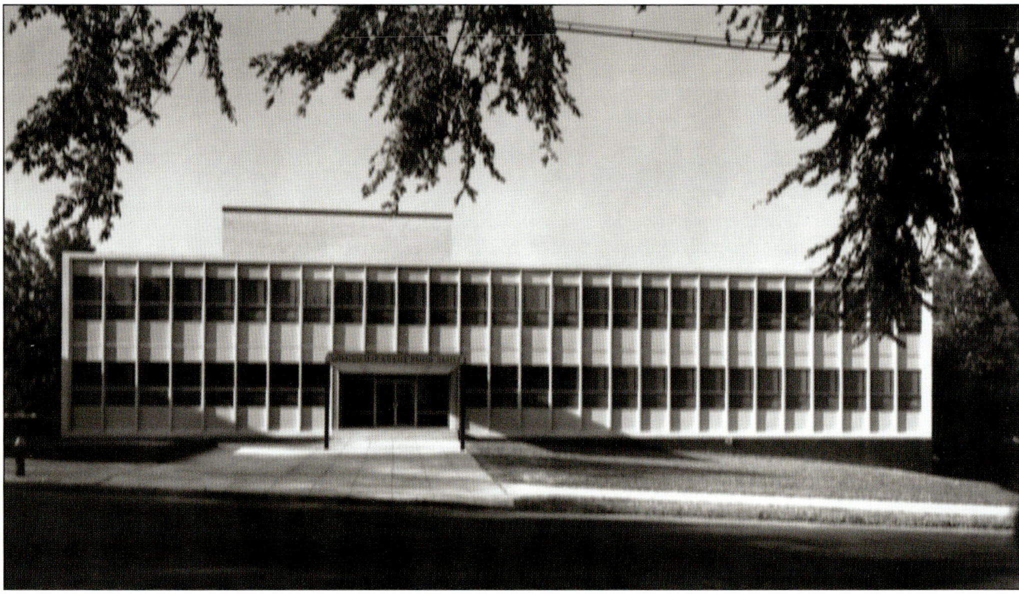

The Montgomery County Health Department, located on West Jeff Davis Avenue, was a new, modern building designed by Sherlock, Smith & Adams in 1963. (Courtesy Sherlock, Smith & Adams.)

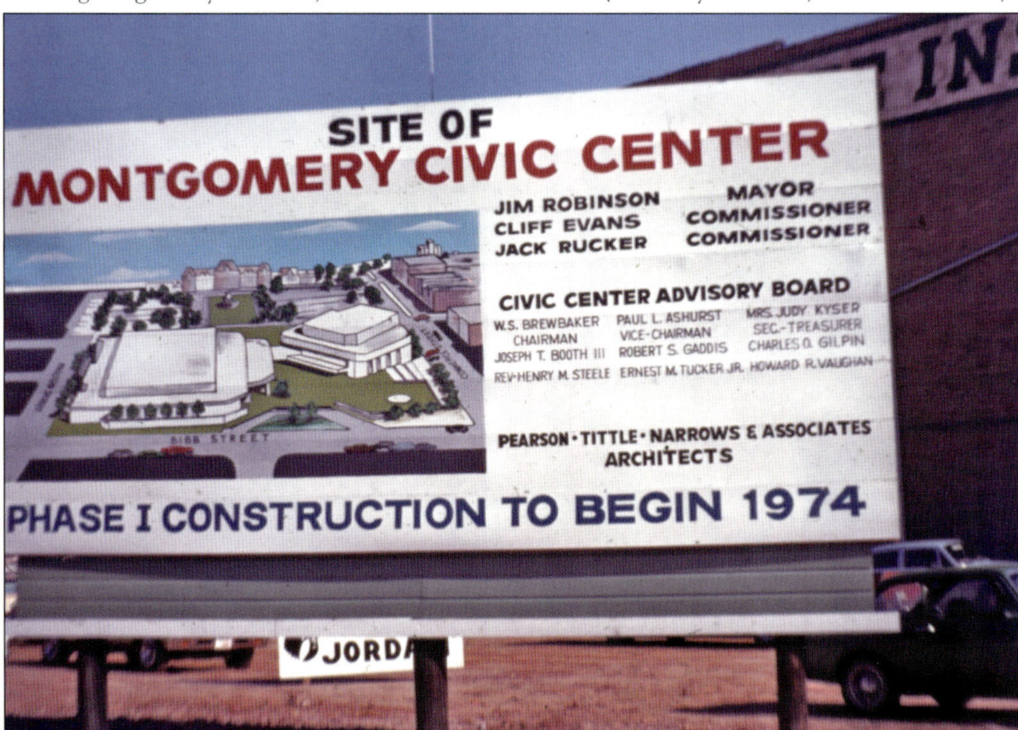

The Montgomery Civic Center, announced and advertised in this 1974 construction sign, was a venue that allowed Montgomery to become a destination for both tourists and business travelers. The civic center was adapted and expanded to create the Montgomery Convention Center, the Montgomery Performing Arts Center, and the Renaissance Montgomery Hotel and Spa. (Courtesy Landmarks Foundation.)

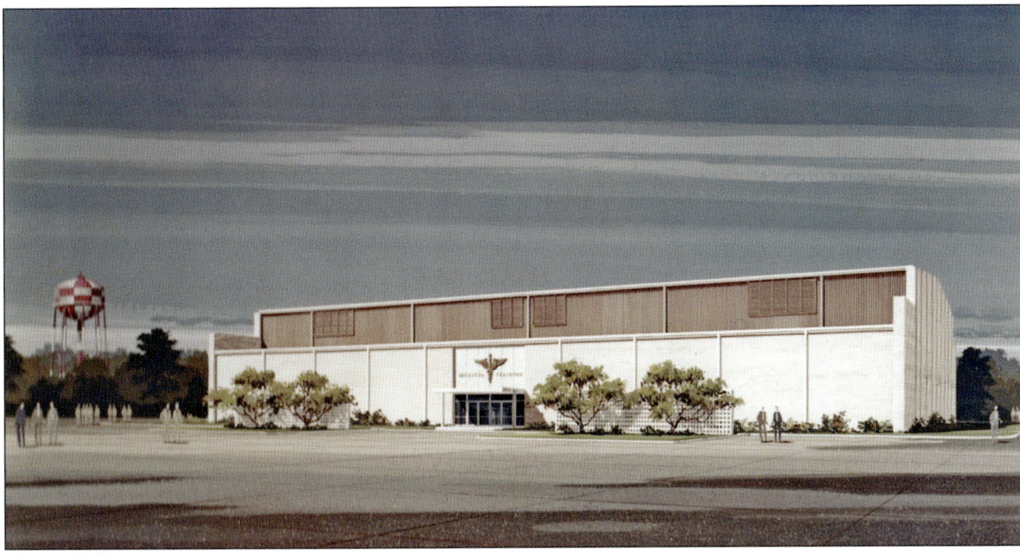

Maxwell Air Force Base and Gunter Annex continue to be an important part of Montgomery's growth. In the 1980s, Gunter Air Force Base contracted some major construction. This architectural drawing shows the building used today as the Air Force Data Systems Design Center. (Courtesy Sherlock, Smith & Adams.)

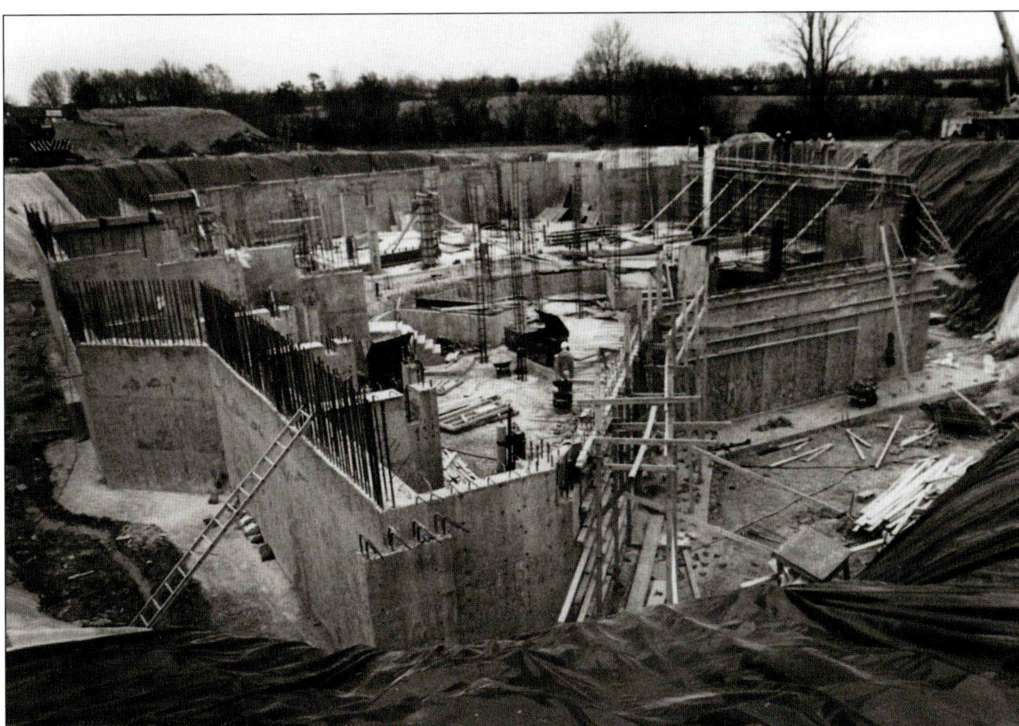

The Alabama Shakespeare Festival (ASF), the state theater, is seen here well under construction on December 21, 1983. Built within the beautiful 250 acres of Wynton M. Blount Cultural Park, ASF houses two theaters, production shops, rehearsal halls, and administrative workspace. ASF, open year-round, undertakes at least 10 productions a year. (Courtesy *Montgomery Advertiser*.)

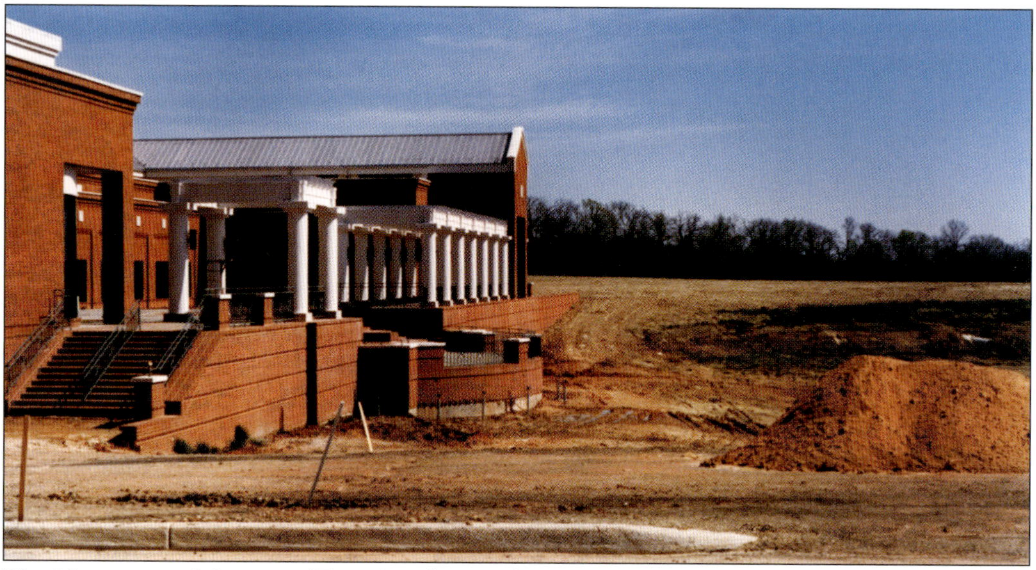

The Montgomery Museum of Fine Arts (MMFA) is shown under construction at the Wynton M. Blount Cultural Park in 1988. Note the plaza overlooking the yet-to-be-created lake that residents, geese, ducks, and the occasional dog enjoy today. Upon the MMFA's 25th anniversary at the Blount Cultural Park, director Mark M. Johnson wrote that the museum had welcomed three million visitors, evolved into a recognized collecting institution, hosted 360 special exhibitions, and published 34 scholarly catalogs. (Courtesy Montgomery Museum of Fine Arts.)

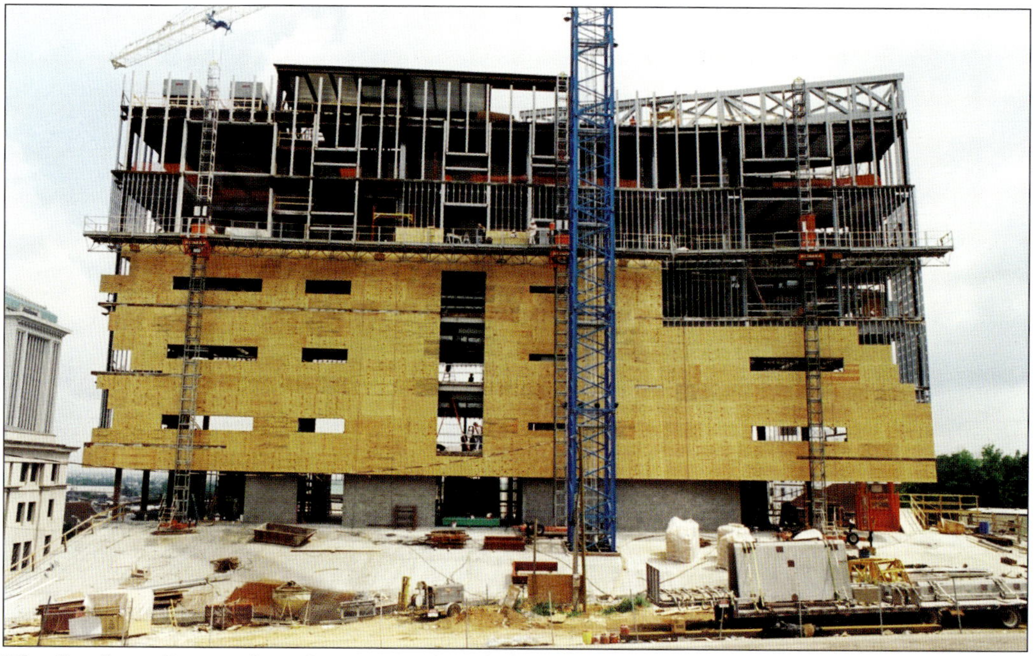

The Southern Poverty Law Center was founded in 1971 by Morris Dees and Joseph J. Levin Jr. to "ensure that the promises of the civil rights movement became a reality for all." In July 1983, the center's office on South Hull Street was firebombed. A new, more fortified center was built on Washington Street. Then the current center, with a modern and even more fortified design, was begun in 1999 and finished in 2001. (Courtesy Southern Poverty Law Center.)

Three

Events and Everyday Life

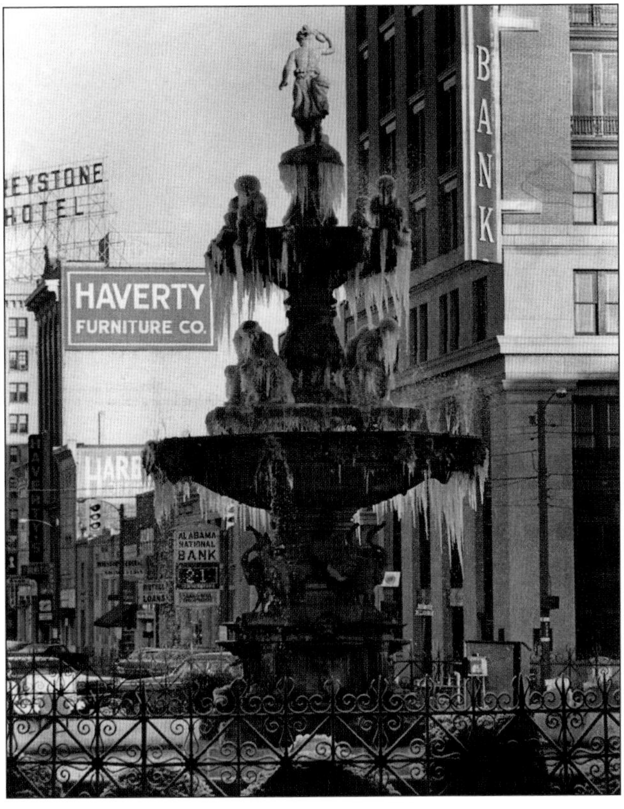

Events are moments to remember, occasions that mark a special time. Unusual for Montgomery, cold weather produced a frozen Hebe in 1967. The First Alabama Bank is also visible in this photograph, taken from Commerce Street. (Courtesy *Montgomery Advertiser.*)

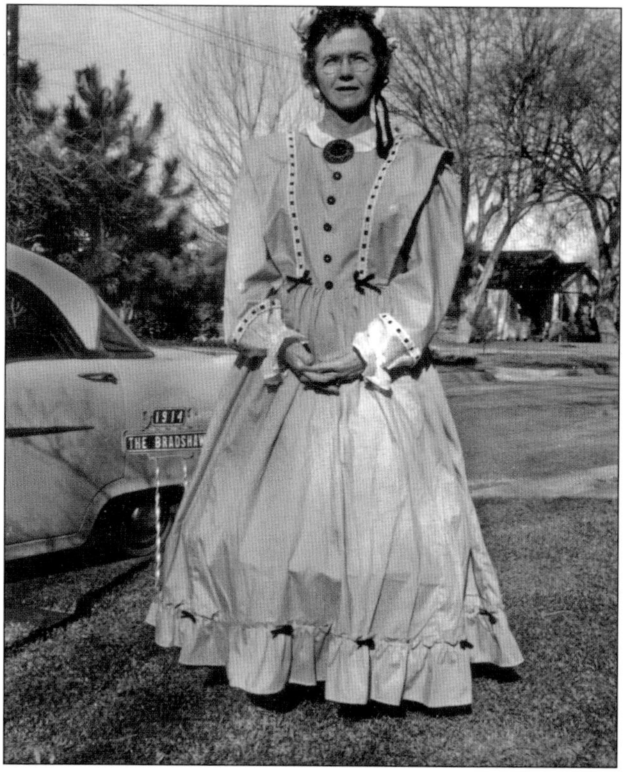

In 1961, city residents dressed in period costumes for the observation of the Civil War's centennial. (Courtesy Bradshaw family.)

In 1971, when the Ringling Bros. and Barnum & Bailey Circus came to town, the animals in the "Greatest Show on Earth" were unloaded and paraded downtown. In Montgomery, the day was so hot even the camels needed water. (Courtesy *Montgomery Advertiser*.)

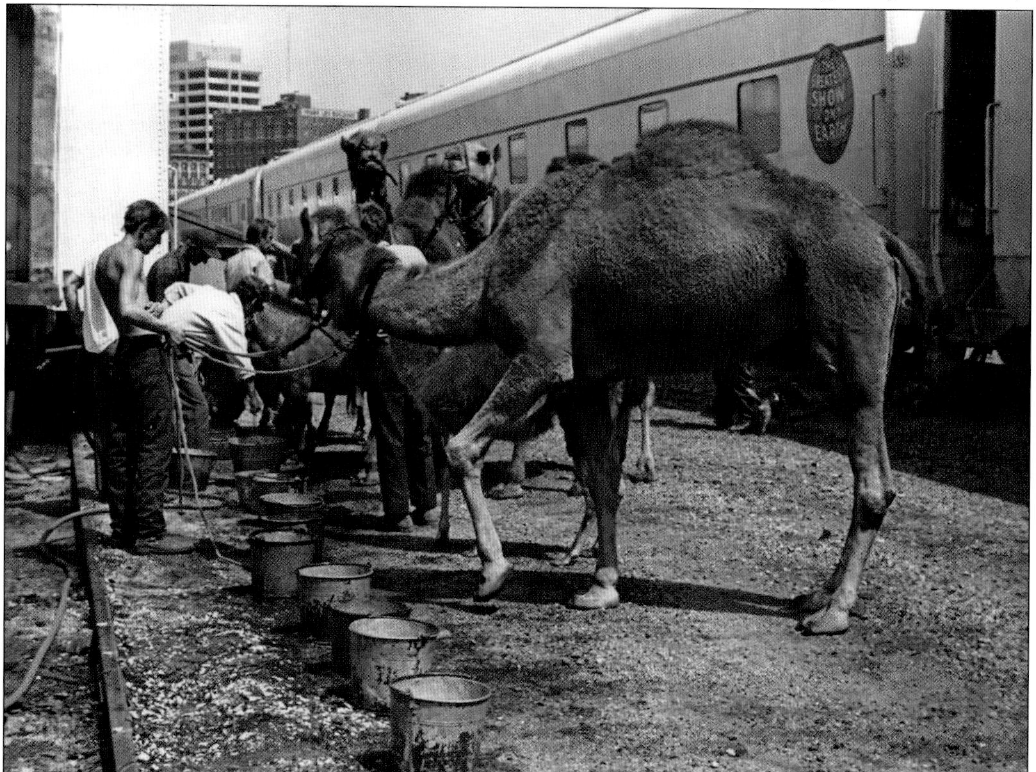

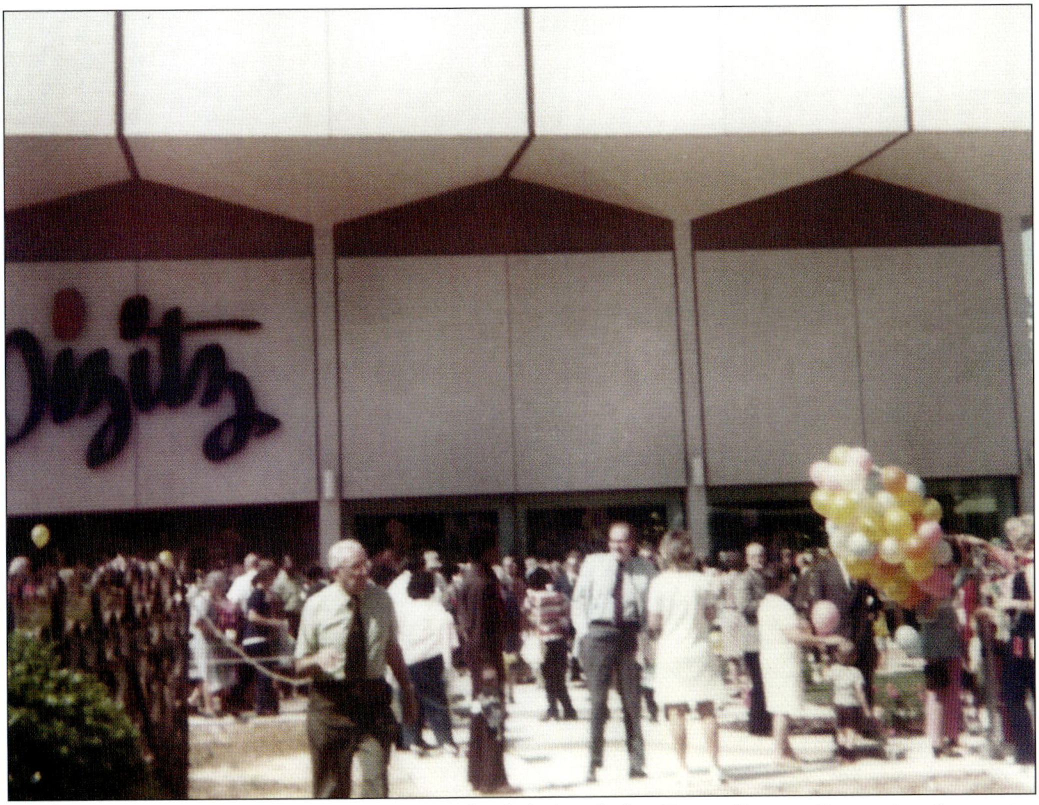

In 1972, the Pizitz Department Store was built behind the Court Square Fountain. An entire block of historic buildings was demolished in the era of urban renewal. The store's grand opening celebration in April of that year included a parade in downtown Montgomery. The building, currently empty, is known as One Court Square. (Courtesy Faye Foster Singleton.)

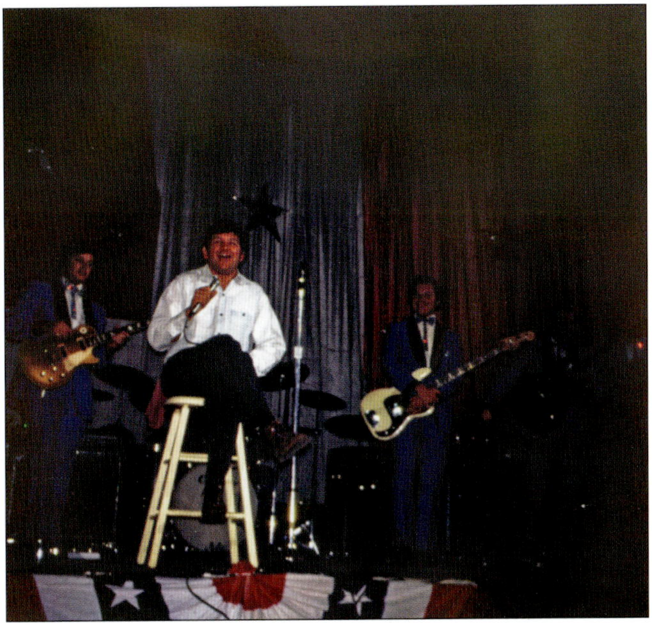

This photograph shows television star and Alabama native George Lindsey, best known as "Goober Pyle," during the Alabama Stars Show at the Coliseum in May 1973. In addition to his appearances at the Alabama Stars Show, Lindsey raised over $1 million for the Alabama Special Olympics during the 17 years he sponsored the George Lindsey Celebrity Weekend Golf Tournament in Montgomery. (Courtesy Landmarks Foundation.)

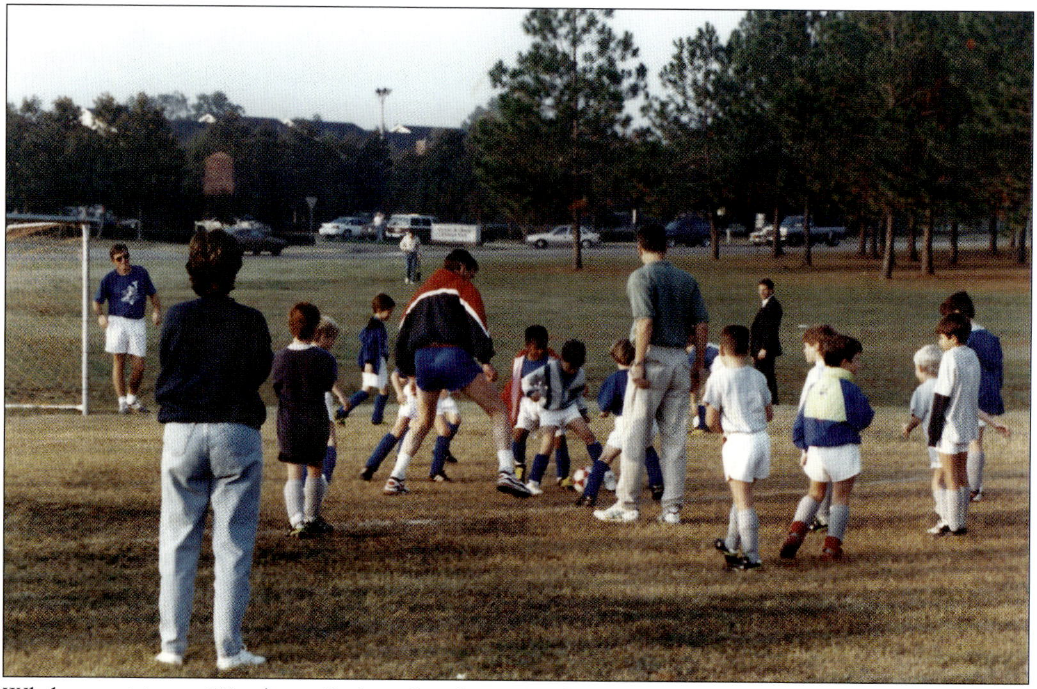

While practicing at Woodmere Park in October 1993, the Genpac soccer team acquired a temporary player when former president George H.W. Bush, who was visiting Montgomery and out on his morning run, joined in the action. (Courtesy Crowley family.)

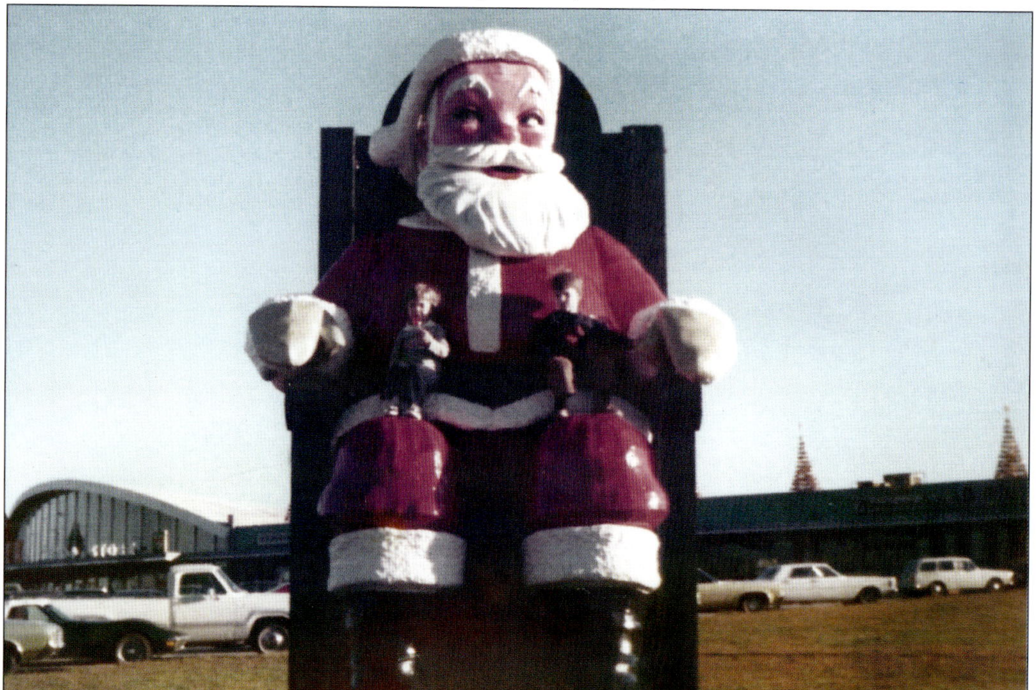

Matt Dickson and Allison Trego perch on a big Santa's lap at the Normandale Shopping Center in 1974. (Courtesy Faye Foster Singleton.)

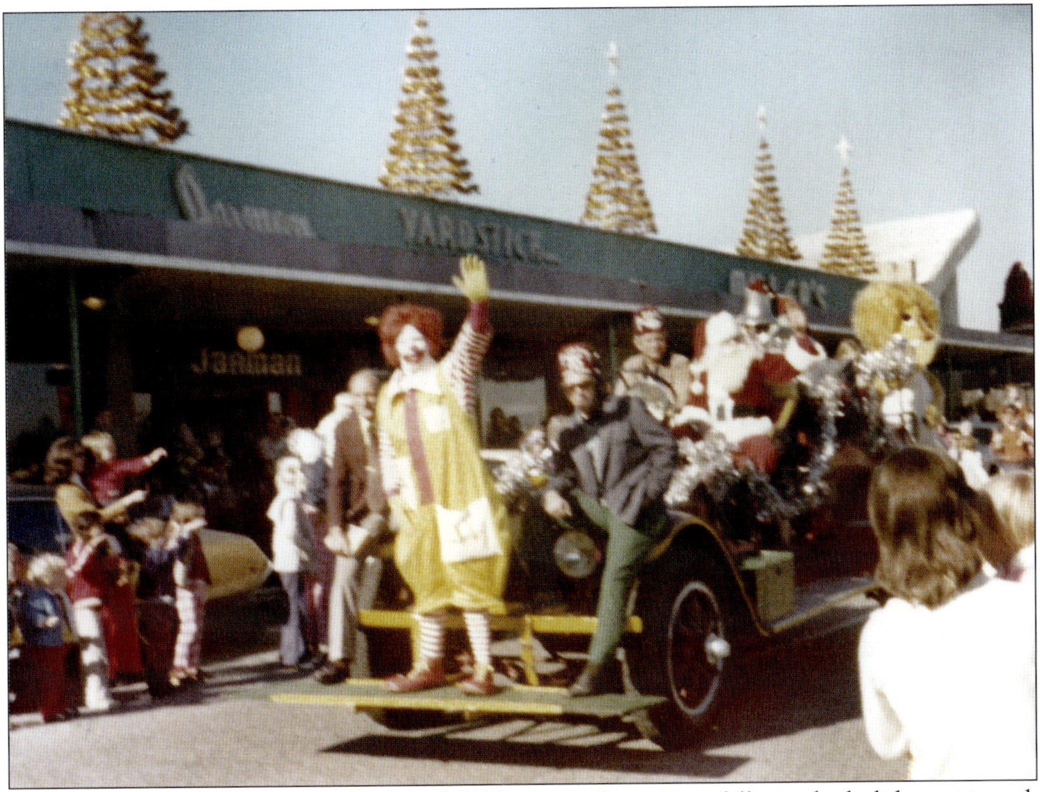

The 1974 Christmas parade in Normandale Shopping Center put folks in the holiday spirit and, merchants hoped, in a shopping mood. (Courtesy Faye Foster Singleton.)

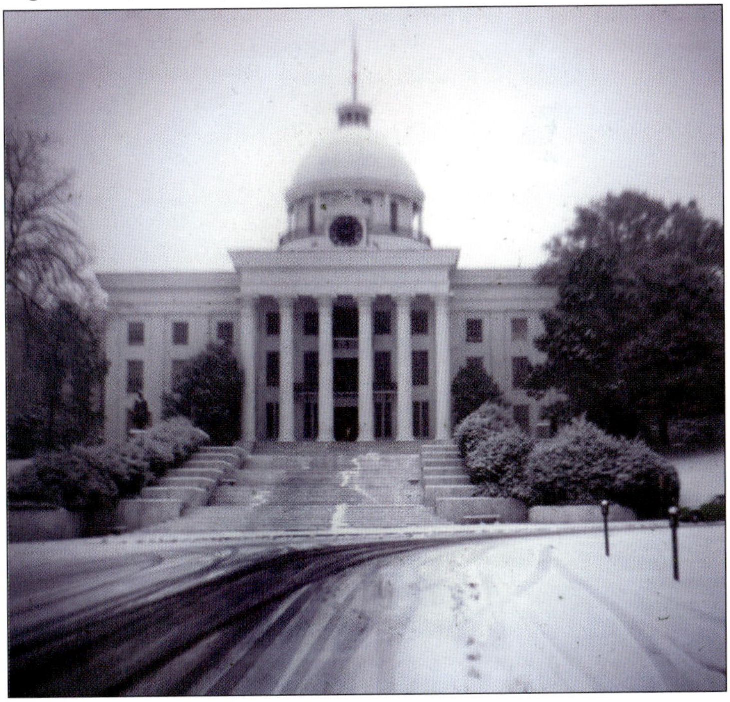

In March 1977, residents were surprised with snow. Here, the Alabama State Capitol remains elegant at the top of snowy "Goat Hill," the folk history name of Capitol Hill, where the capitol building stands. (Courtesy Landmarks Foundation.)

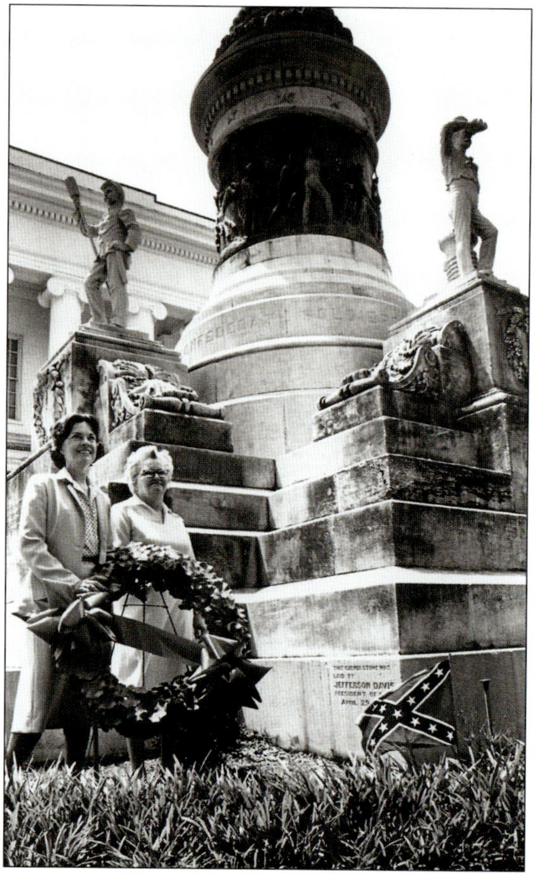

Anita Folmar (left) and Mrs. Edward H. Macon (right), both of the Sophie Bibb Chapter of the United Daughters of the Confederacy, lay a wreath to commemorate Confederate Memorial Day on April 26, 1978. The 88-foot monument on the grounds of the Alabama State Capitol was dedicated in 1898. (Courtesy *Montgomery Advertiser*.)

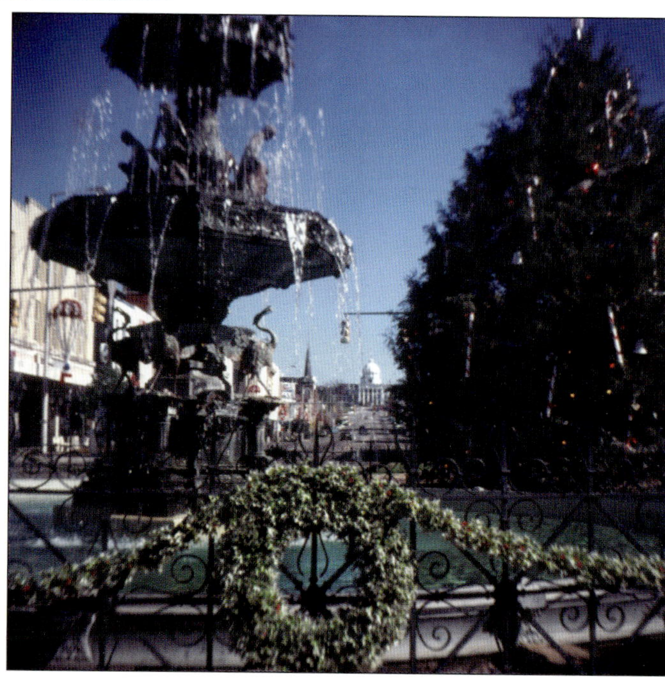

Here, Hebe enjoys Christmas decorations in December 1979. A Christmas tree on the capitol lawn and one at Court Square allow Dexter Avenue to begin and end with a lovely decorated tree. (Courtesy Landmarks Foundation.)

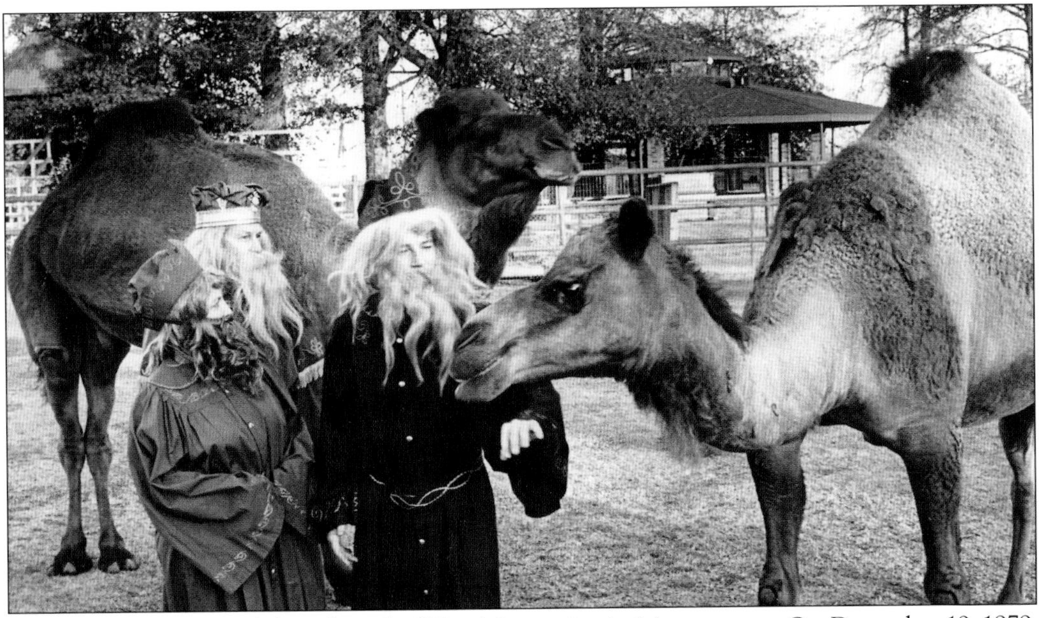

Certainly, it is a special day when the Wise Men arrive in Montgomery. On December 19, 1979, zookeepers, from left to right, Mike McGough, David Sangster, and Mark Ratliff, costumed for the Montgomery Zoo Christmas program, pose with camels, who needed no costume. (Courtesy *Montgomery Advertiser.*)

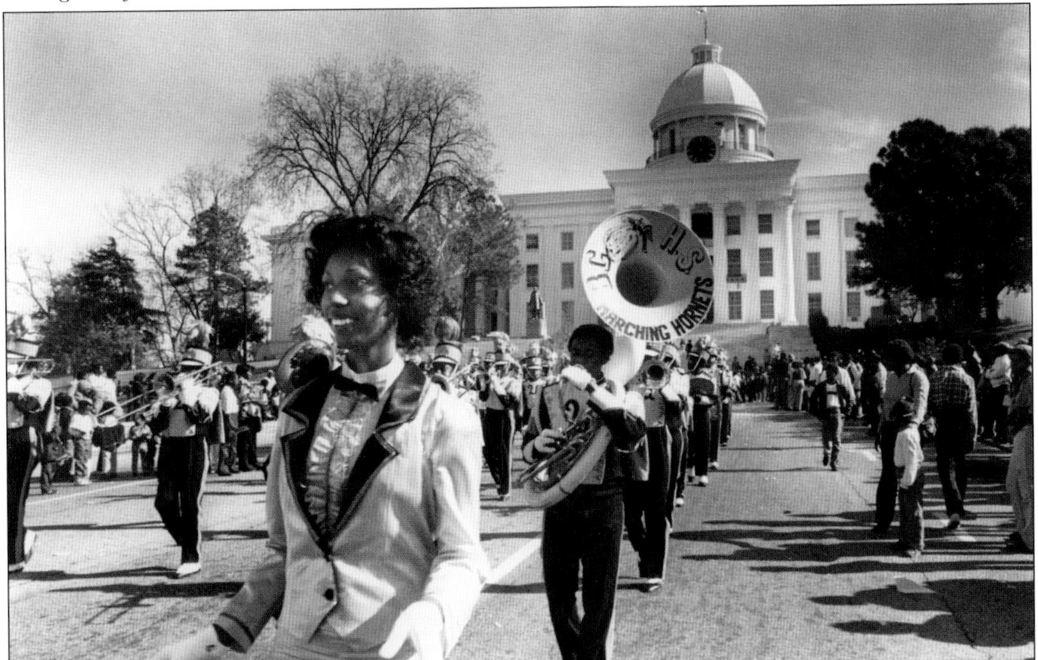

The annual Turkey Day Classic Parade was held the morning of the football game between Alabama State University and Tuskegee Institute. In this photograph from November 26, 1981, the Marching Hornets Band struts down Dexter Avenue from the capitol building. (Courtesy *Montgomery Advertiser.*)

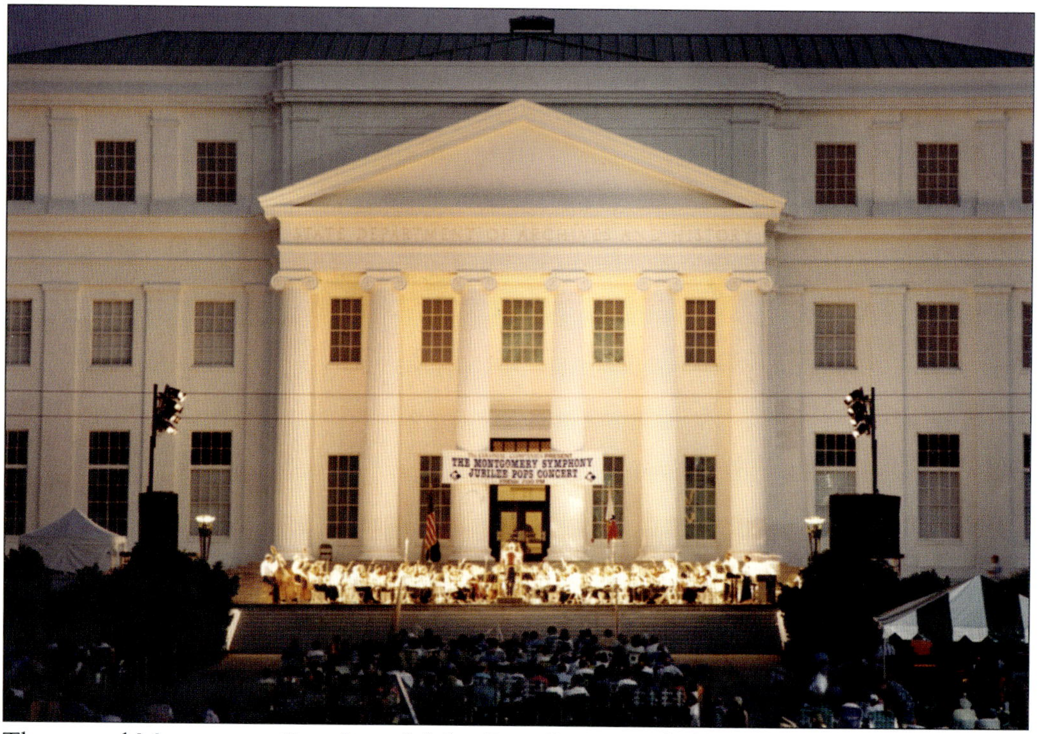

The annual Montgomery Symphony Jubilee Pops Concert is held on the steps of the Alabama Department of Archives and History Building. The event serves as the kickoff to Memorial Day weekend. The 2013–2014 season of the Montgomery Symphony Orchestra marked Maestro Thomas Hinds's 31st year on the MSO podium as musical director and conductor. (Courtesy *Montgomery Advertiser*.)

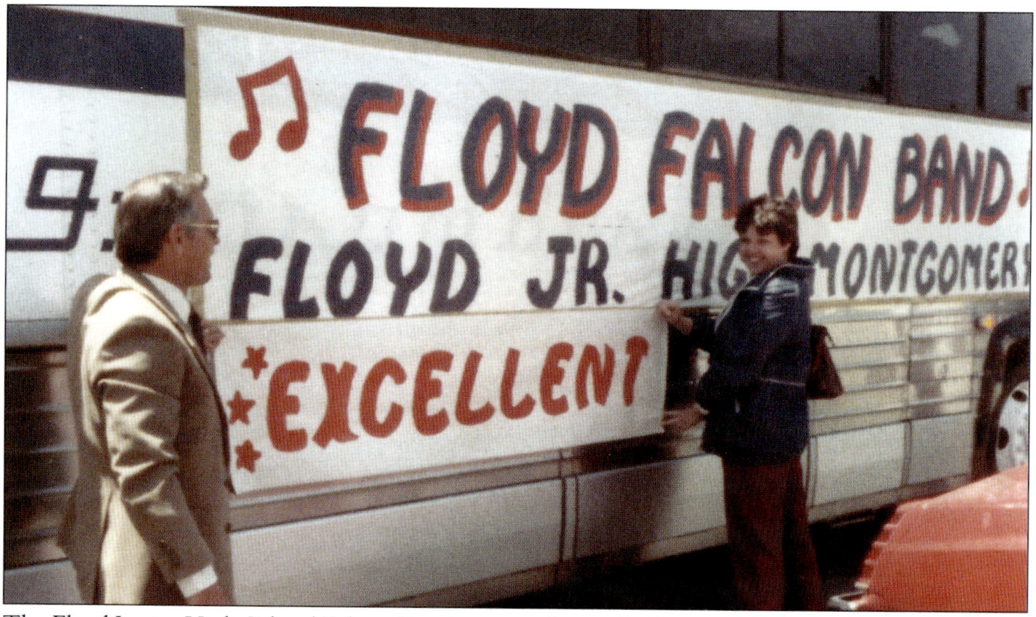

The Floyd Junior High School Falcon Band returns from a 1982 competition at which they earned the rating of "Excellent," as seen on the side of their bus. (Courtesy Faye Foster Singleton.)

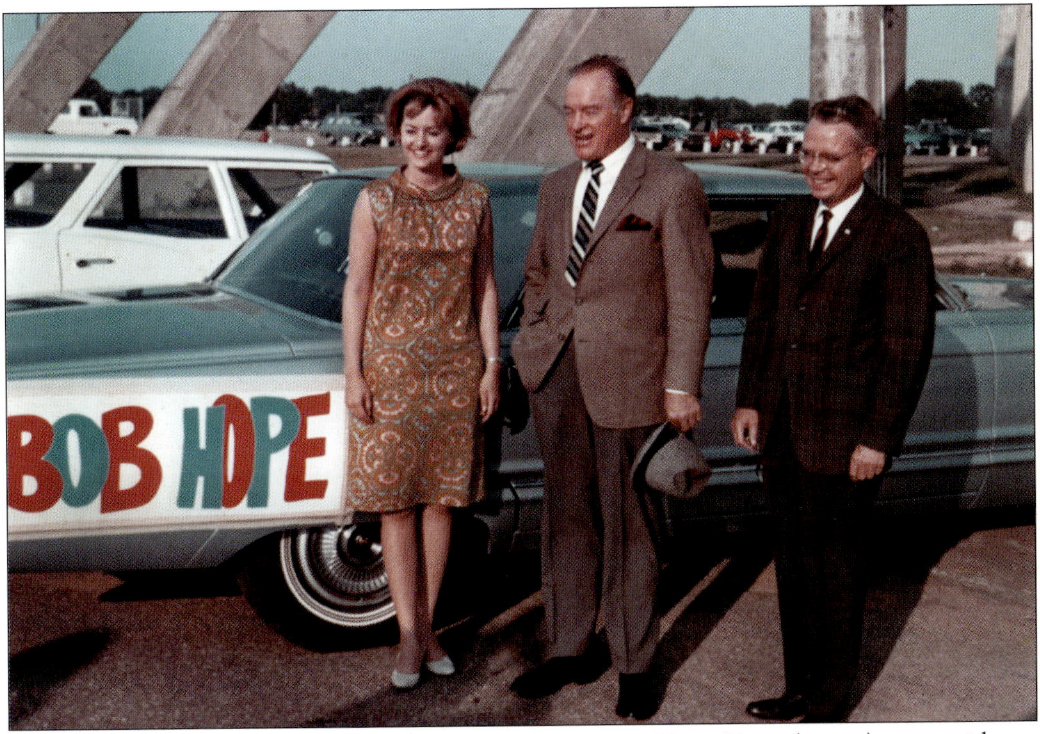

Bob Hope often visited Montgomery for his charity event. Here, Hope (center) poses with car dealership owner J.L "Jimmy" Rouse and an unidentified woman. Note the base of the Coliseum in the background. (Courtesy Rouse family.)

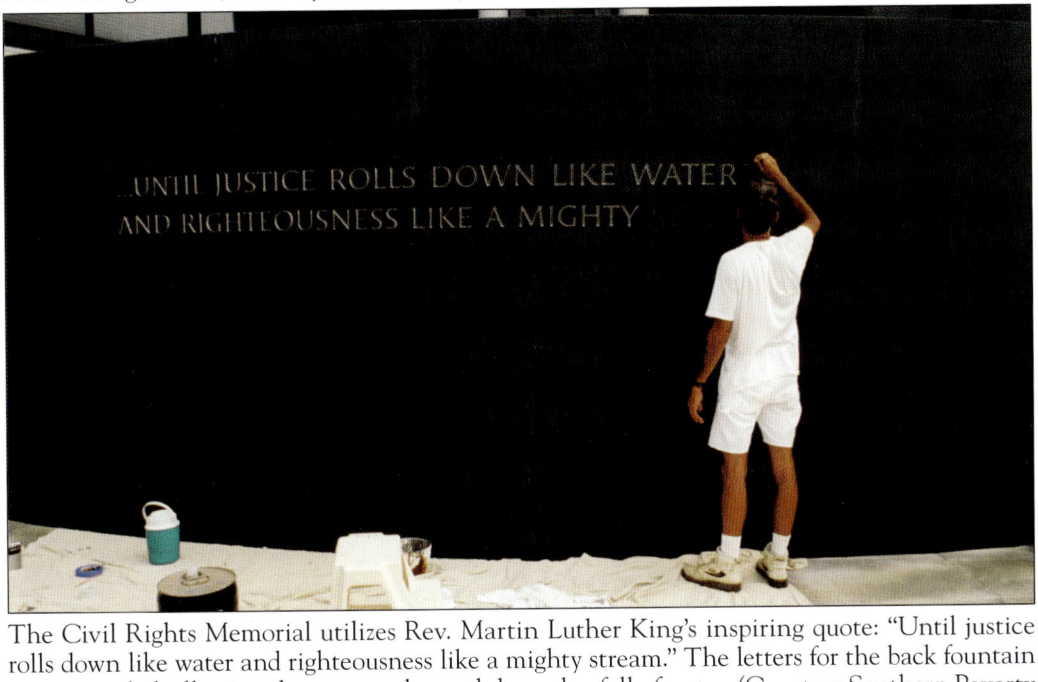

The Civil Rights Memorial utilizes Rev. Martin Luther King's inspiring quote: "Until justice rolls down like water and righteousness like a mighty stream." The letters for the back fountain were stenciled, allowing the quote to be read through a fall of water. (Courtesy Southern Poverty Law Center.)

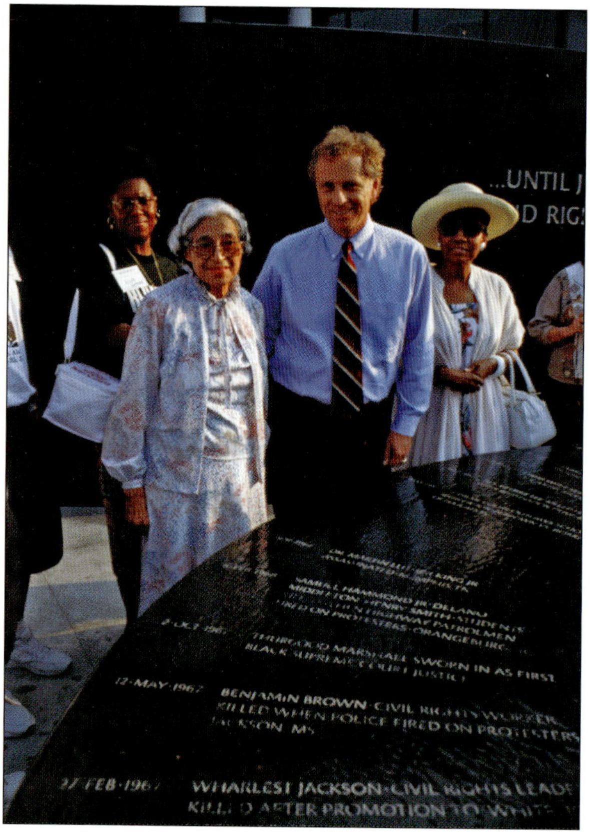

The Civil Rights Memorial was dedicated in 1989. Many dignitaries attended the ceremony. Standing closest to the monument are civil rights pioneer Rosa Parks and Southern Poverty Law Center founder Morris Dees. (Courtesy Alabama Department of Archives and History.)

The Civil Rights Memorial honors the achievements and memory of those who died during the civil rights movement. The names on the granite are specifically from 1954 to 1968. These years were also chosen for their special significance: in 1954, the US Supreme Court ruled against school segregation, and 1968 marked the assassination of Dr. Martin Luther King. The Civil Rights Memorial is located at 400 Washington Avenue, across the street from the Southern Poverty Law Center. It is open to the public 24 hours a day, seven days a week. (Courtesy Southern Poverty Law Center.)

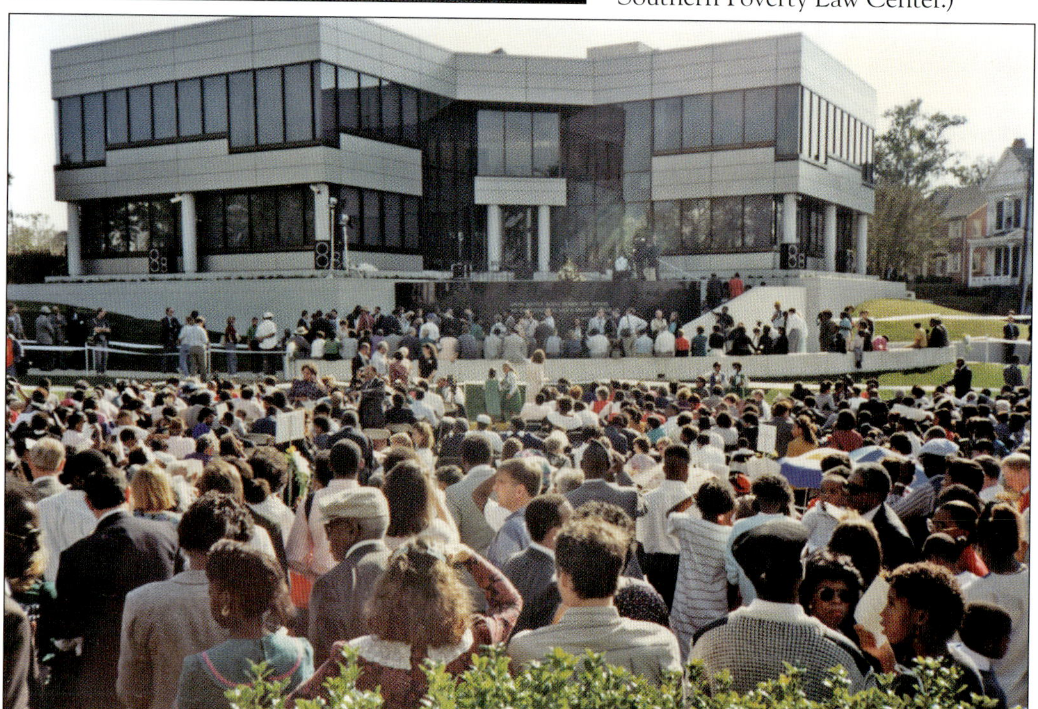

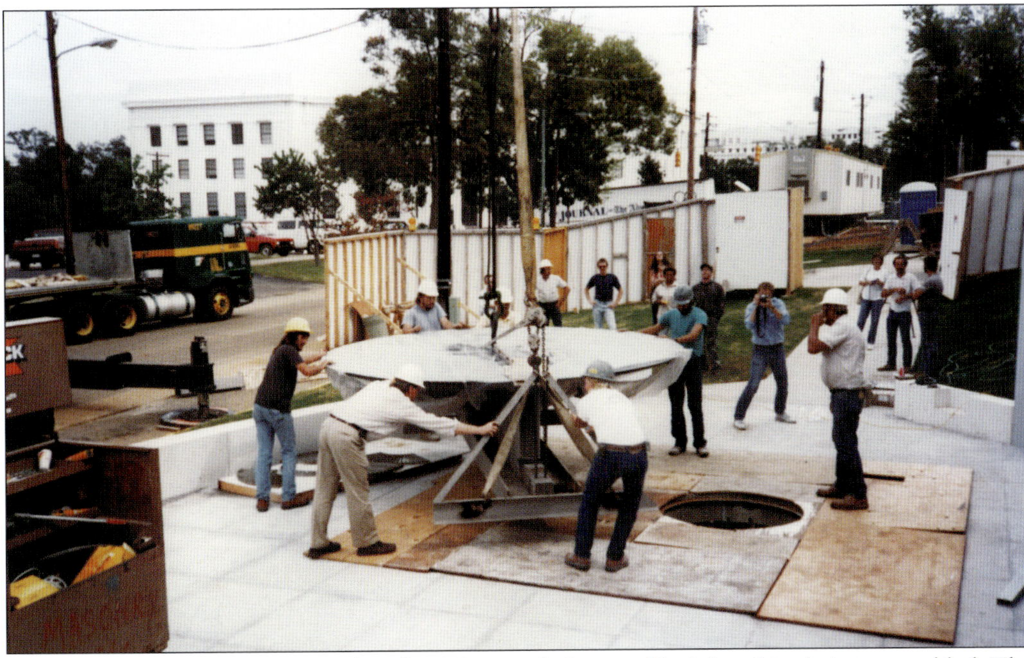

This photograph shows the Civil Rights Memorial, designed by Maya Lin, being assembled. The base, shown here, encourages visitor interaction. As the water pours over the black granite and the names of those who gave their lives in the civil rights struggle, visitors can place their hands on the names. (Courtesy Southern Poverty Law Center.)

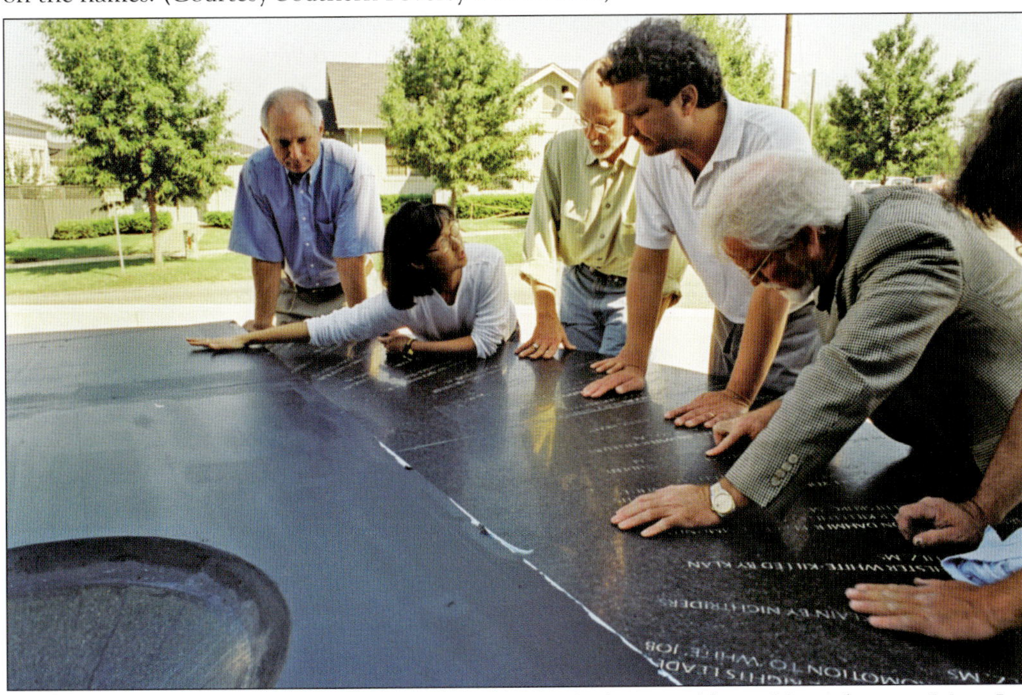

In 1995, the Civil Rights Memorial developed water leakage problems. Here, designer Maya Lin (second from left) discusses repair plans with administrators at the Southern Poverty Law Center. (Courtesy Southern Poverty Law Center.)

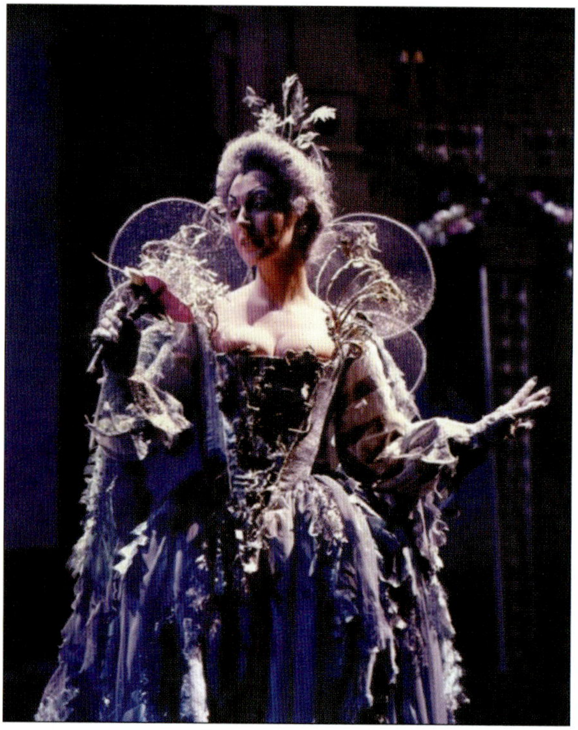

In 1985, the Alabama Shakespeare Festival's first production in its new theater at the Wynton M. Blount Cultural Park featured Montgomery's most popular actress, Greta Lambert, as Titania in William Shakespeare's *A Midsummer Night's Dream*. (Courtesy Greta Lambert and Alabama Shakespeare Festival.)

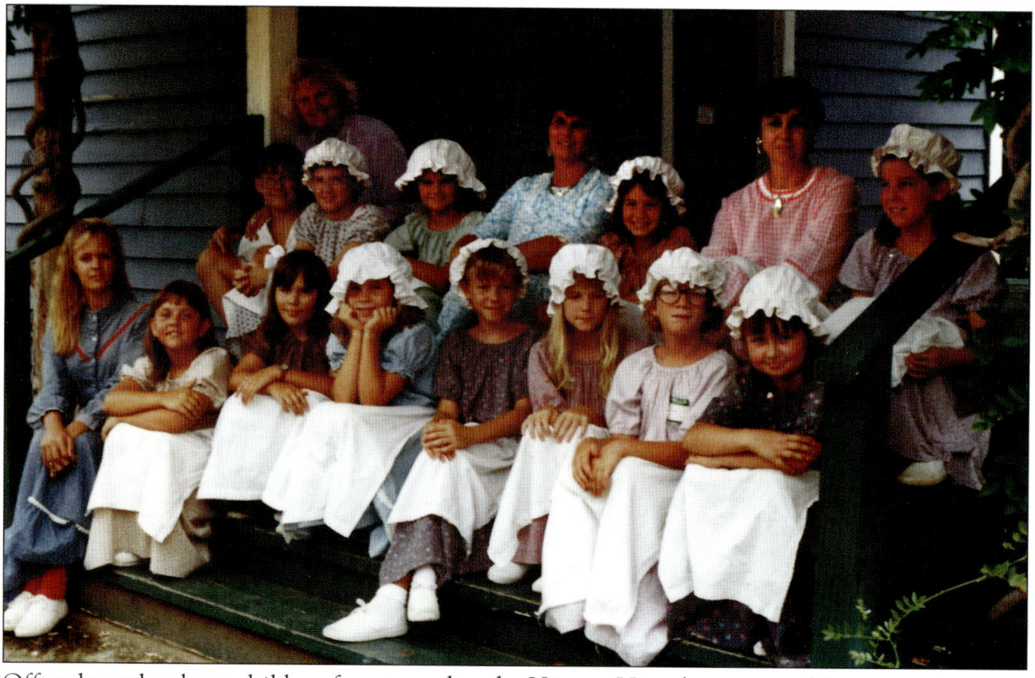

Offered to school-age children for over a decade, History Hurrah was a weeklong summer camp that explored historical tradition. This late-1980s photograph shows a collection of happy campers sitting on the steps of the Dogtrot building. They are dressed in 19th-century attire. Of these smiling faces, only two people are identified: at far left in the back row is Anneé Caspari, and at far left in the first row is her granddaughter Rachel Caspari. (Courtesy Landmarks Foundation.)

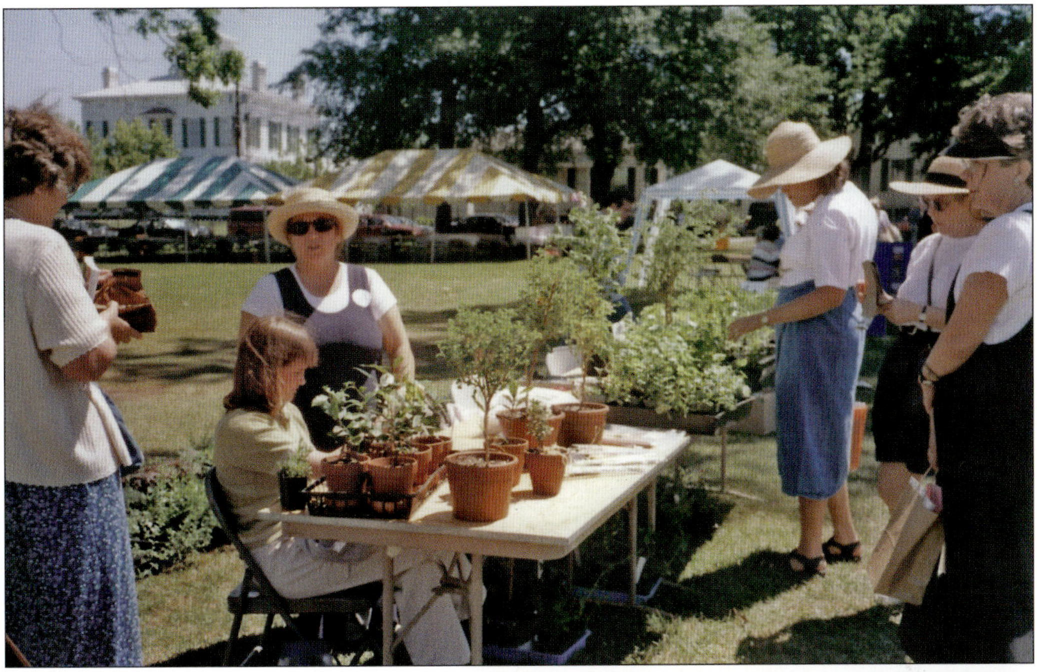

In 1999, the popular Herb Day began in Kiwanis Park, in Old Alabama Town. It later moved to the Living Block of Old Alabama Town. The Old Alabama Town Herb Society (OATHS) sponsors the annual event, which offers herbs, plants, and garden accessories for sale, along with workshops and vendor advice. (Courtesy Landmarks Foundation.)

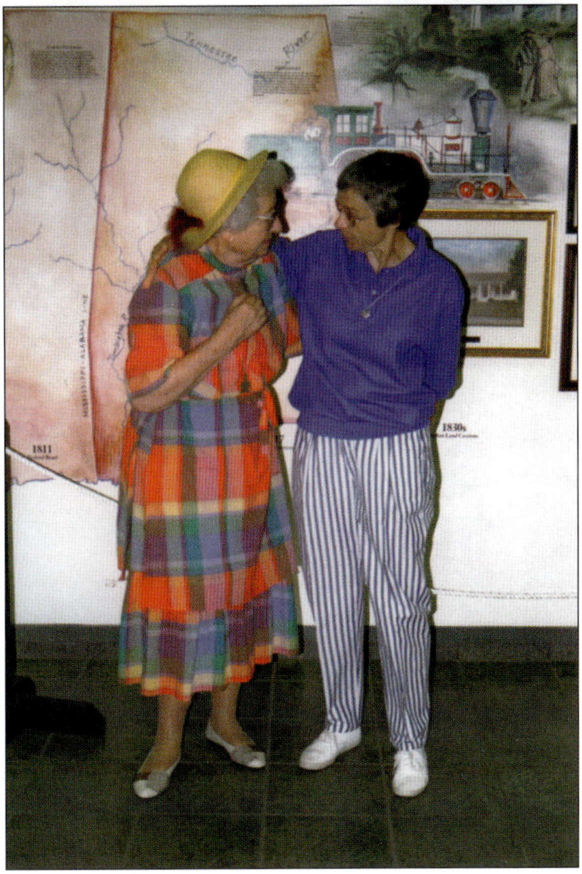

The Old Alabama Town and Landmarks Foundation hosted a storytelling festival at Old Alabama Town in 1999. This photograph shows two of the most established historians and storytellers in Alabama, Kathryn Tucker Windham (left) and Mary Ann Neeley (right). (Courtesy Landmarks Foundation.)

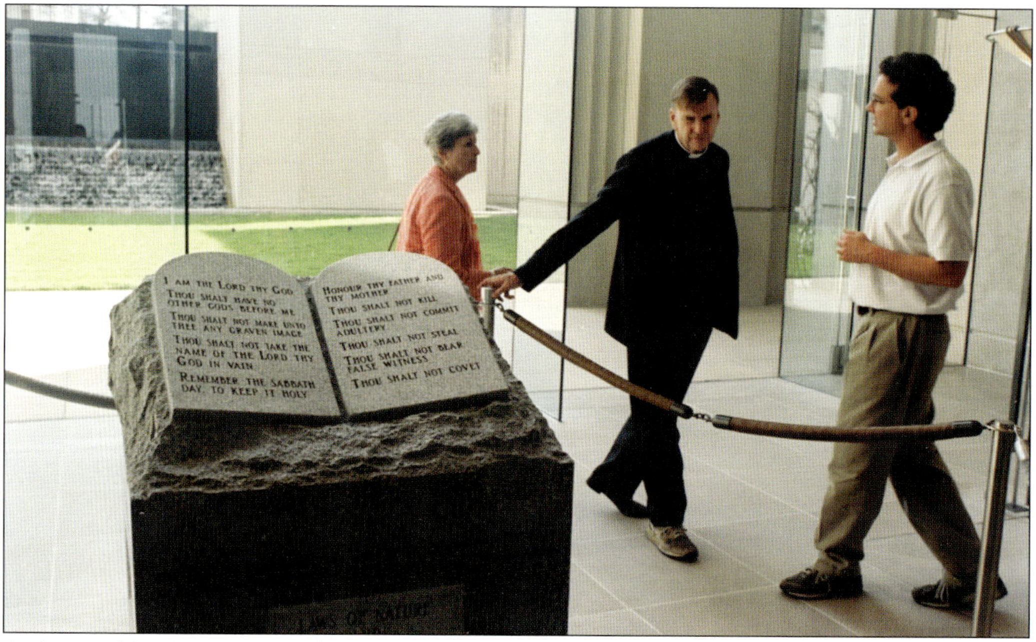

In August 2003, Roy Moore, chief justice of the Alabama Supreme Court, refused a federal court order to remove the Ten Commandments monument that he had placed in the Alabama Judicial Building. A federal judge cited the monument's placement as a violation of the separation of church and state. The monument was removed. Richard Cohen (right) of the Southern Poverty Law Center is pictured here with an unidentified clergyman. (Courtesy Southern Poverty Law Center.)

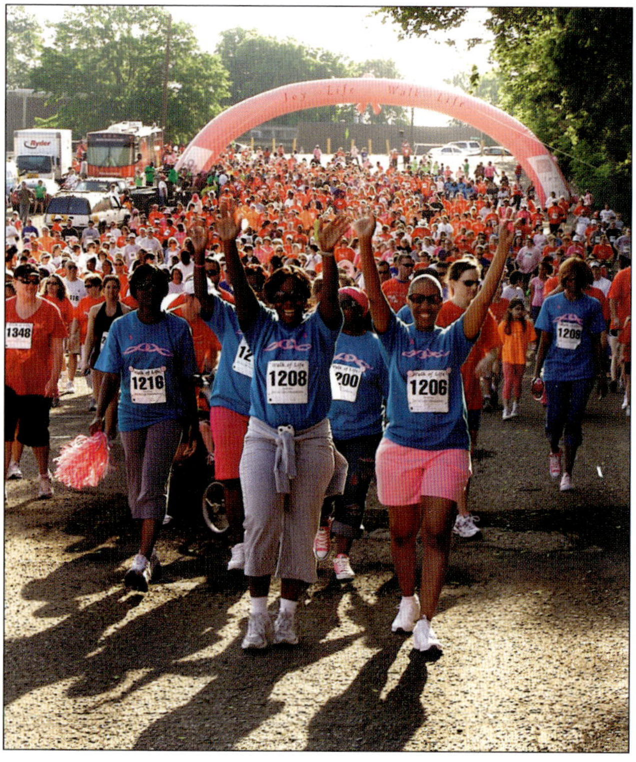

Breast cancer survivor Joy Blondheim and her husband, Dickie Blondheim, established the Joy to Life Foundation in 2001. Their mission is to provide free mammograms to underserved women in Alabama and to increase breast cancer awareness. Thanks to Joy to Life, over 10,000 mammograms have been provided, and over 80 women have been successfully treated. Each year, the community has great fun participating in the Walk of Life. Held downtown in April, the event includes a 5K run/walk, as well as a kids' dash. After the race, participants gather at Riverfront Park for a party featuring entertainment, food, and vendors. (Courtesy Dreemz Production and Joy to Life Foundation.)

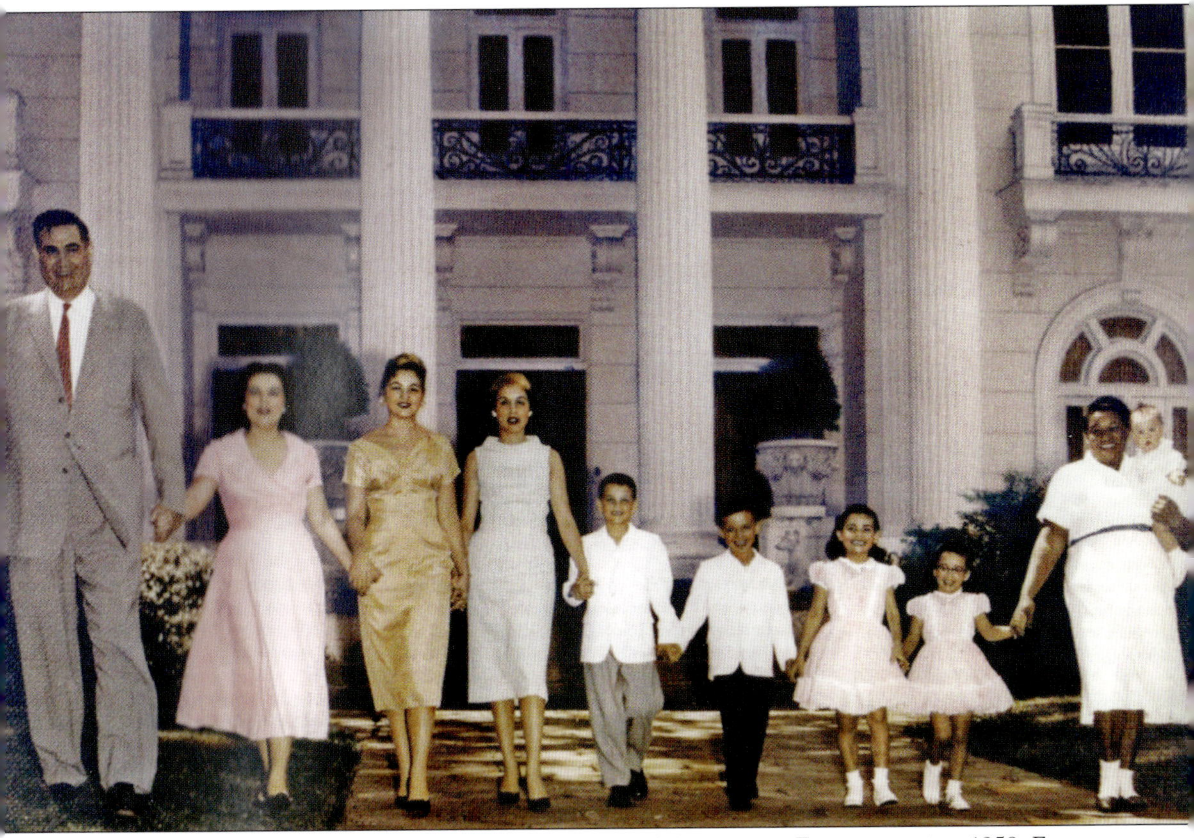

Alabama's first family poses in front of the Governor's Mansion on Easter morning 1958. From left to right are Governor James "Big Jim" Folsom, Janielle Moore Folsom, Rachel, Melissa, James Elisha Jr., Andrew Jackson, Jamelle Alabama, Thelma Ebelene, and Joshua Melvin, held by an unidentified caregiver. (Courtesy Alabama Department of Archives and History.)

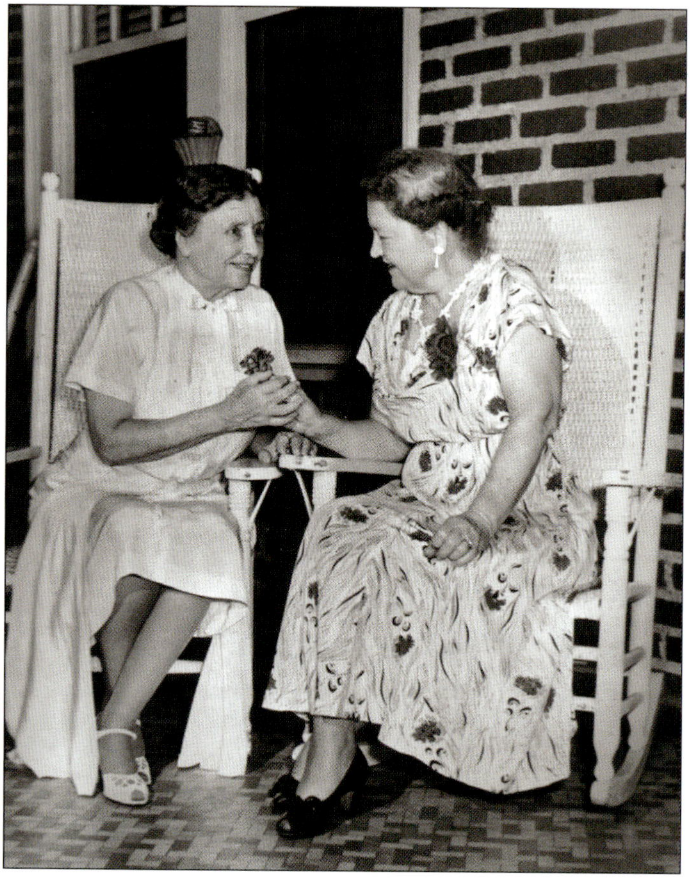

Events are special times, but people's lives are lived from day to day. Helen Keller (left) and her sister, Mildred Keller Tyson, sit on the front porch of 831 Felder Avenue in 1955. Helen, a frequent visitor, enjoyed the company of her nieces, Mildred's three daughters, Patty, Mildred, and Katherine. (Courtesy Leslie McPhillips.)

Everyday traffic moves along Bainbridge Street in front of the Alabama State Capitol. The bus in this late-1950s photograph is an example of those used during the Montgomery Bus Boycott, when Rosa Parks refused to give up her seat. (Courtesy Landmarks Foundation.)

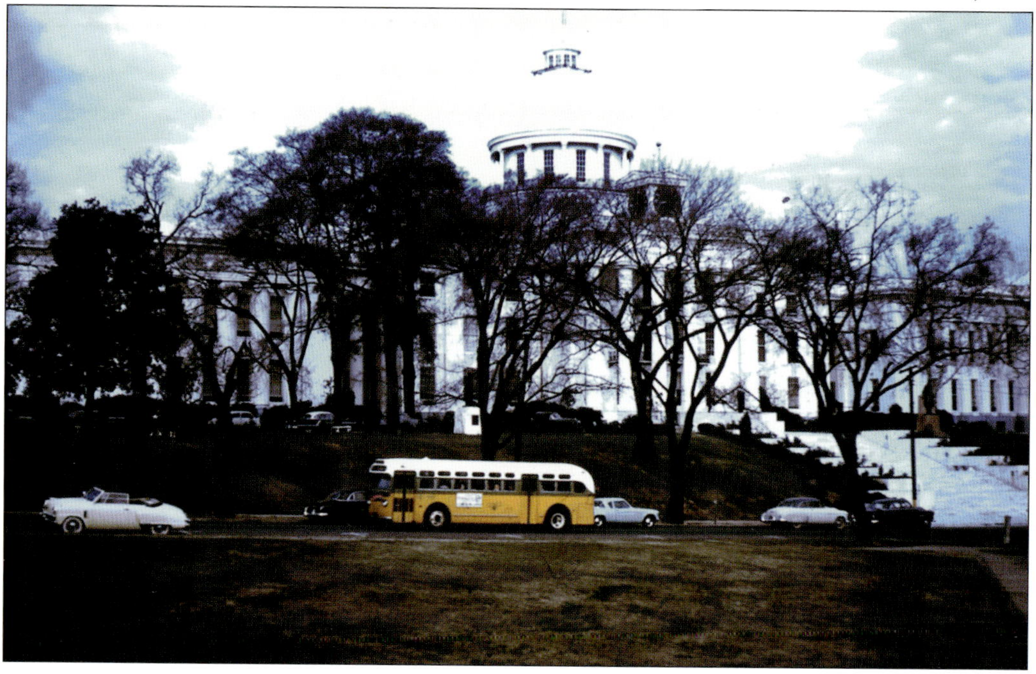

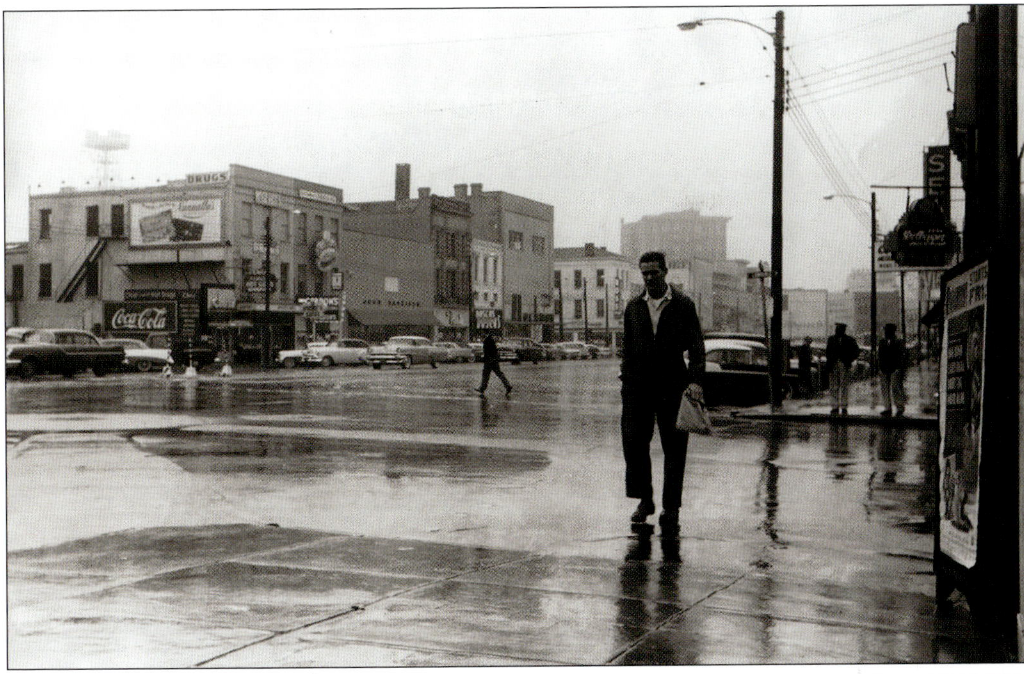

This photograph of a rainy day in the late 1950s shows Montgomery residents going about daily routines on the corner of Dexter Avenue and Lawrence Street. Across the street, note Chris' Hot Dogs and the wedding rings on the facade of the 19th-century building next door. (Courtesy Landmarks Foundation.)

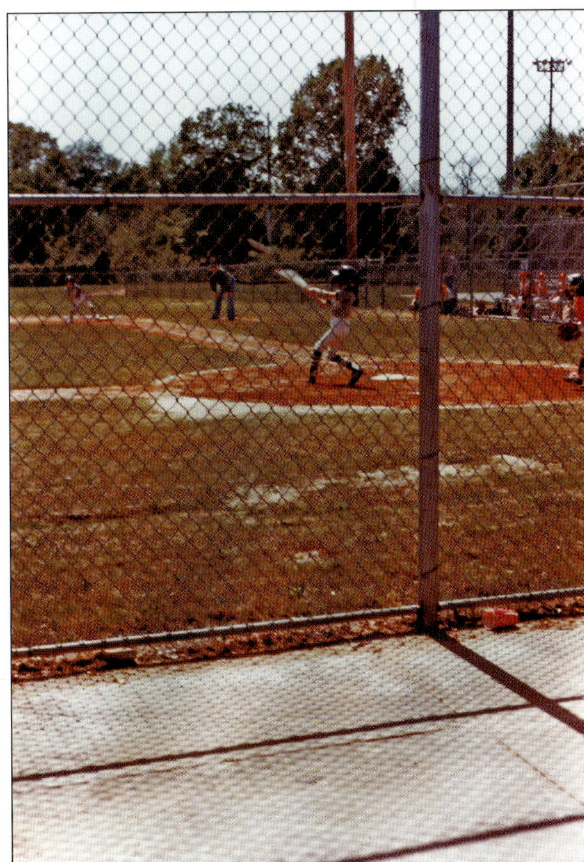

The campus of Auburn University at Montgomery (AUM) moved to its current location in 1971. The school's community outreach includes hosting various teams on the AUM ball fields. Here, the Dixie Youth Ball Team plays a game on the AUM baseball field in 1983. Peter Crowley is up at bat. (Courtesy Crowley family.)

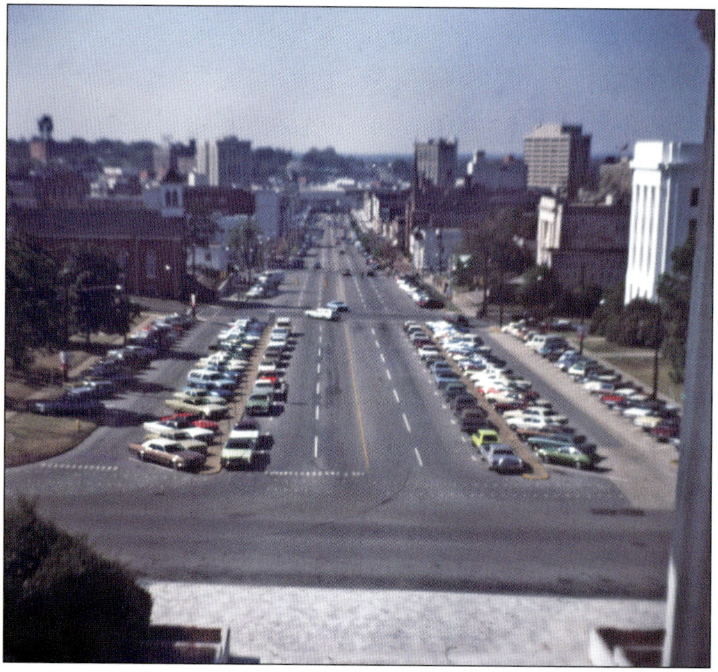

This photograph shows a view of Dexter Avenue from the third floor of the capitol building in November 1976. (Courtesy Landmarks Foundation.)

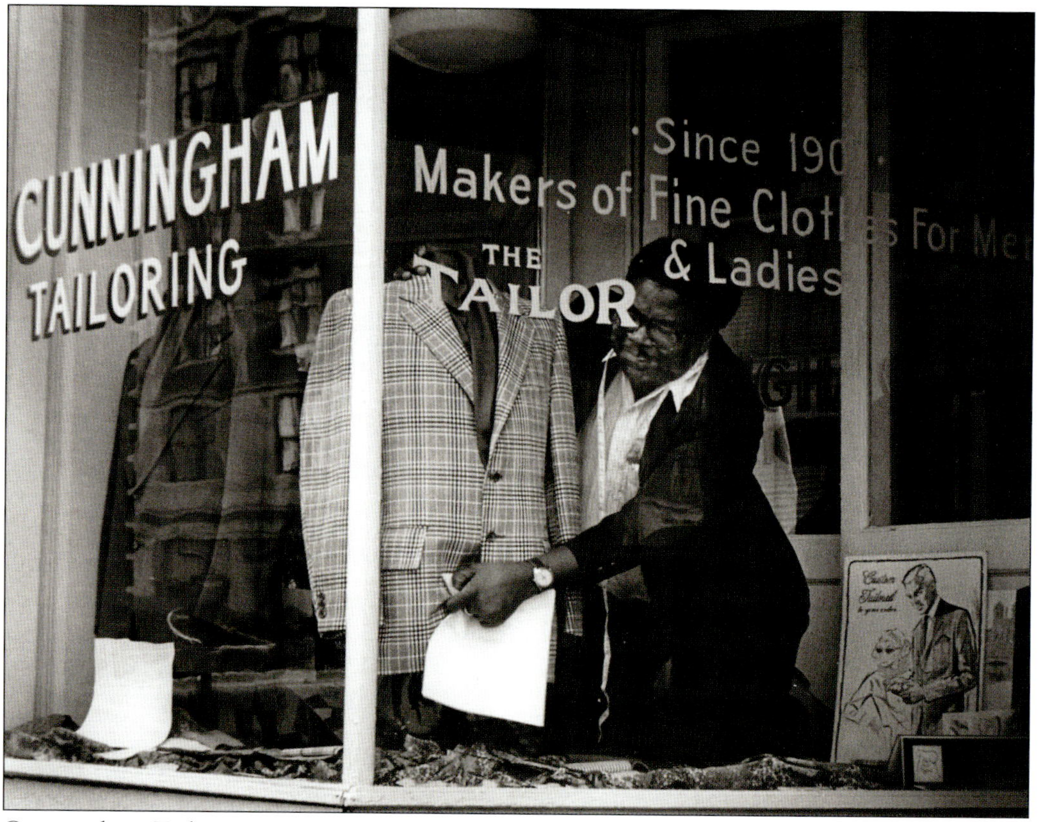

Cunningham Tailors maintained a long-established business on Lee Street, as seen here in 1980. (Courtesy *Montgomery Advertiser*.)

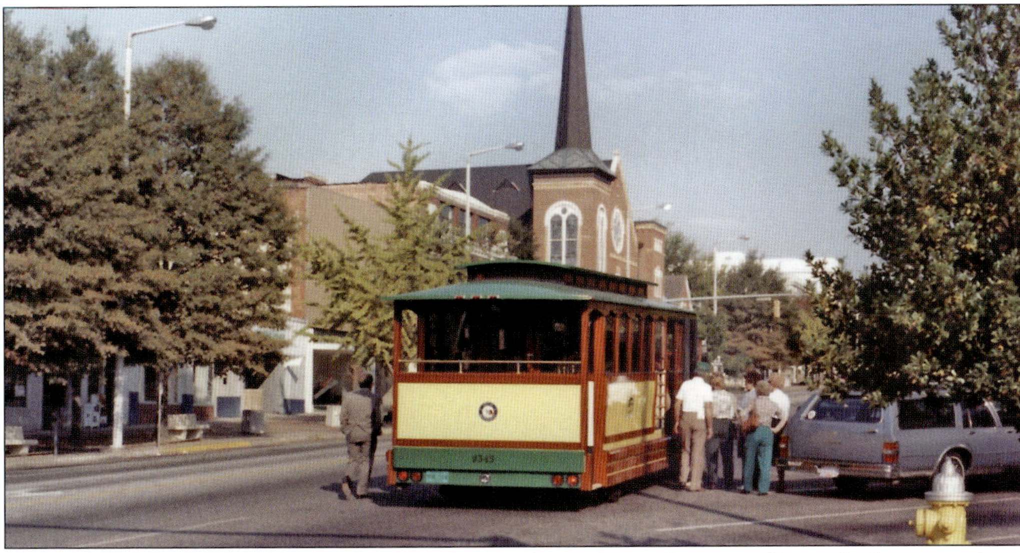

In 1885, Montgomery became the first city in America to have electric trolleys, which were replaced with buses in 1936. In recognition of the trolley's centennial in 1985, a diesel reproduction of the original trolley was reintroduced for downtown transportation. The trolley remained a popular way to get around downtown until the service was retired again in 2014. (Courtesy Landmarks Foundation.)

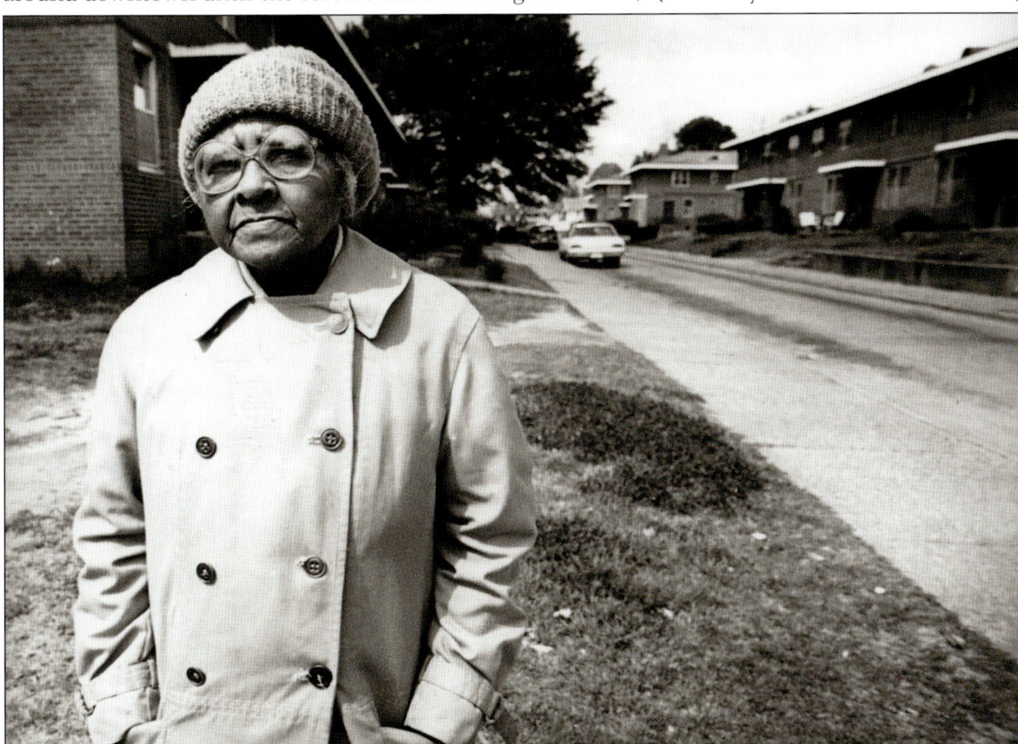

On May 4, 1987, the *Montgomery Advertiser* published an article on the Cleveland Court Federal Housing Project. This photograph of Imener Davis, a resident, standing in front of Cleveland Court accompanied the article. Cleveland Court was home to civil rights pioneer Rosa Parks from 1951 to 1957. (Courtesy *Montgomery Advertiser.*)

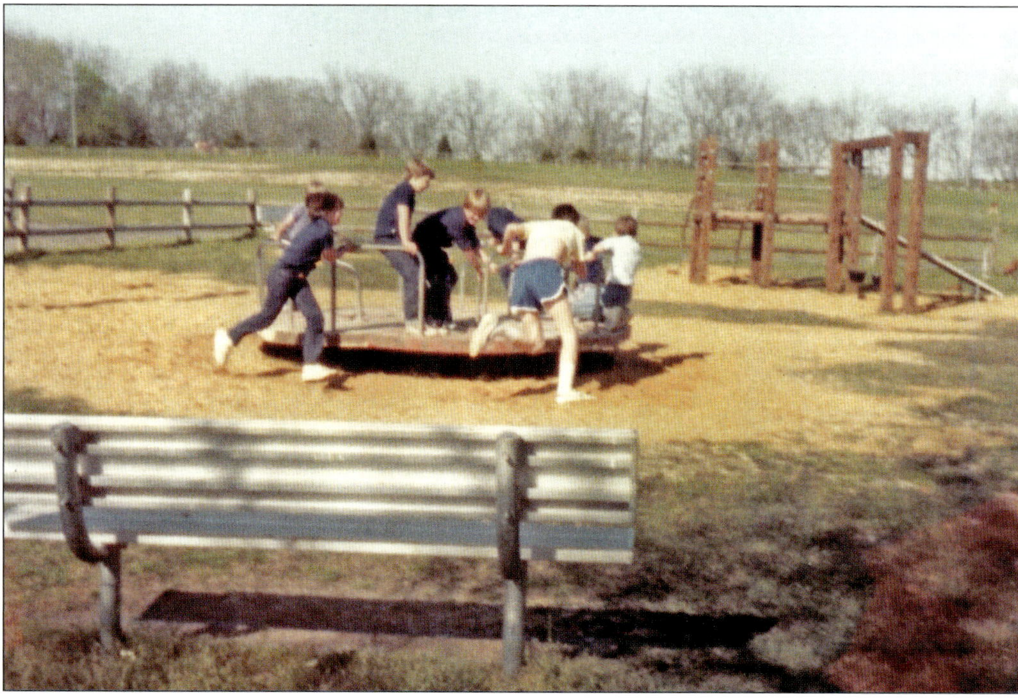

Michael Foster (left) and Keith Hildebrand (right) spin other children on the roundabout, or merry-go-round, at Vaughn Road Park in the late 1980s. (Courtesy Faye Foster Singleton.)

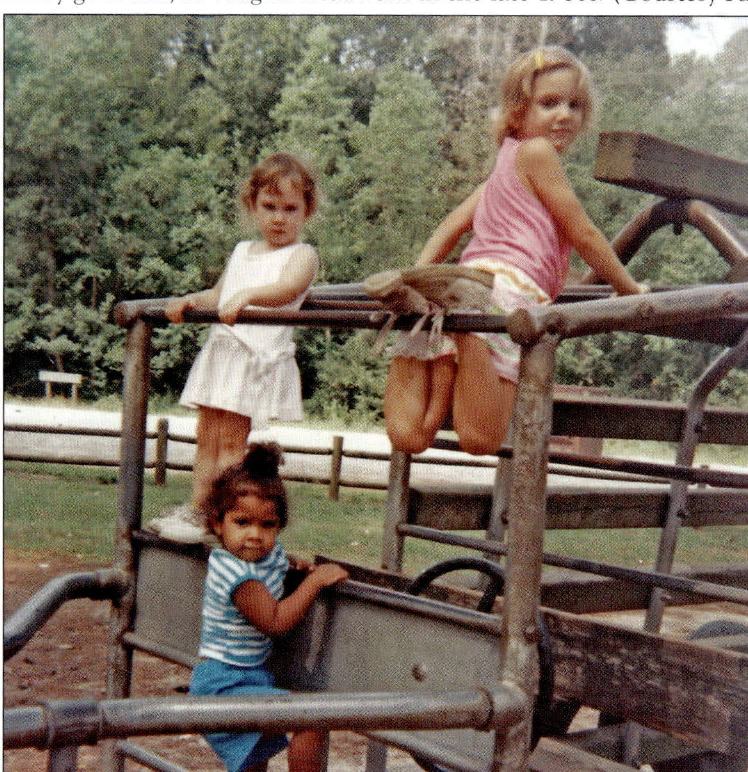

In this 1990 photograph, a group of children play at Lagoon Park. (Courtesy Crowley family.)

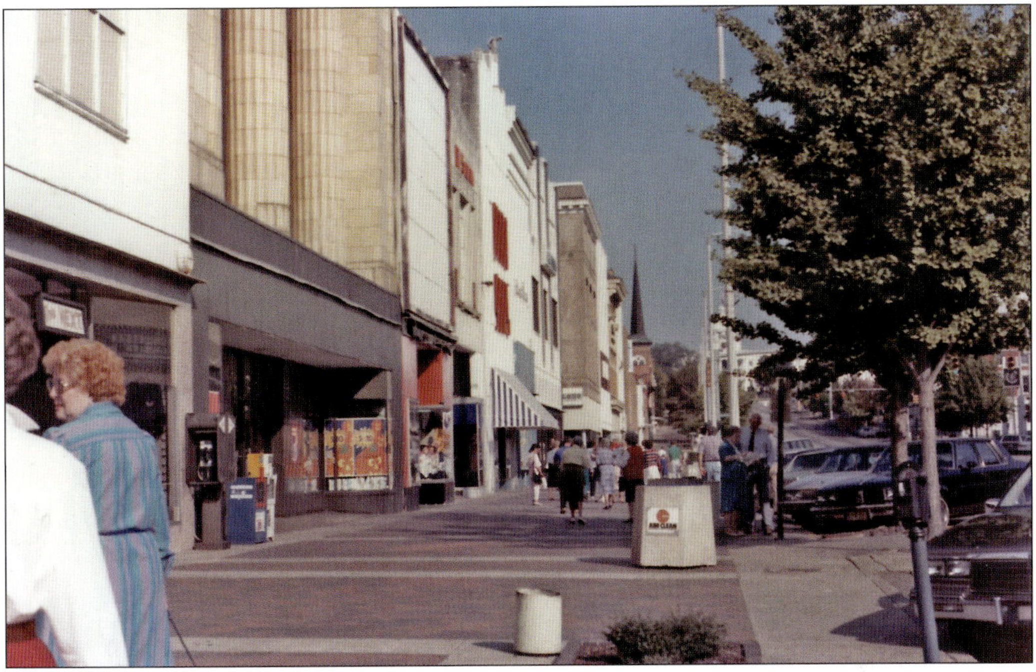

This 1990s street scene shows shoppers and visitors walking down Dexter Avenue on a sunny Alabama day. Note the pay phone at left and the capitol building peeking from under the tree limbs at right. (Courtesy Landmarks Foundation.)

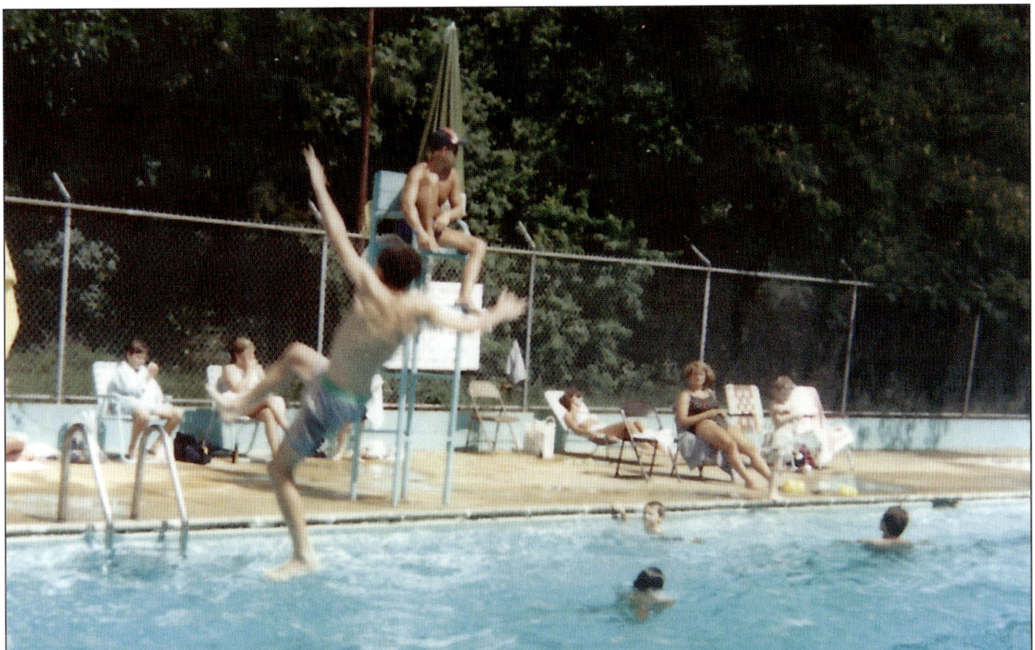

The YMCA has a long history in Montgomery. The first building was constructed in 1906 on Washington Avenue as a residence for men and boys. The YMCA grew and changed with the times and the needs of Montgomery's community. In this 1990 photograph, Peter Crowley gleefully jumps into the pool at East YMCA. (Courtesy Crowley family.)

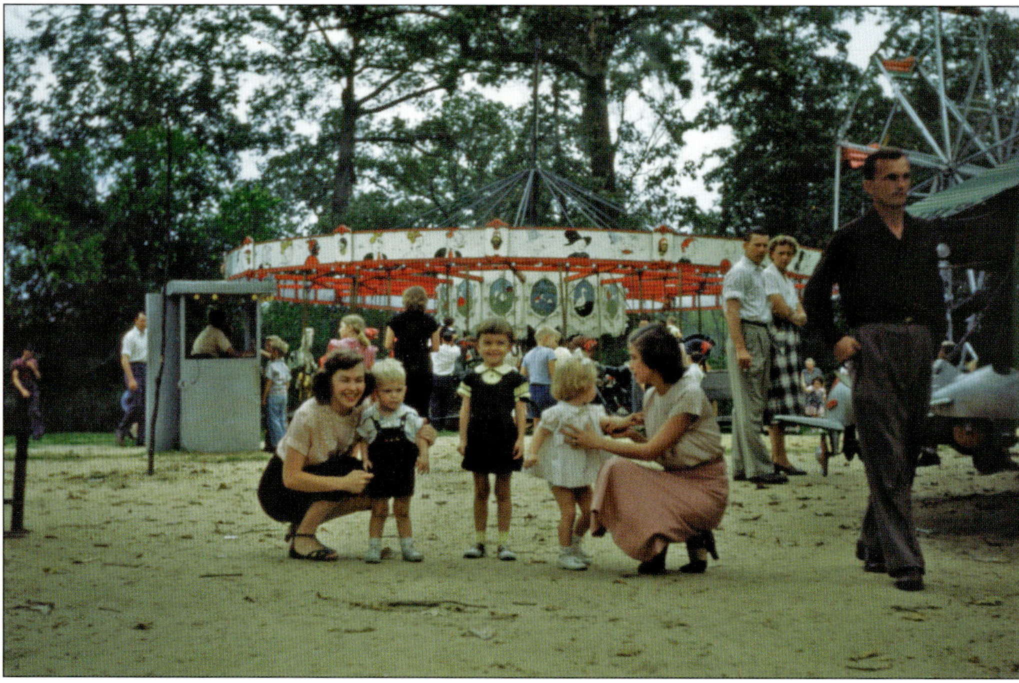

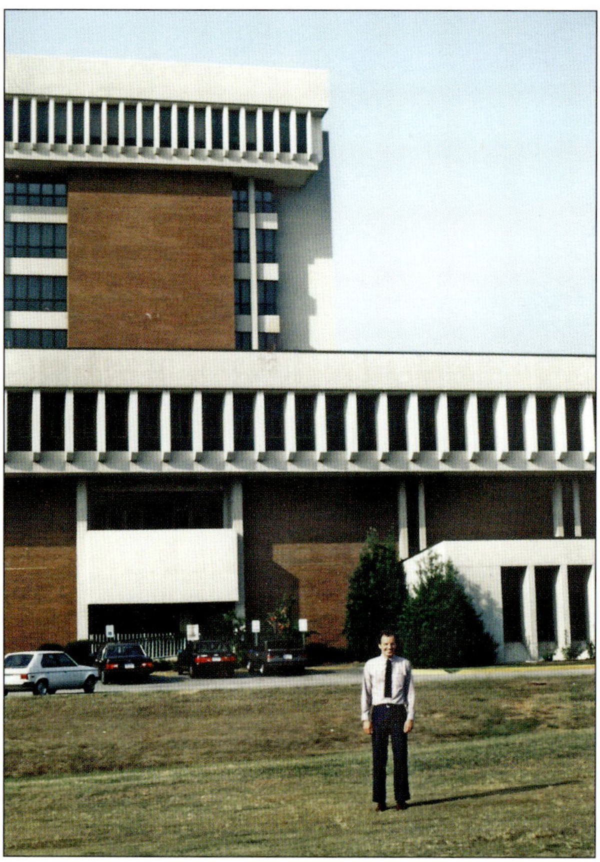

Oak Park was a favorite place for family fun. Shown here in front of the carousel in 1950 are, from left to right, Billie Radford and her daughter Barbara Radford, Vicki Shoults, Randy Shoults, and their mother, Betty Shoults. Vicki and Randy's father, Charlie Shoults, took the photograph. (Courtesy Randy Shoults.)

The 10-story Ida Belle Young Library Tower is an iconic structure on the campus of Auburn University at Montgomery. This 1991 photograph shows Dr. Joe Crowley in front of the AUM Library Tower. (Courtesy Crowley family.)

Four

Sleep and Eats

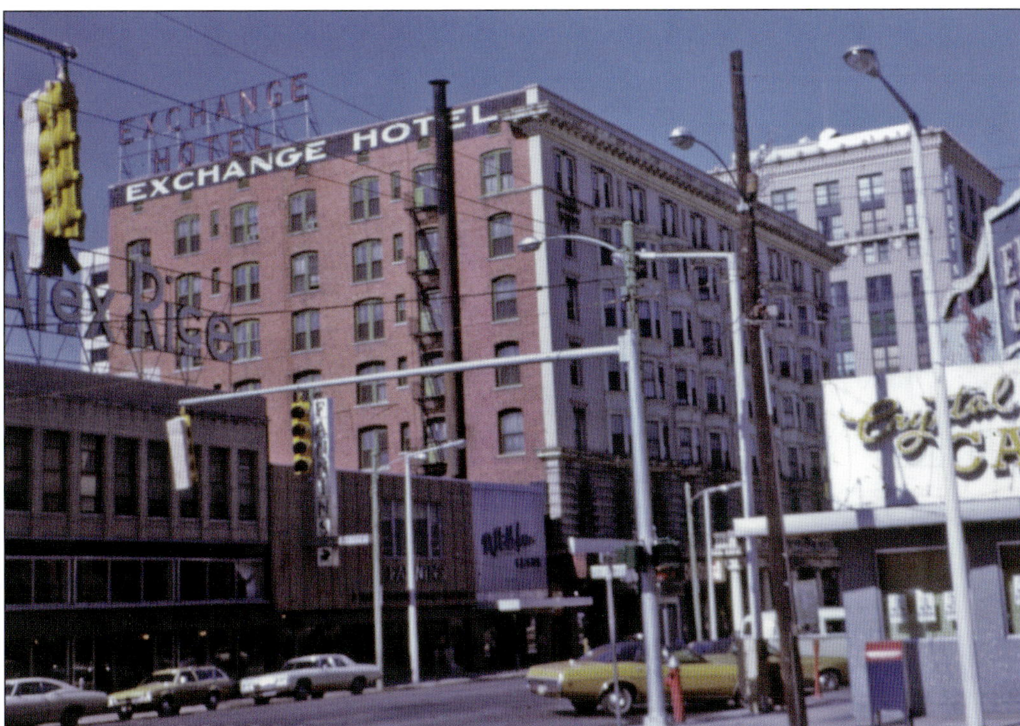

The first Exchange Hotel, built in 1846, is famously known as the residence of Confederate president Jefferson Davis and his wife, Varina, when they first moved to Montgomery. The hotel also provided meeting space for the early Confederate government. In 1905, the old Exchange Hotel was torn down, and the new Exchange Hotel (pictured) served for many years as a popular gathering place for travelers and politicians. The hotel was demolished in 1974, not long after this photograph was taken. Note the popular Elite Café. (Courtesy Landmarks Foundation.)

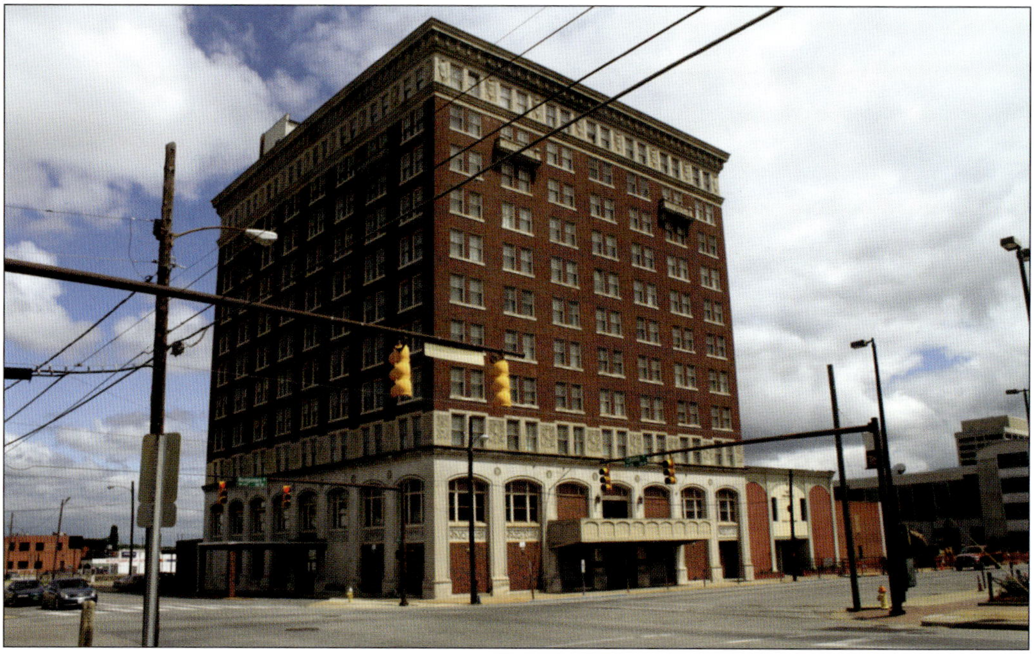

Built by prominent Montgomery architect Frederick Ausfeld in 1928, the Jefferson Davis Hotel remained a popular destination for tourists and business travelers through the 1960s. A 1950s postcard advertised the hotel as a "Dispenser of True Southern Hospitality," with "Two Hundred Fifty Rooms and Two Hundred and Fifty Baths." Today, it functions as subsidized apartments. (Courtesy Landmarks Foundation.)

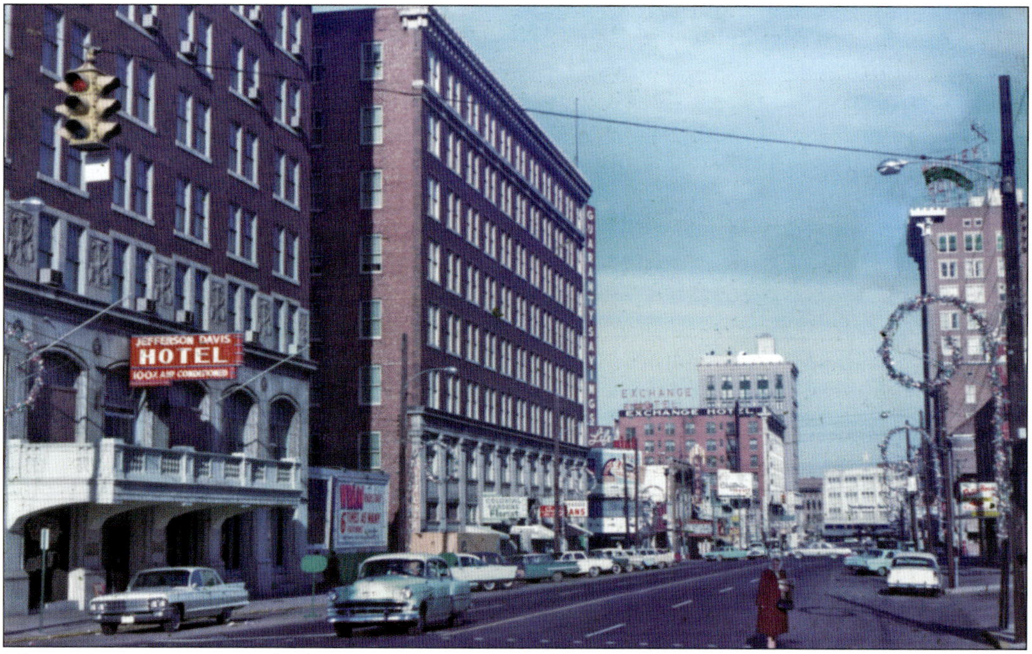

This 1963 street scene includes, from left to right, the Jefferson Davis Hotel, the Exchange Hotel, and the Whitley Hotel. The Selma-to-Montgomery Voting Rights March went by all three hotels in 1965. (Courtesy Landmarks Foundation.)

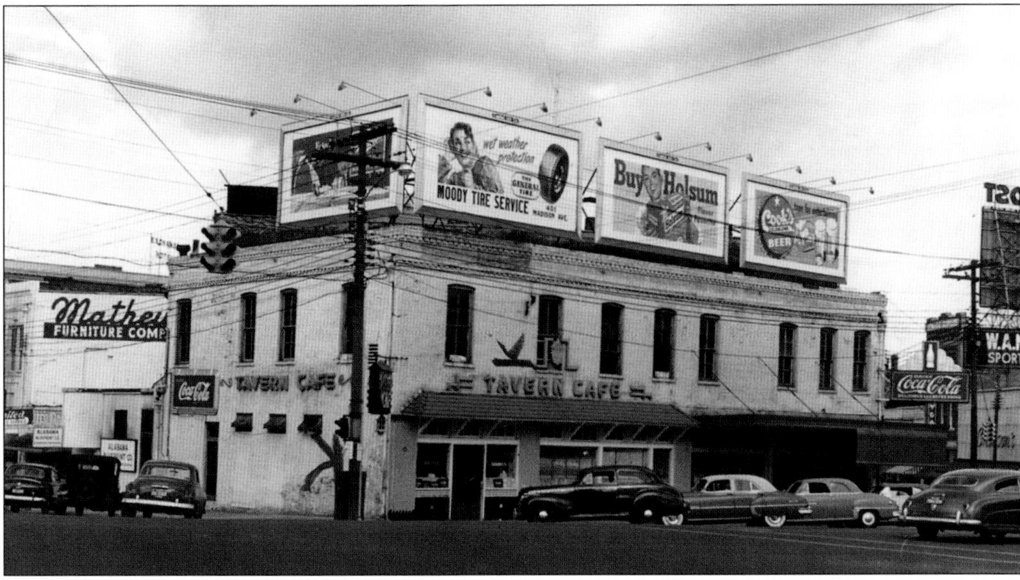

The Tavern Café at the intersection of Washington Avenue, Lee Street, and Court Street was a popular lunch spot for postal workers in the 1950s. (Courtesy Landmarks Foundation.)

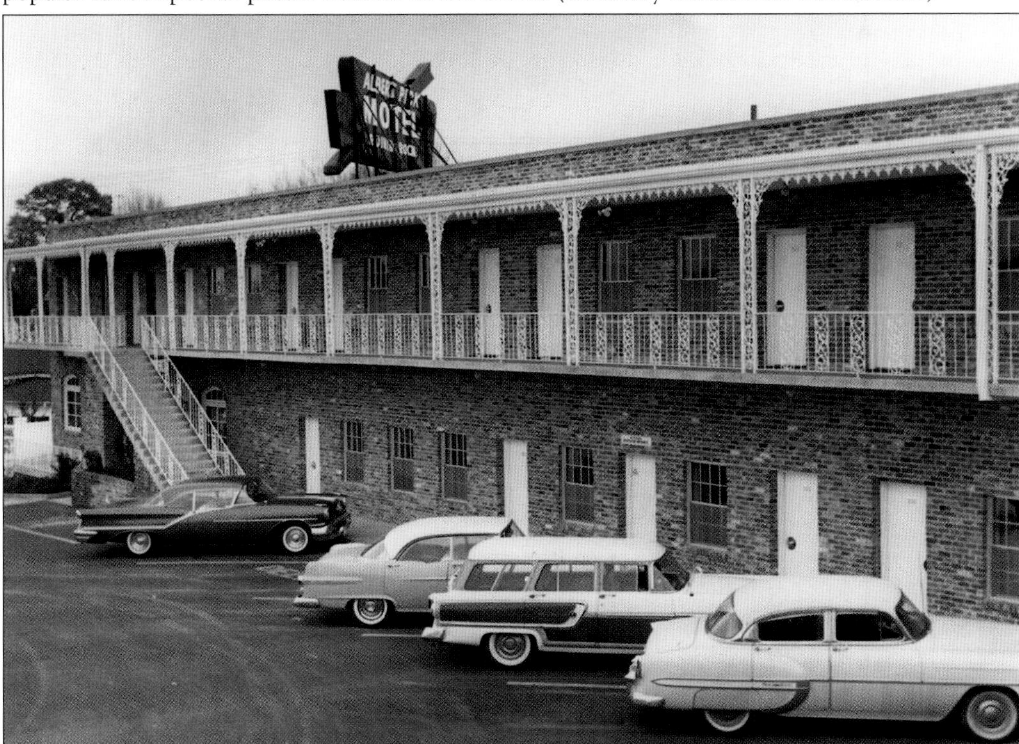

The Albert Pick Motel was built in the 1950s, before the interstate came through. The motel stood on a rise just outside of downtown, at the junction of what was then Highway 31. Its lacy ironwork was Montgomery's nod to the ever-romantic New Orleans style. The new owners later renamed the motel the Capitol Inn. The restaurant and tavern, Goat Hill, remained popular until the early 1990s. The Capitol Inn is currently closed. (Courtesy Landmarks Foundation.)

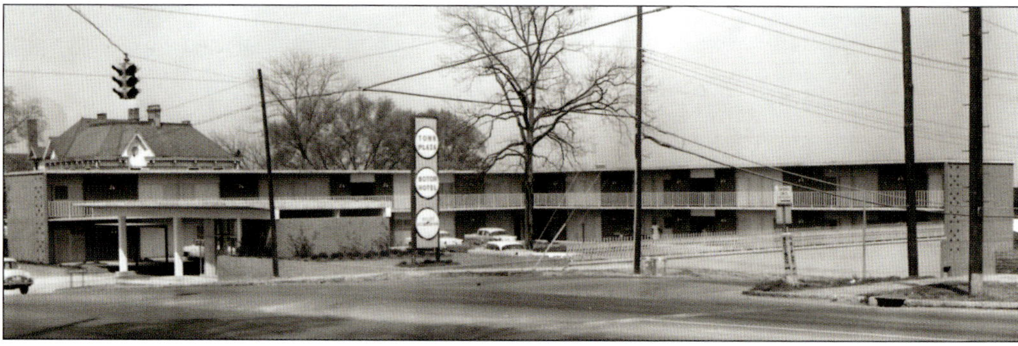

This 1950s photograph shows the Town Plaza Motel at the corner of Madison Avenue and North Ripley Street. Economical and convenient, it was popular among frequent travelers to the capital city. When the original Capitol Inn closed, the owners of this motel, which is still in business, adopted the same name due to its proximity to the capitol building. (Courtesy *Montgomery Advertiser*.)

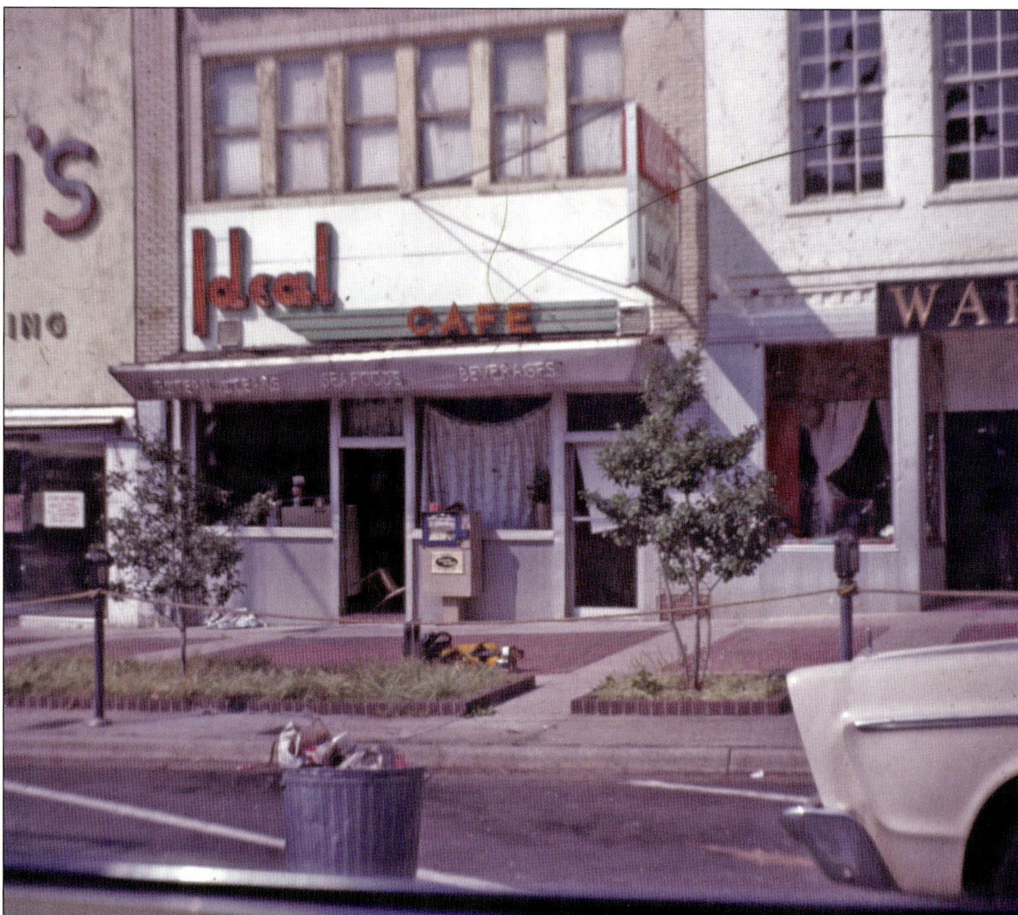

The Ideal Café, seen here in 1974, was located next to WAPX Radio on Dexter Avenue. (Courtesy Landmarks Foundation.)

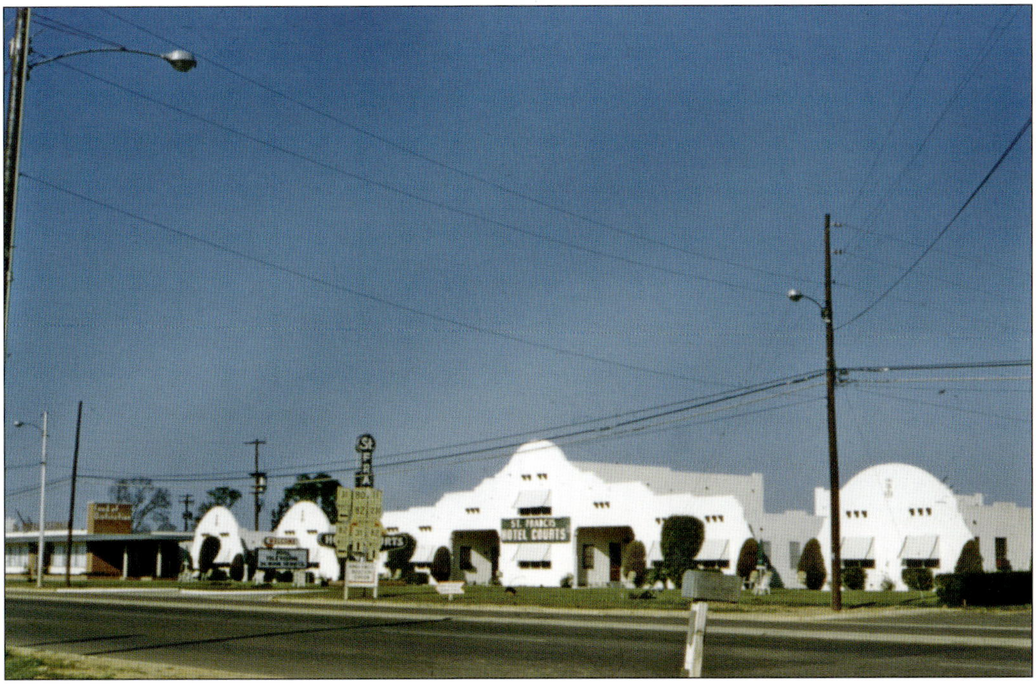

Located at the convergence of US Highways 80, 31, and 82 (known as Mobile Highway), the St. Francis Hotel Court was billed as the "Traveler's Home of Distinction," boasting "Seventy-Three Rooms and Baths." In the 1960s, innkeeper Revis Allen advised, "Don't take chances. Stay at St. Francis." (Courtesy Landmarks Foundation.)

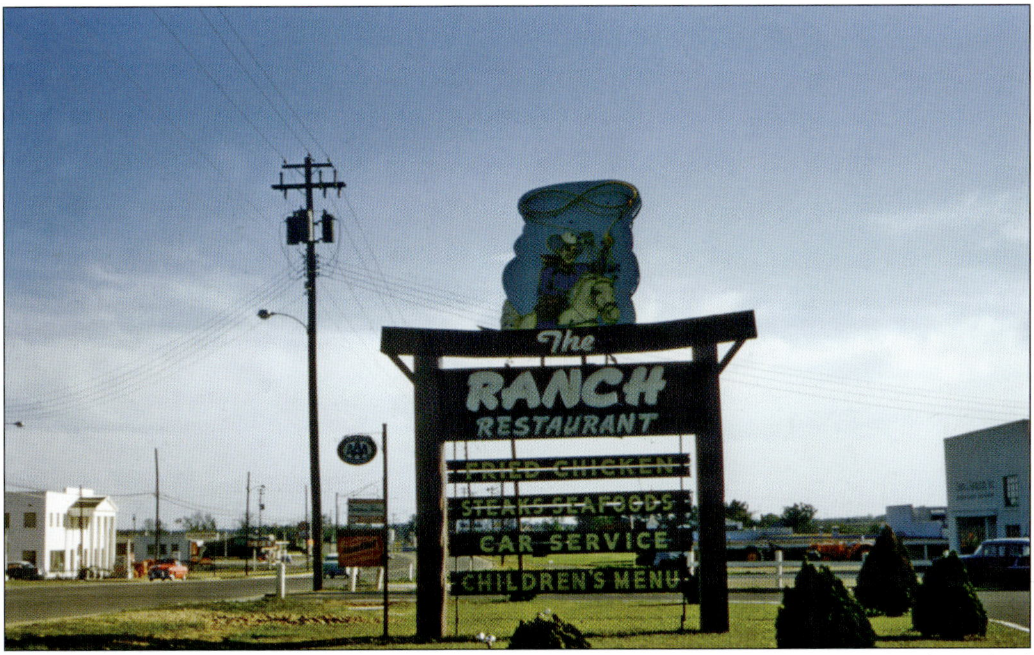

The Ranch Restaurant stood across from the St. Francis Hotel Court. Featuring Southern food and a popular 1950s version of a Western cowboy theme, the eatery was a favorite of the Maxwell Air Force Base crowd. (Courtesy Landmarks Foundation.)

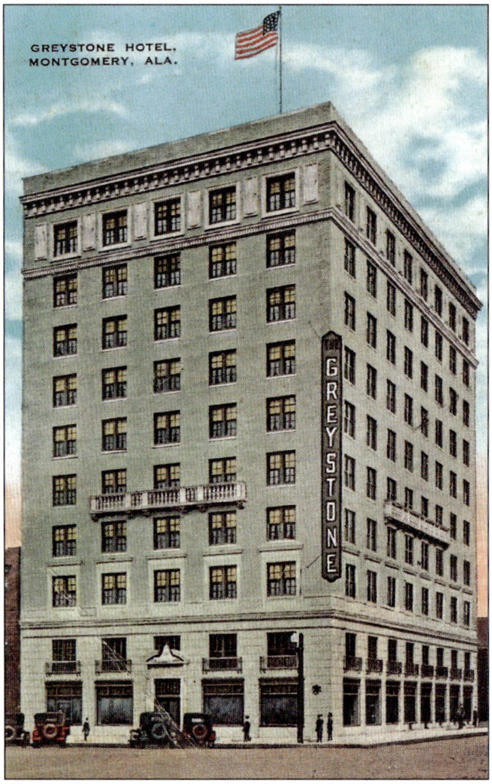

The Greystone Hotel, at the corner of Commerce Street and Bibb-Madison Avenue, was built in 1927. It is seen here in a vintage postcard. The Greystone, now the Hampton Inn, has remained an icon of downtown. (Courtesy Landmarks Foundation.)

This July 1974 photograph shows the Holiday Inn Downtown on Madison Avenue. Guests often included lobbyists and lawyers who were in Montgomery for business connected to state offices. The Top of the Star nightspot on the top floor was popular with the "capital crowd" and with residents of the nearby Capitol Heights neighborhood. (Courtesy Landmarks Foundation.)

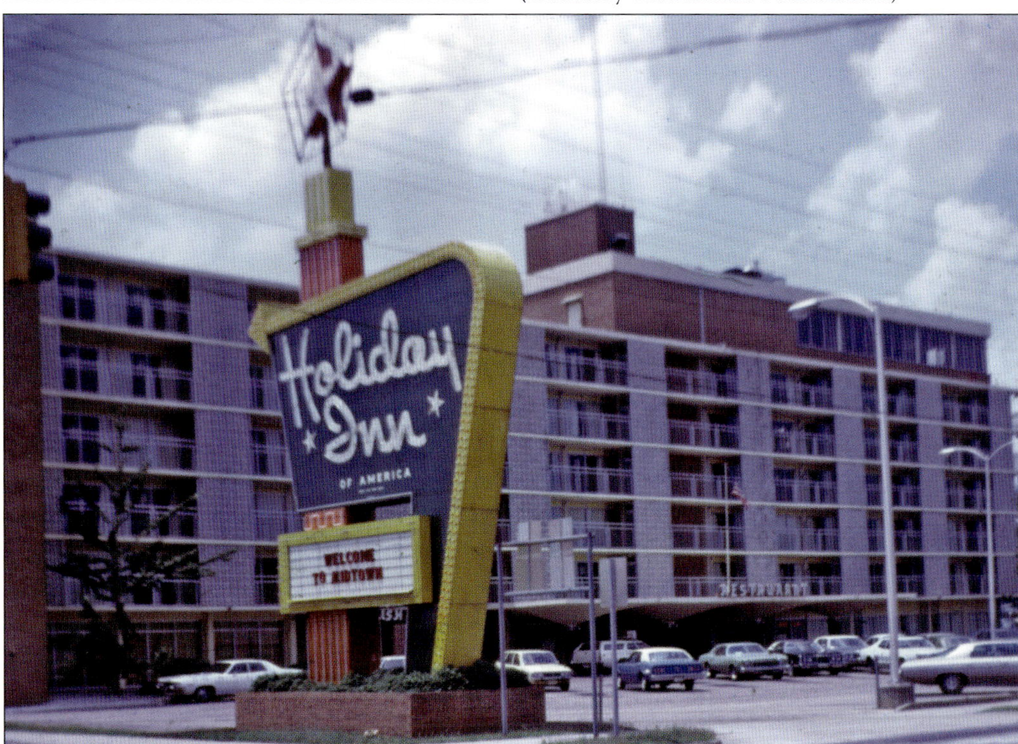

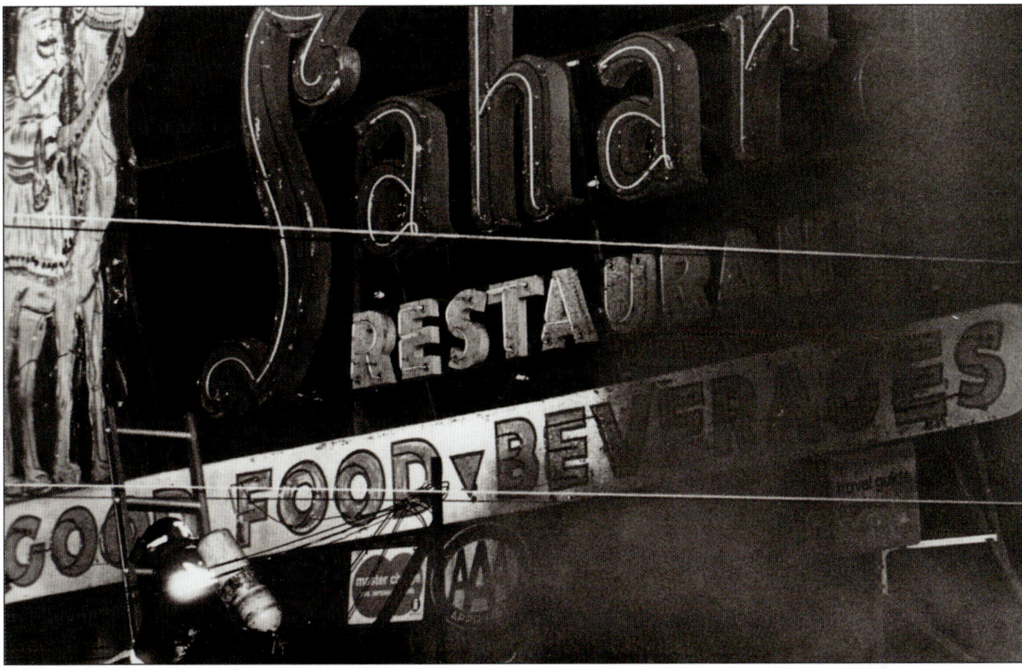

Joe and Toofie Deep owned and operated the Sahara Restaurant on Edgemont Avenue at Norman Bridge Road. The menu featured Southern food; its most popular entrée was "Shrimp Athena." The servers wore white jackets, and the ambiance was completely suited to business and ladies' lunches. This 1987 photograph was taken during the Sahara Restaurant fire. The owners rebuilt following the blaze. (Courtesy *Montgomery Advertiser*.)

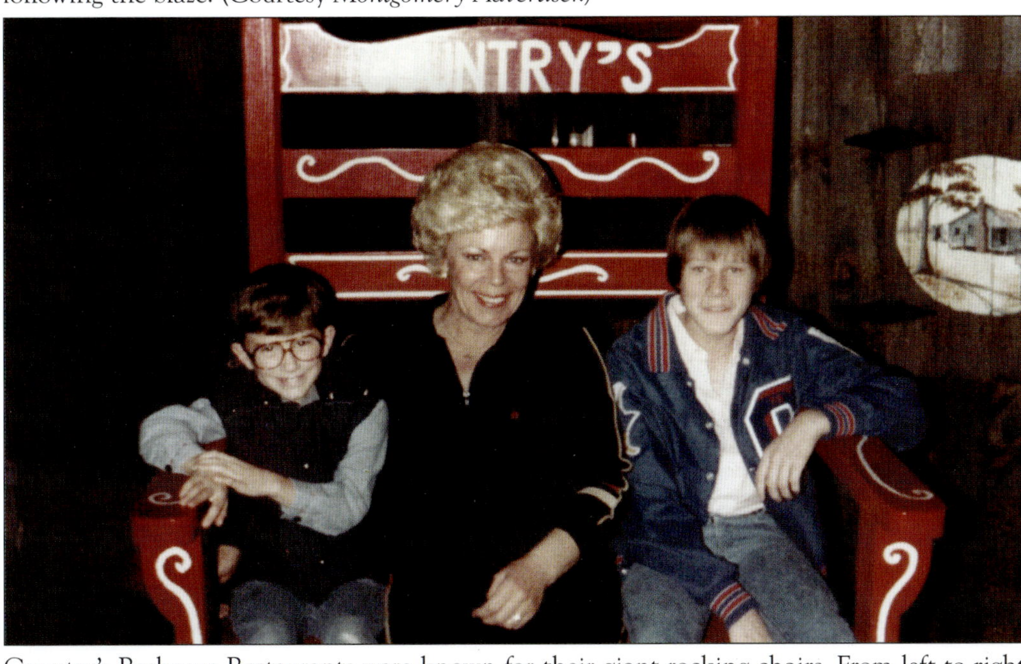

Country's Barbecue Restaurants were known for their giant rocking chairs. From left to right, Foster Dickson, Lilly Foster, and Jeff Foster share a seat at the Eastdale location in February 1983. (Courtesy Faye Foster Singleton.)

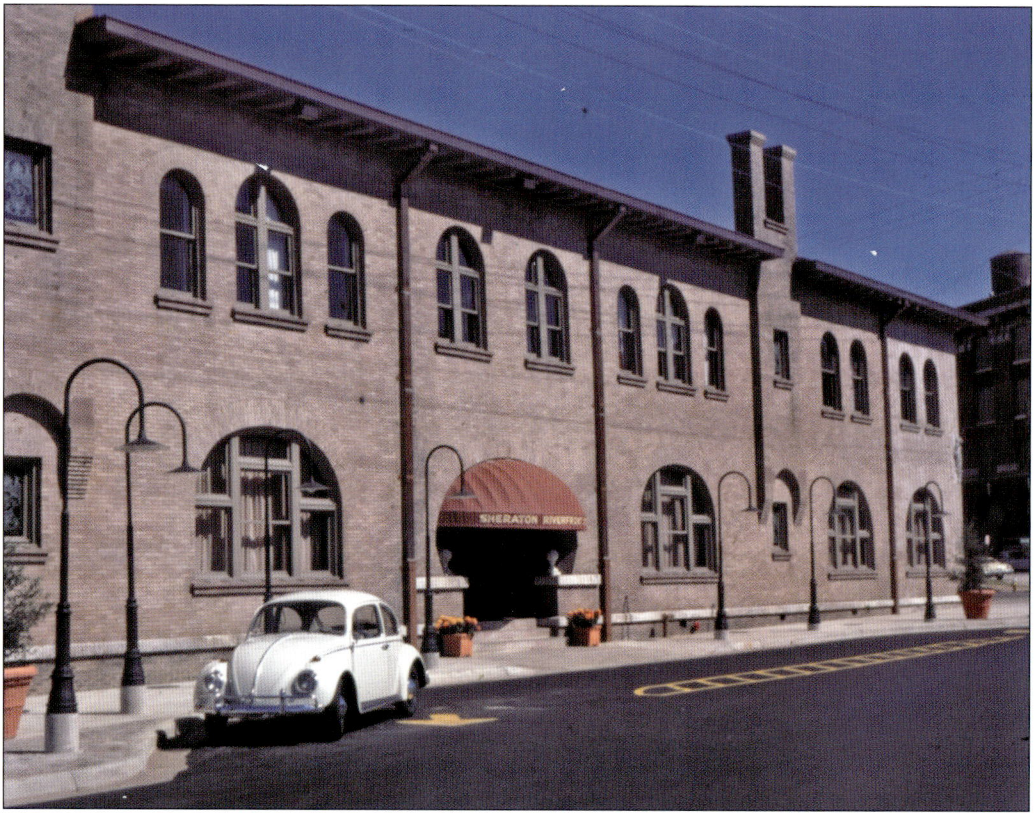

These November 1981 photographs show the Sheraton Riverfront Hotel shortly after it opened. A $6 million renovation transformed the Great Western Railway of Alabama freight terminal, built in 1898, into a 131-room hotel. The U-shaped wings that once had railroad tracks and loading platforms became a pool and leisure area. This building is now Riverwalk Stadium. (Both, courtesy Landmarks Foundation.)

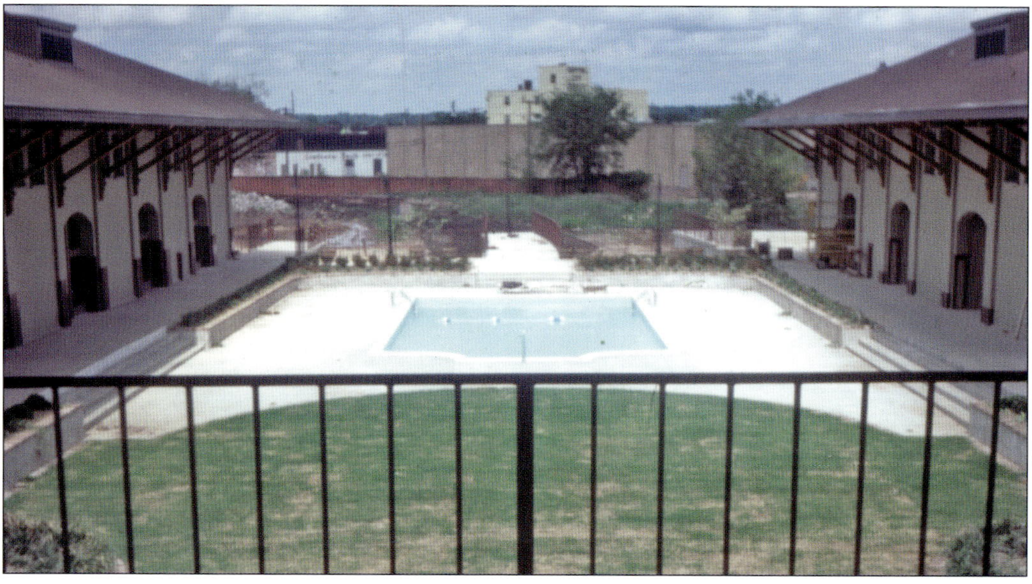

Five

THE DREAM BEGINS

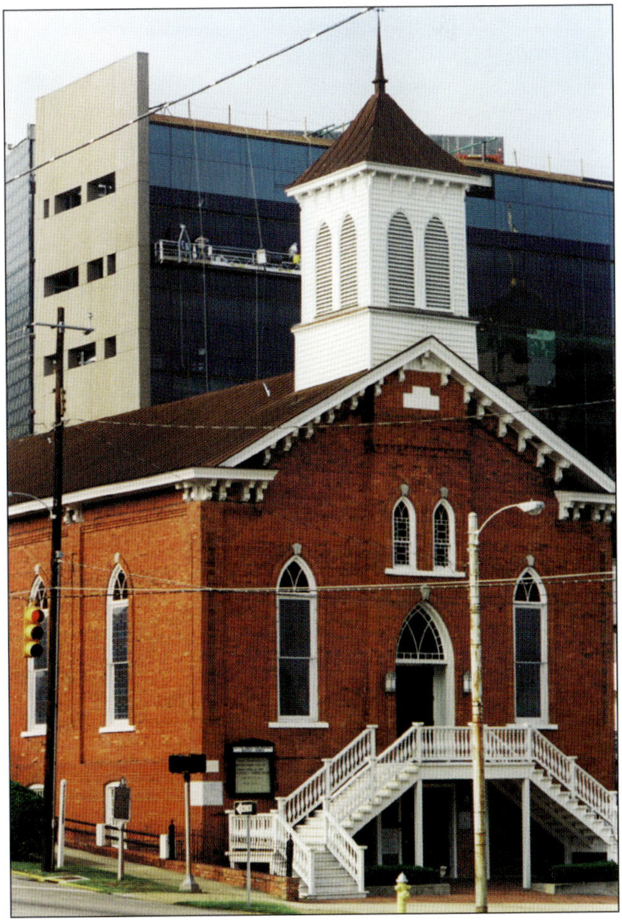

This current photograph shows the Dexter Avenue King Memorial Baptist Church, built in the 1880s on the former site of a slave trader's pen. Rev. Martin Luther King served as pastor of this church from 1954 to 1960. From this pulpit and with that congregation, he began the civil rights movement. The church was designated a National Historic Landmark on June 3, 1974. (Courtesy Southern Poverty Law Center.)

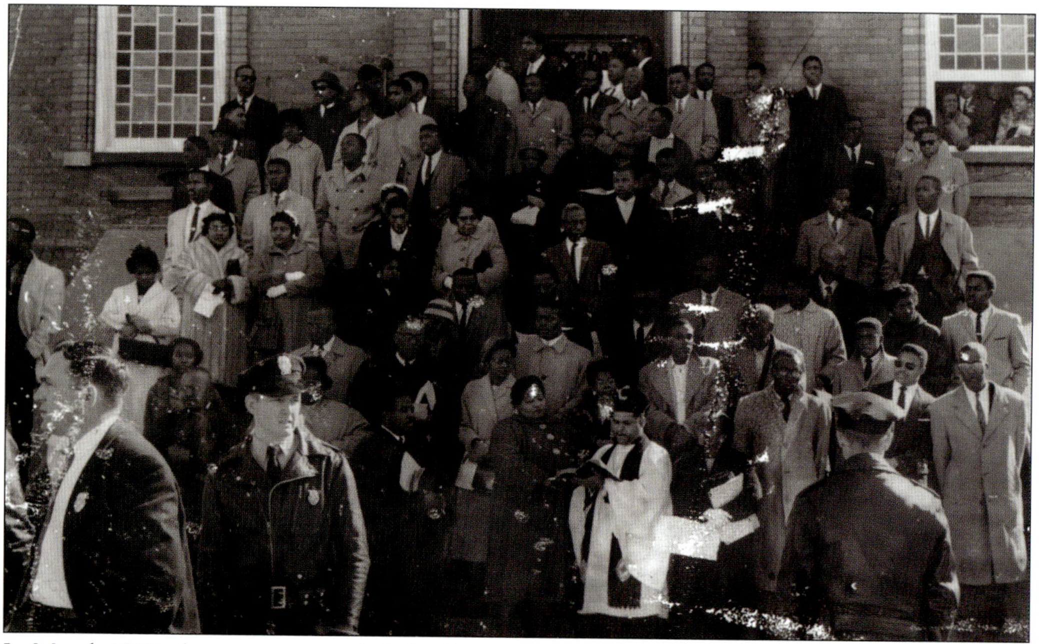

In March 1960, the congregation left the Dexter Avenue Baptist Church, expecting to see other black church congregations joining them to walk peaceably a few steps to the capitol to pray for social change. However, white police officers blocked their way. Home to an active congregation, the church remains a popular and beloved civil rights landmark. (Courtesy Nelson Malden and Alabama Department of Archives and History.)

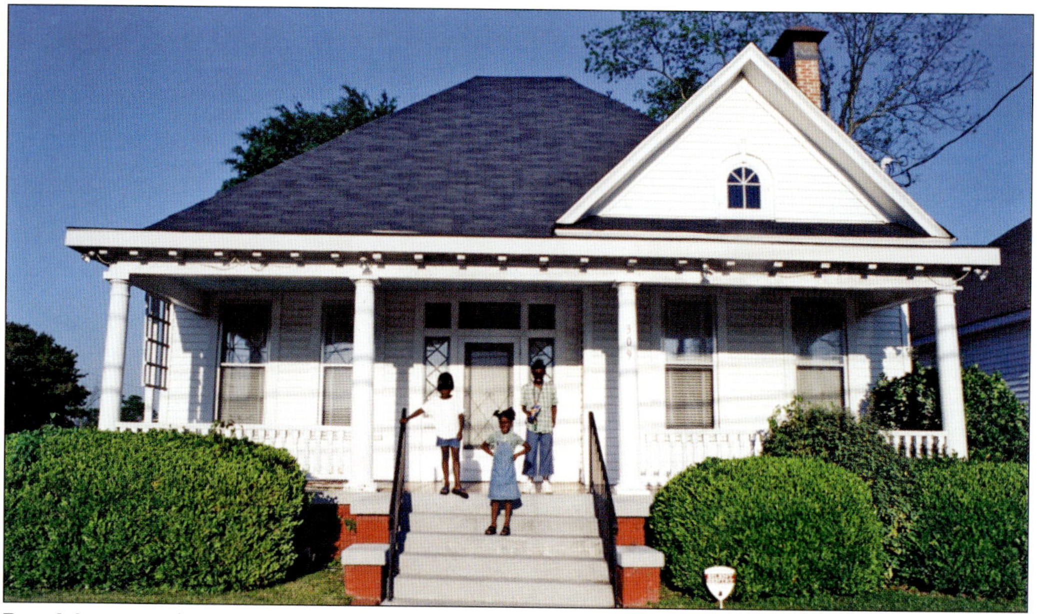

Rev. Martin Luther King and his wife, Coretta Scott King, lived in the Dexter Avenue Baptist Church Parsonage (pictured) with their young children from 1954 to 1960. The parsonage was bombed on January 31, 1956. Coretta and her 10-week-old daughter, Yolanda, were home at the time; luckily, neither was injured. An angry crowd gathered, but Reverend King dissuaded them of perpetrating any violence. (Courtesy Southern Poverty Law Center.)

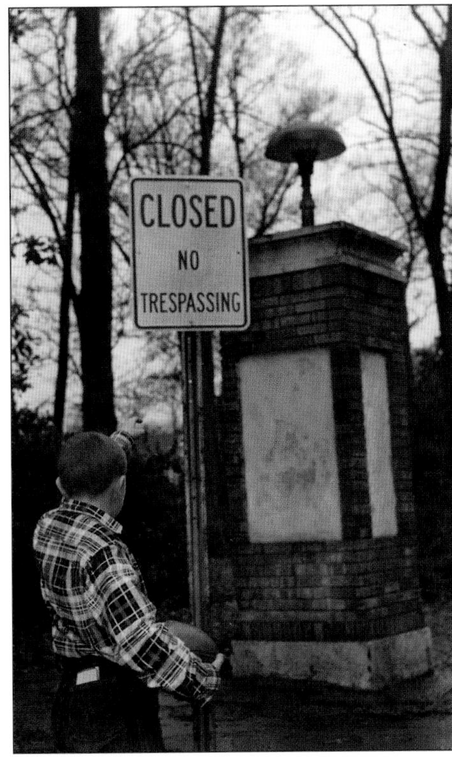

After federal legislation declared segregation illegal, the City of Montgomery closed all municipal parks rather than integrate them on January 1, 1959. At Oak Park, swimming and wading pools were drained; lions, alligators, monkeys, and deer from the Oak Park Zoo were either given away or sold. The gates were closed and locked. (Both, courtesy *Montgomery Advertiser*.)

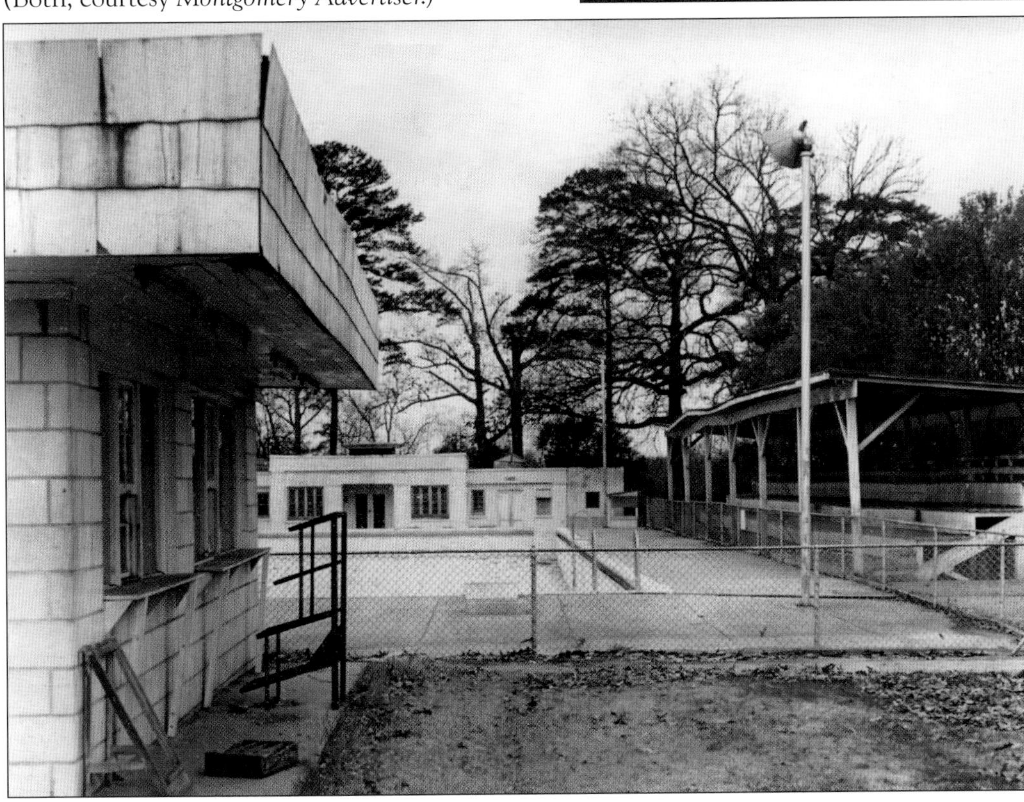

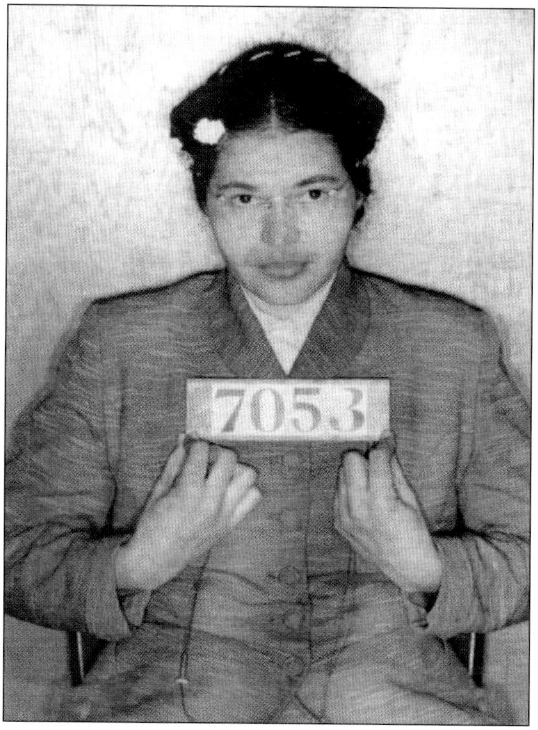

These police photographs, or mug shots, were taken during the Montgomery Bus Boycott. On December 1, 1955, Rosa Parks refused to give up her seat on a city bus to a white man. As a result, she was arrested. Rev. Martin Luther King was arrested later, on February 22, 1956. These photographs, along with 13 others, were found in 2004, stored in the basement of the old Montgomery Courthouse. The notation across Reverend King's photograph was made by an unknown hand. (Both, courtesy Montgomery County Archives.)

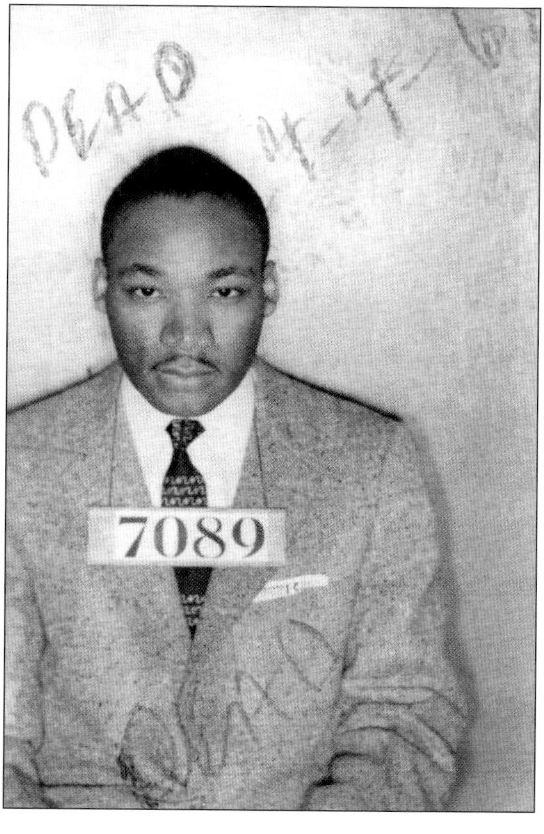

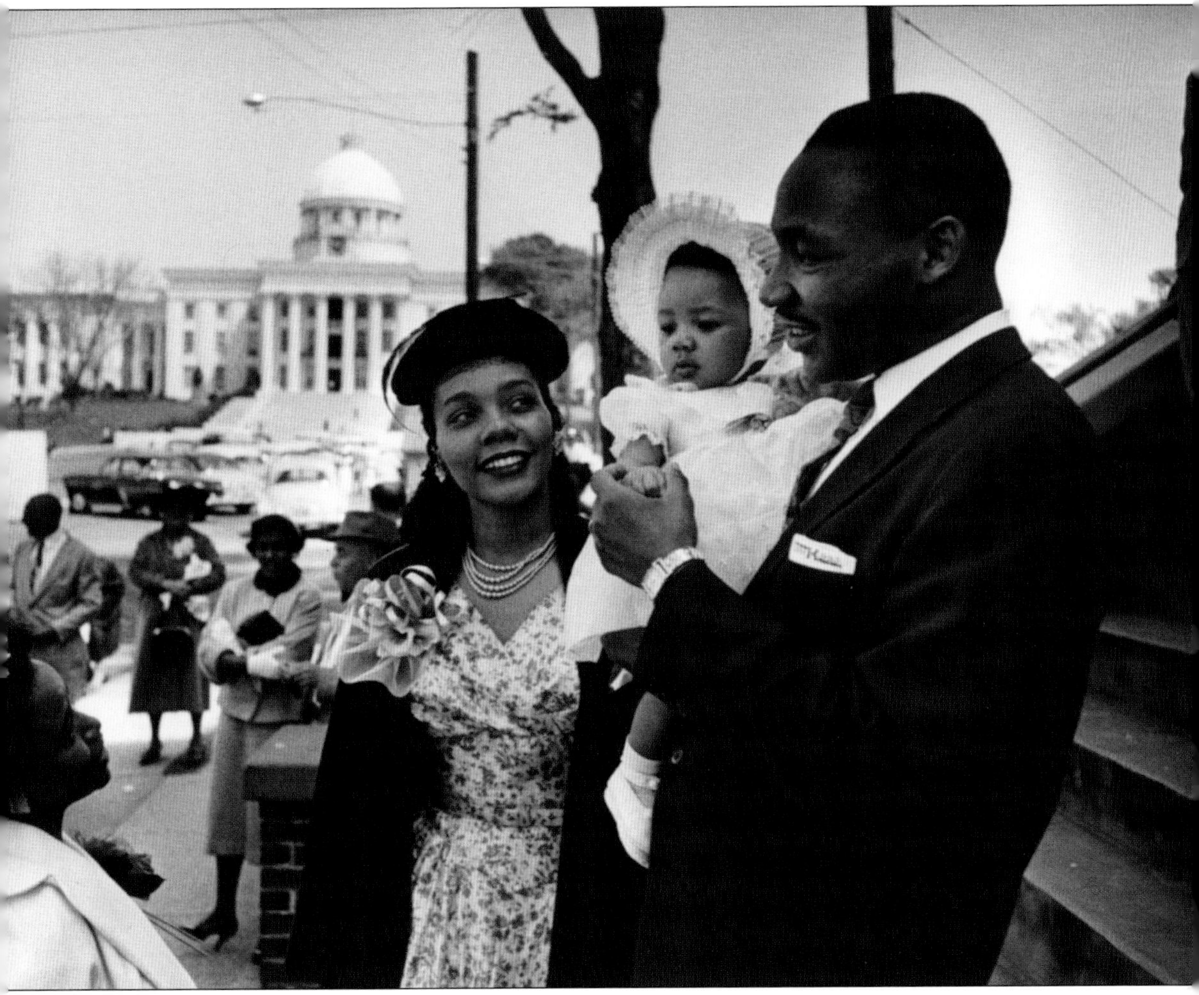

Coretta Scott King, Rev. Martin Luther King Jr., and their daughter Yolanda pause on the steps of the Dexter Avenue Baptist Church (now Dexter Avenue King Memorial Baptist Church) in 1956. The capitol stands in background. Yolanda was born two weeks before Rosa Park's refusal to give up her seat on a Montgomery city bus to a white man, beginning the Montgomery Bus Boycott. Yolanda was only 10 days old when their home, the Dexter Parsonage, was bombed. This photograph, taken by Dan Weiner, is part of the National Portrait Gallery collection. (Courtesy National Portrait Gallery, Smithsonian Institute; Art Resource, New York.)

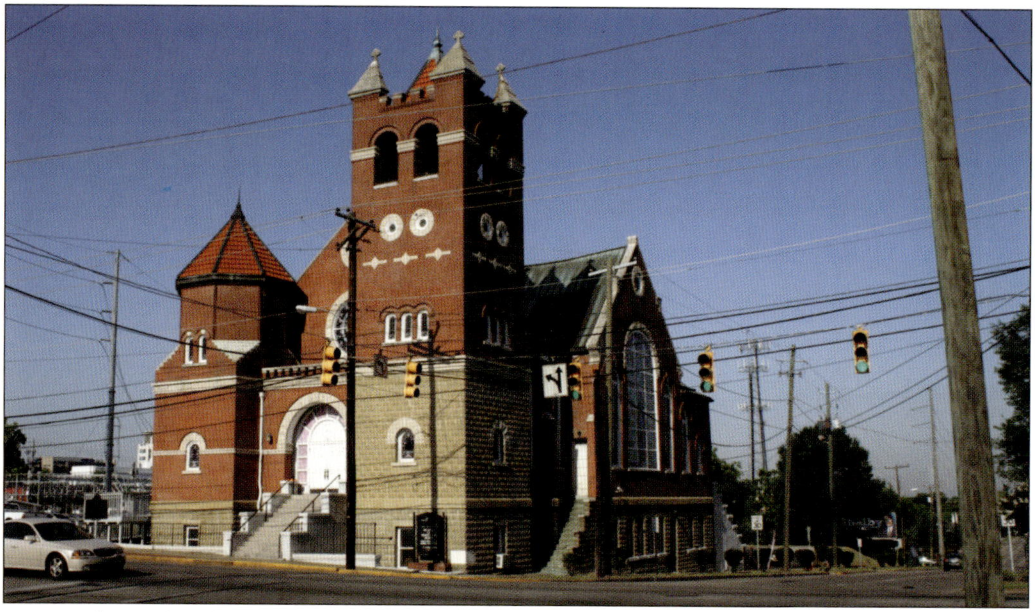

During the civil rights movement, Rev. Ralph Abernathy was pastor at the First Baptist Church on North Ripley Street. The church was active in the Montgomery Bus Boycott in 1955, and it supported the Freedom Riders on May 20, 1961. The Freedom Riders met at the church on May 21, which was then attacked by a white mob. Today, the church and its members, noted as the largest black Baptist congregation in America, stand as a testament to faith and freedom. (Courtesy Landmarks Foundation.)

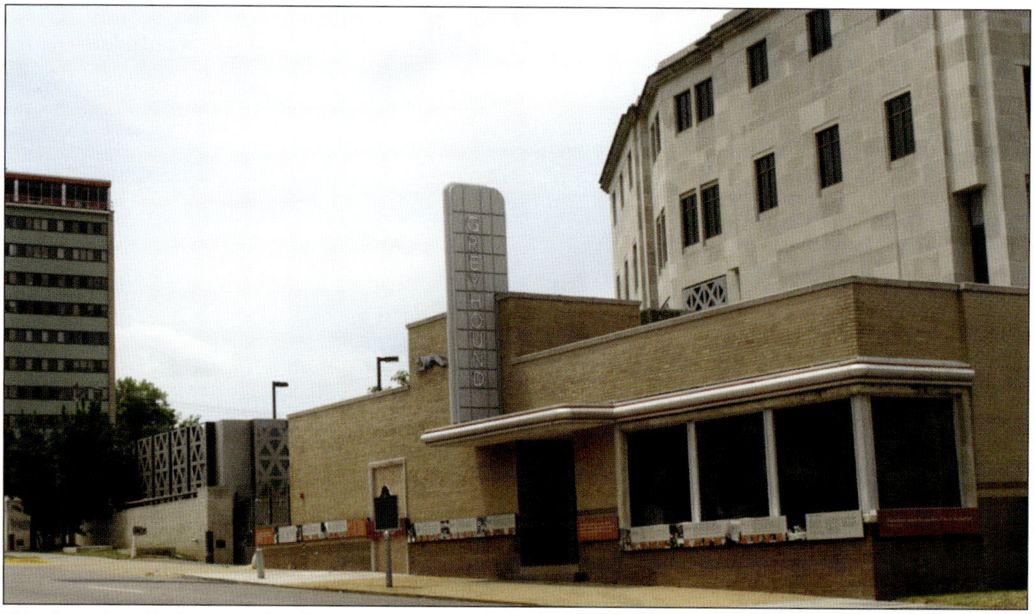

The Freedom Riders sought the enforcement of the US Supreme Court ruling to outlaw segregated transportation. As they arrived at the Greyhound Bus Station in Montgomery on May 20, 1961, their police escort disappeared. A violent crowd of white protestors attacked them, and several Freedom Riders were seriously injured. In 2011, the building was opened as a museum. It is listed in the National Register of Historic Places. (Courtesy Landmarks Foundation.)

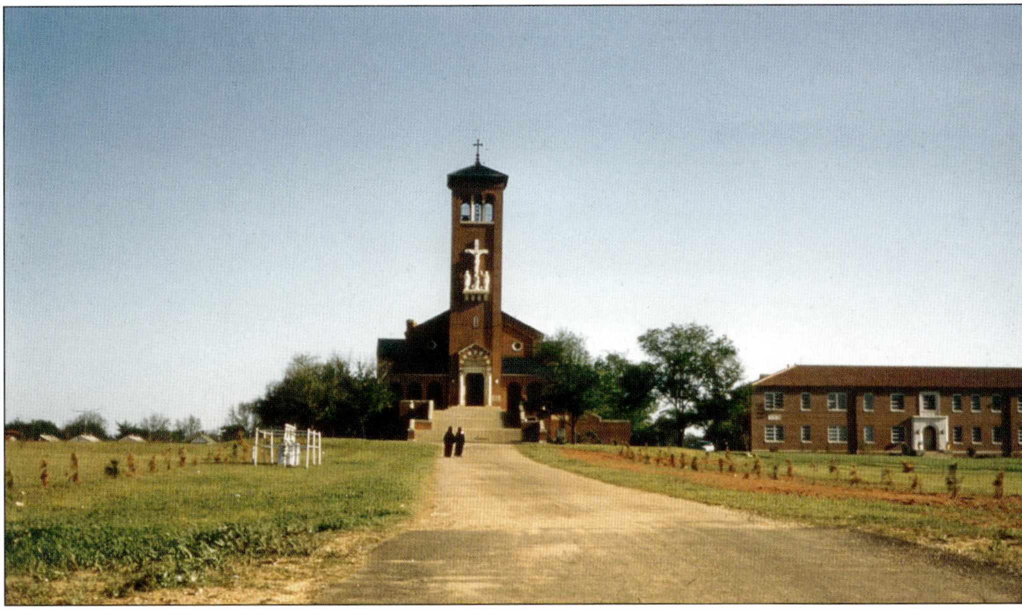

The city of St. Jude is a black Catholic community a few miles from downtown. On March 24, 1965, the night before the march to the capitol, participants of the Voting Rights March camped on 36 acres of an athletic field. A Stars of Freedom rally kept spirits up that night. The event featured Odetta, Harry Belafonte, Pete Seeger, and Joan Baez. At the end of the march, St. Jude Hospital tried to save the life of Viola Liuzzo, who was shot by Klansmen as she was driving marchers back to Selma. (Courtesy Landmarks Foundation.)

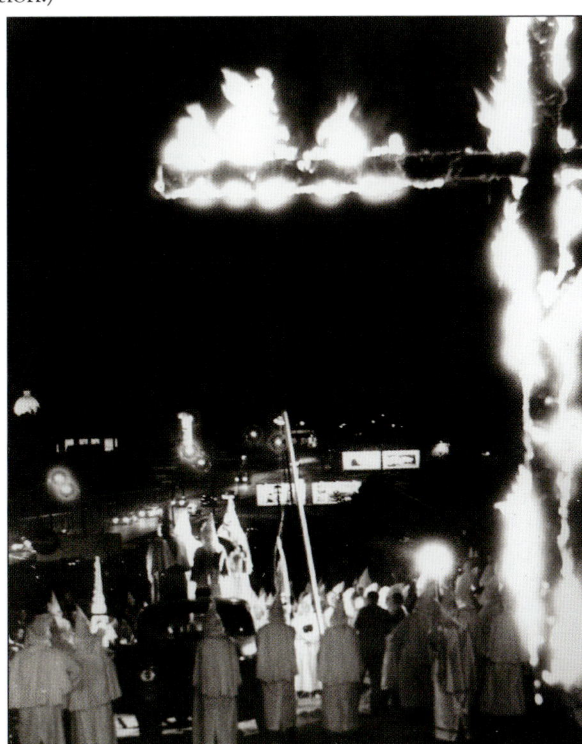

Here, Klansmen burn a cross in downtown Montgomery. Burning crosses was intended to frighten the black community and deter protests or marches. The Klansmen were allowed to erect the cross and set it on fire; no city officials prohibited these actions or interrupted the actual burning. The message from municipal government was clear. (Courtesy Landmarks Foundation.)

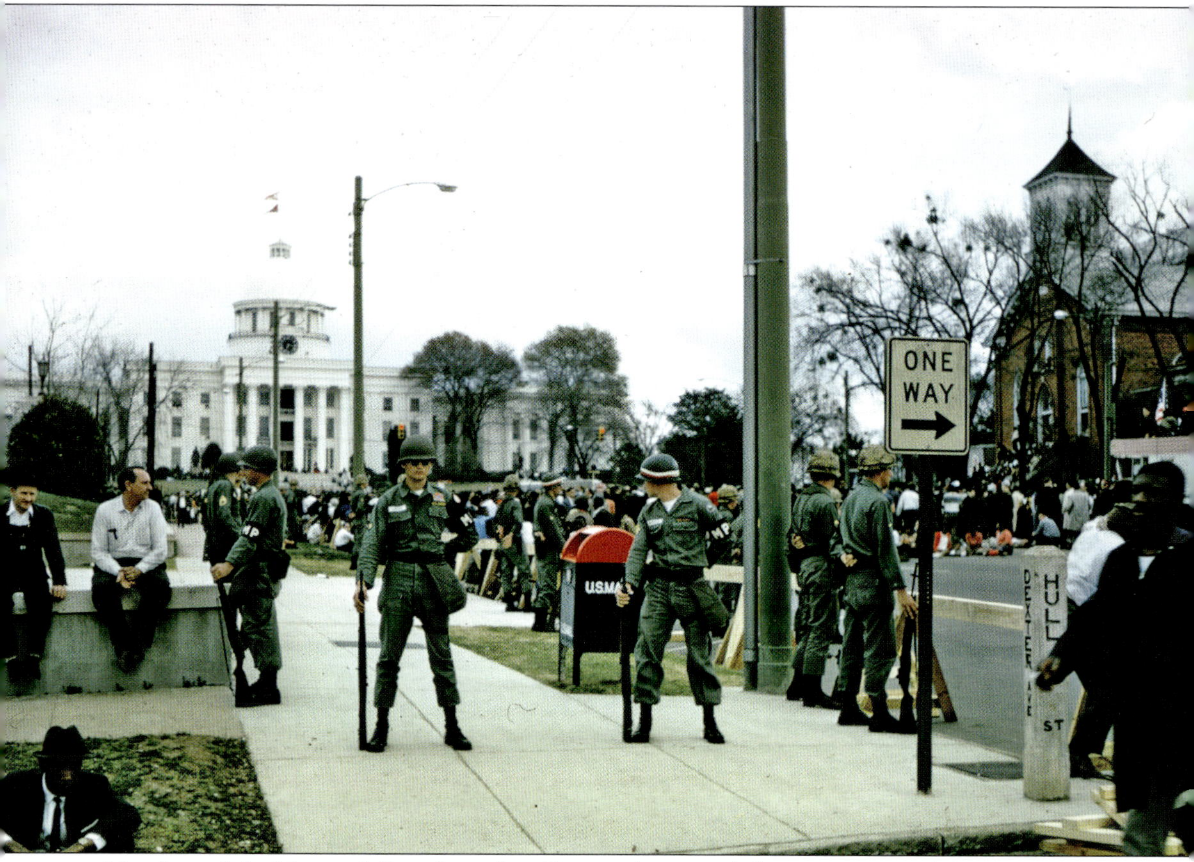

Members of the National Guard stand on Dexter Avenue while participants of the Voting Rights March proceed to the capitol on March 25, 1965. On the steps of the capitol, Dr. Martin Luther King delivered his "How Long, Not Long" speech. He then attempted to hand-deliver a petition to Gov. George Wallace. Although Wallace refused to come to the door, Dr. King stood patiently, and after a while, the governor's secretary came to the door and took the petition. (Courtesy Alabama Department Archives and History.)

Six

DOWN AND BACK

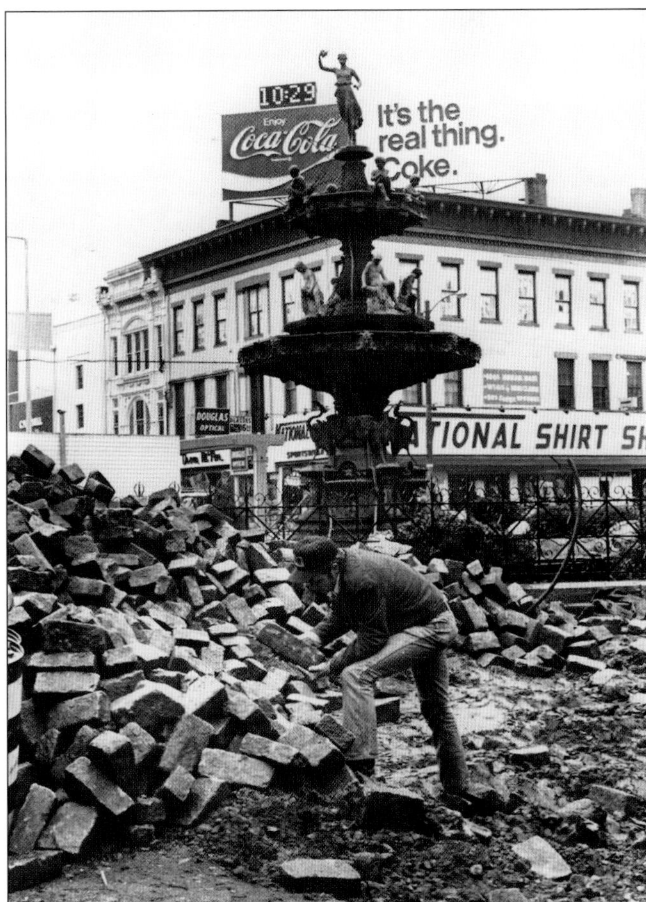

During the period of urban renewal, this January 24, 1972, photograph by Phillip Sheffield was featured in the *Montgomery Advertiser*. The accompanying article stated the following: "Montgomery's urban renewal workers have pulled hundreds of antique granite blocks from the soil in the heart of town where they have lain since 1854. Director Elizabeth Wright says Montgomery streets were paved with the block after merchants took them from ships' holds to make room for cotton exports. At the heap's bottom, Dwight Miniard inspects one of the imports." (Courtesy *Montgomery Advertiser*.)

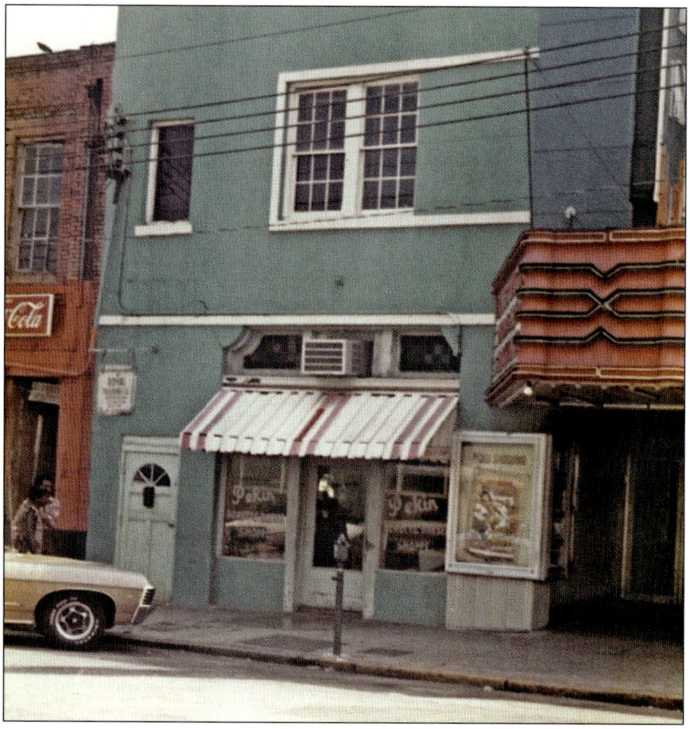

This photograph of the Pekin Barbershop was taken in 1973 for a real estate appraisal in preparation for urban renewal projects. Visible at right is part of the marquee of the Pekin Theatre. (Courtesy Landmarks Foundation.)

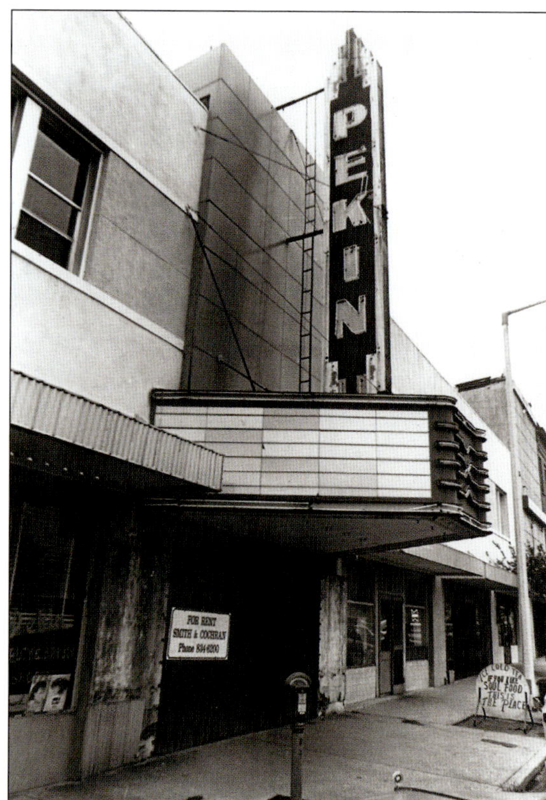

The Pekin Theatre at 30 Lawrence Street was built in 1911. In addition to movies, the facility was designed to host vaudeville shows, with a full orchestra pit and a backstage area. By the time of this 1989 photograph, it had lost its glamor. The Pekin Theatre closed in 1985 and was demolished in 1995. (Courtesy *Montgomery Advertiser*.)

From the era of urban renewal, this 1973 photograph of 18 North Court Street shows bricks being excavated from the streets. This building, with its handsome mansard roof and arched windows, still stands. It currently faces Klein Park. (Courtesy Landmarks Foundation.)

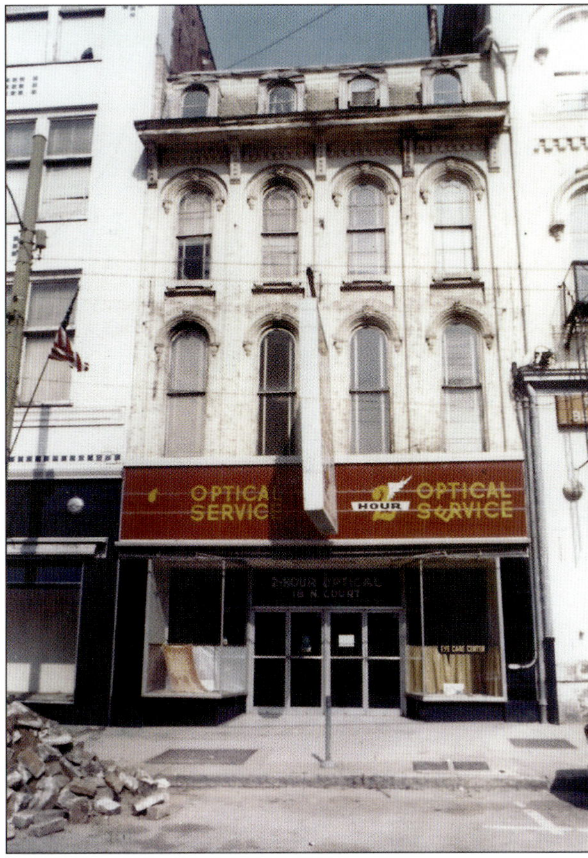

Another 1973 urban renewal photograph shows buildings on South Court Street. Previously, another building stood to the right of Shinbaum's. When it was demolished, Shinbaum's moved next door. (Courtesy Landmarks Foundation.)

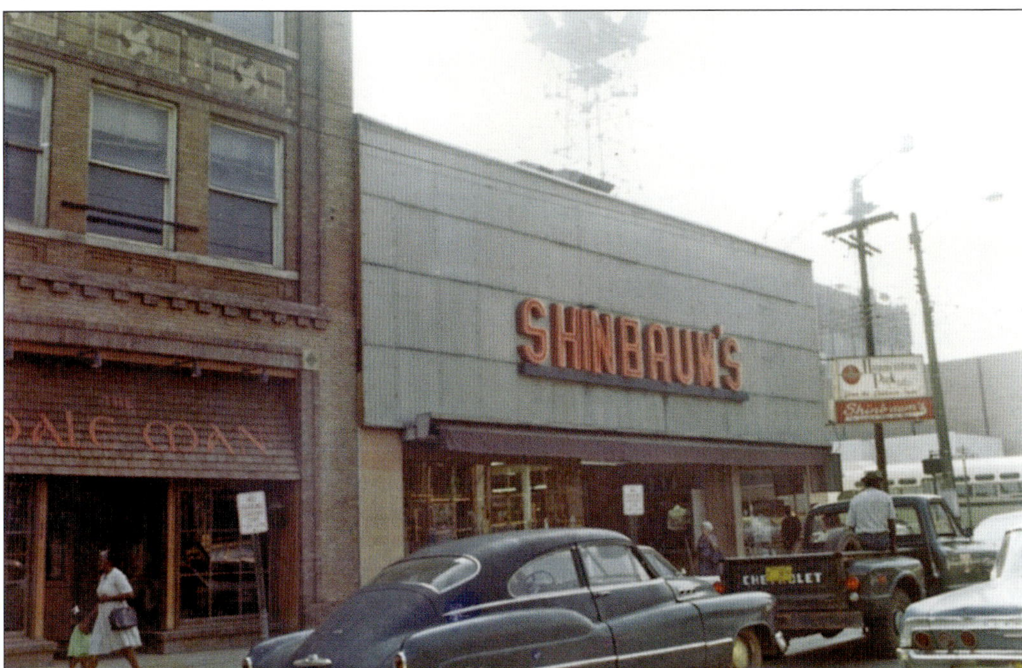

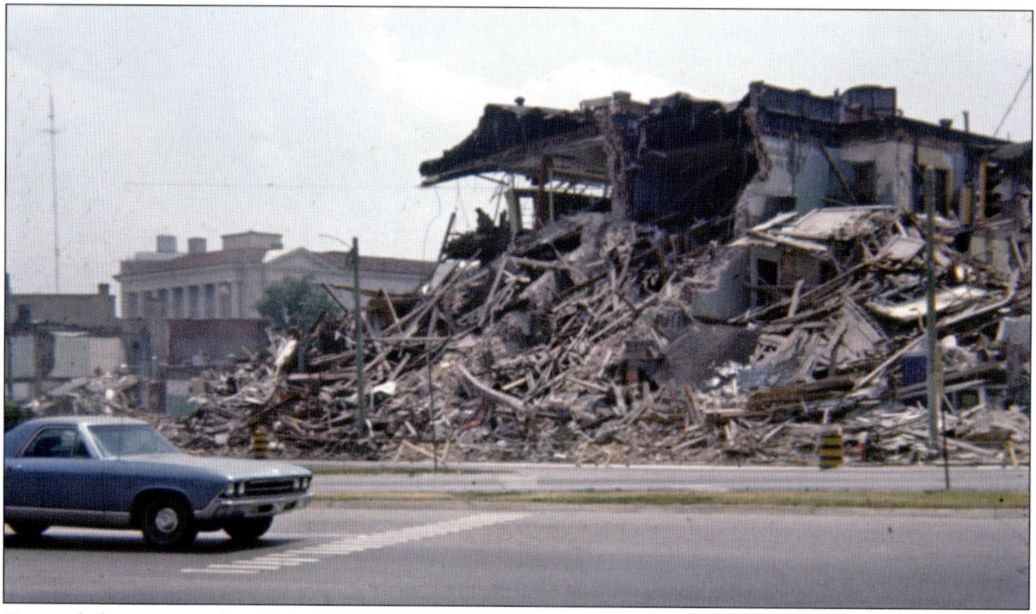

For a while, it seemed as if every building with some history was in jeopardy. A desire for a modern image dominated the mood of the era, causing many Montgomery residents to turn their backs on the city's architectural history. These photographs from June 1970 were labeled simply as "Demolition Downtown." (Both, courtesy Landmarks Foundation.)

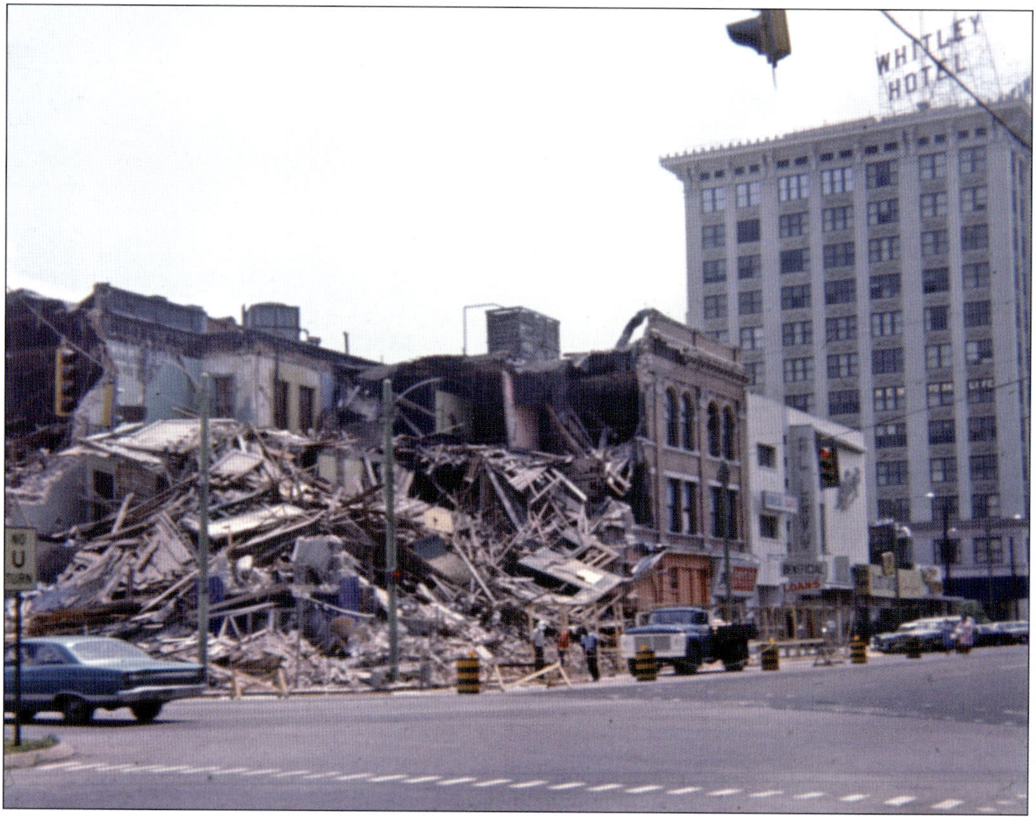

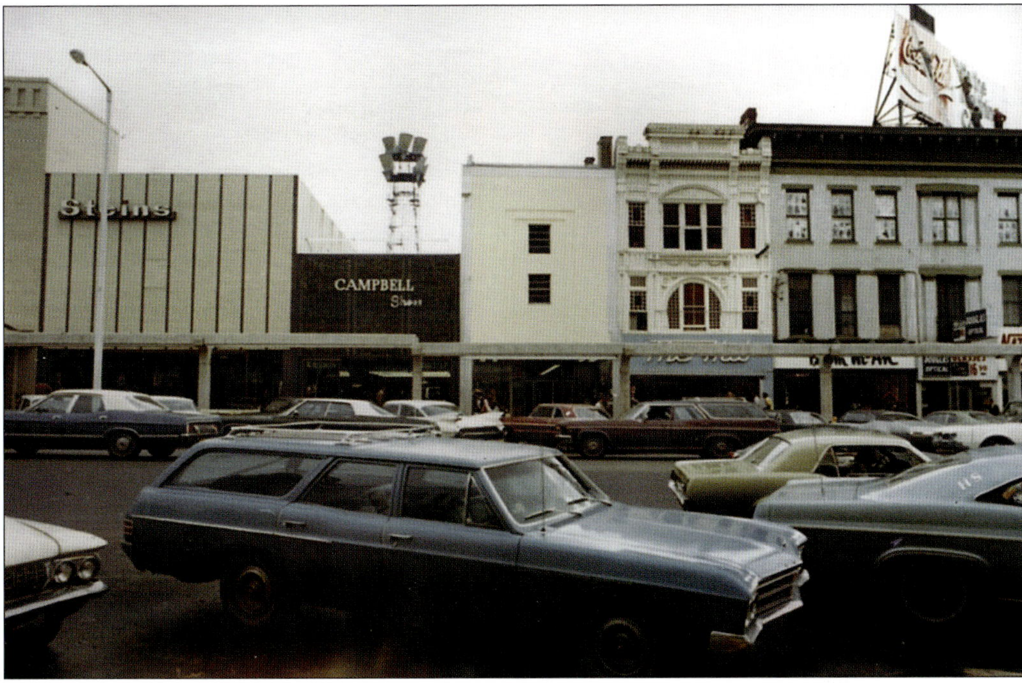

One urban renewal project was the construction of concrete canopies. Seen here in 1973, the canopies line the sidewalks of Dexter Avenue. The canopies were designed to modernize the streetscape and protect pedestrians from the elements. (Courtesy Landmarks Foundation.)

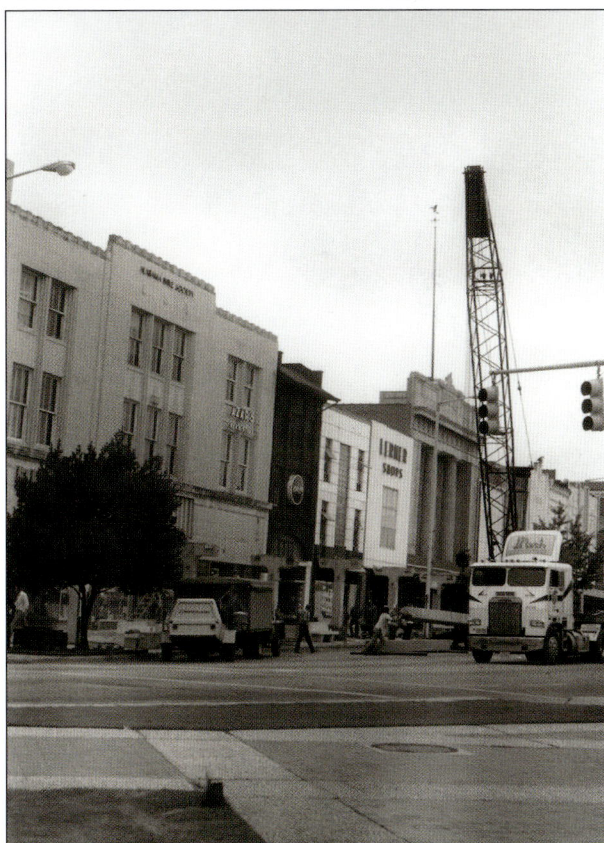

Change is evident as the canopies come down in the 1980s. Their removal signaled a shift in the attitude toward historic preservation. The canopies were removed to enable the repair of upper building facades. (Courtesy Landmarks Foundation.)

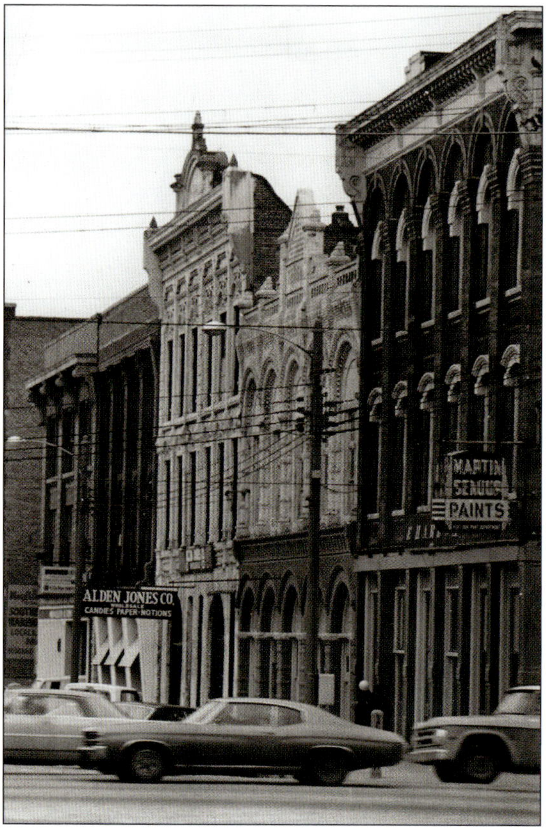

This photograph, taken on January 7, 1973, shows a strip of 19th-century buildings on Commerce Street. While a few are gone, those that have survived have been restored. Today, they are beautiful and appreciated. (Courtesy *Montgomery Advertiser.*)

Several 19th-century buildings were demolished to make way for the new civic center on Commerce Street in May 1974. The city's objective was to attract revenue from conventions. (Courtesy Landmarks Foundation.)

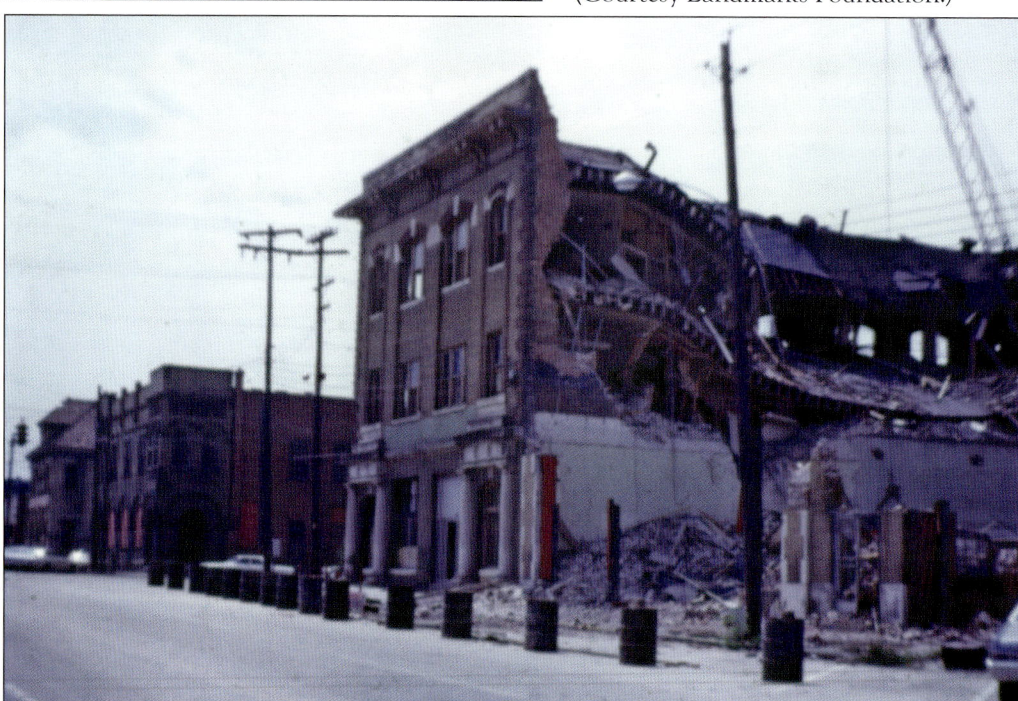

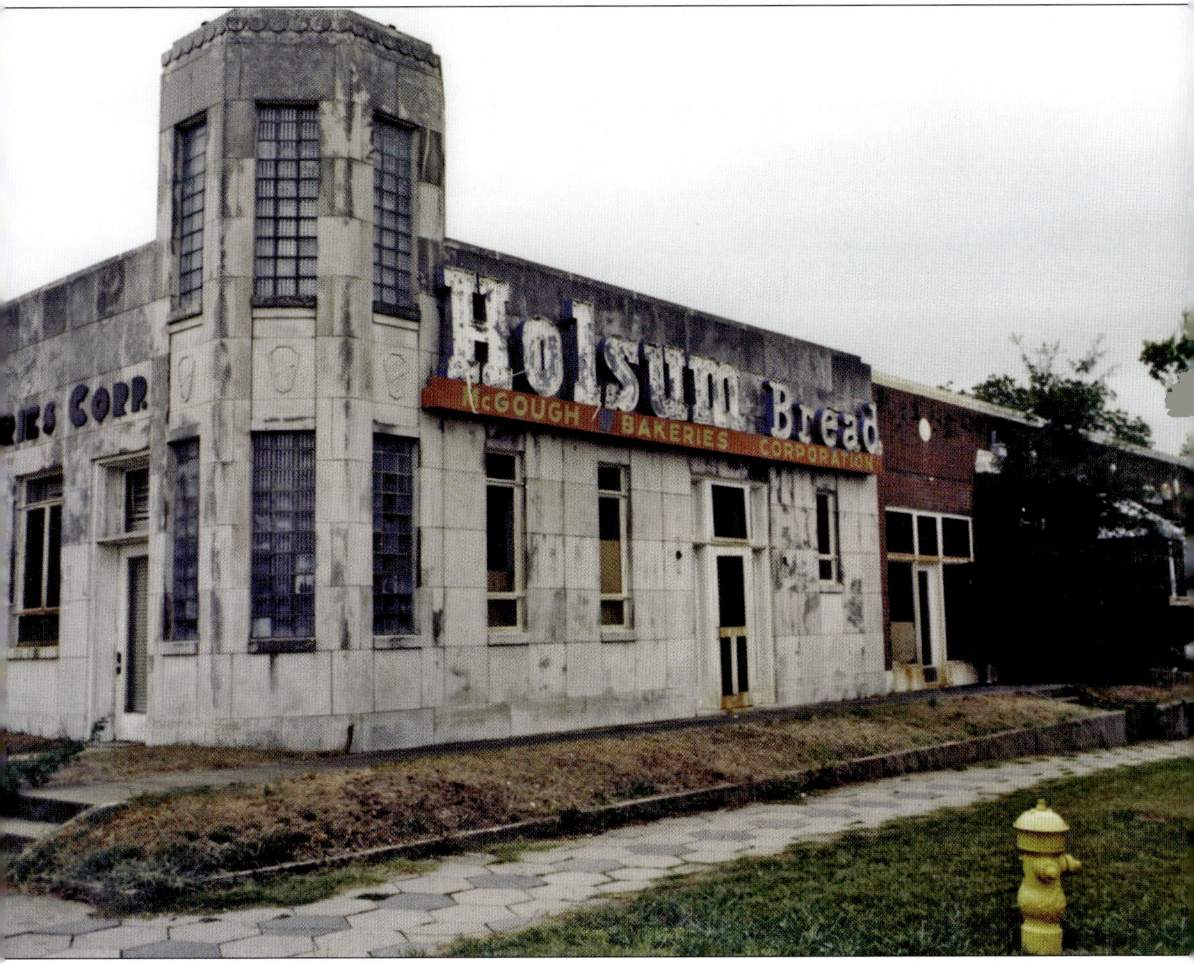

This 1977 photograph shows Holsum Bread, a local bakery and distributor at Monroe and Jackson Streets. The building, which also housed McGough Bakeries Corporation and Betsy Ross Bread, was one of the last classic Art Deco buildings with glass bricks in Montgomery. Note the hex-block sidewalk. (Photograph by R. Baxley; courtesy Landmarks Foundation.)

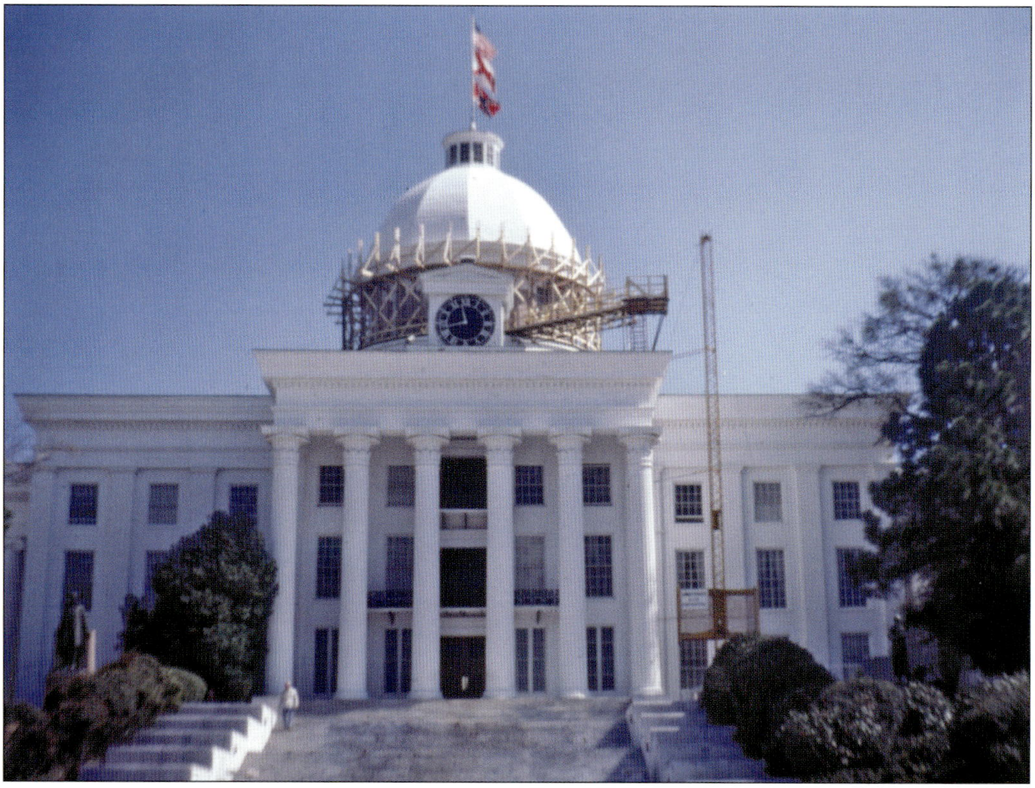

In March 1978, the capitol dome received a face-lift as the first phase of an extensive exterior renovation. The project was carried out under the direction of Nicholas H. Holmes Jr., in association with the Montgomery firm of Seay & Seay Architects. (Courtesy Landmarks Foundation.)

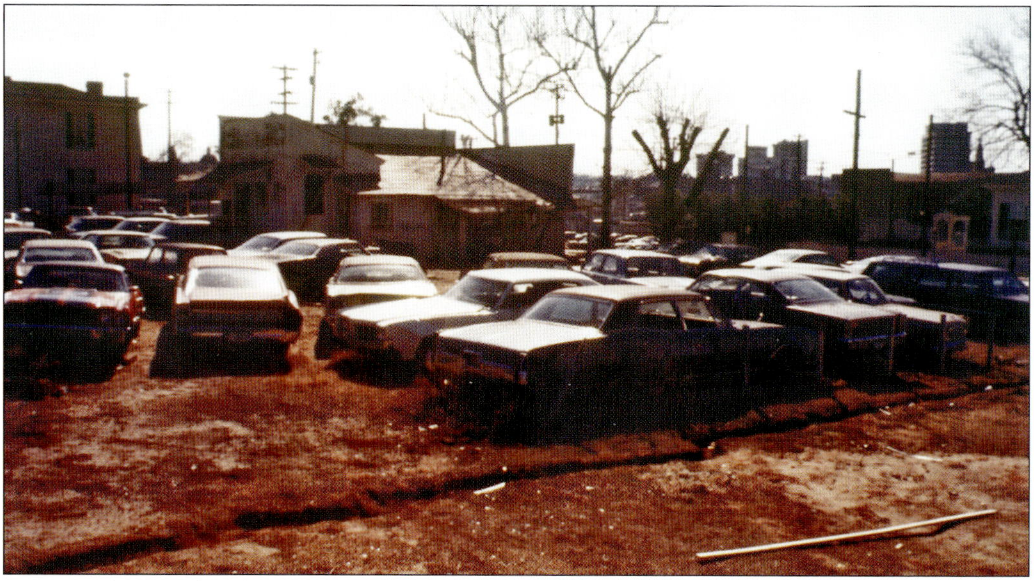

In 1970, the Landmarks Foundation of Montgomery purchased a lot filled with old cars and transformed it into the Living Block of Old Alabama Town. Note the absence of all Retirement Systems of Alabama (RSA) towers on the horizon. (Courtesy Landmarks Foundation.)

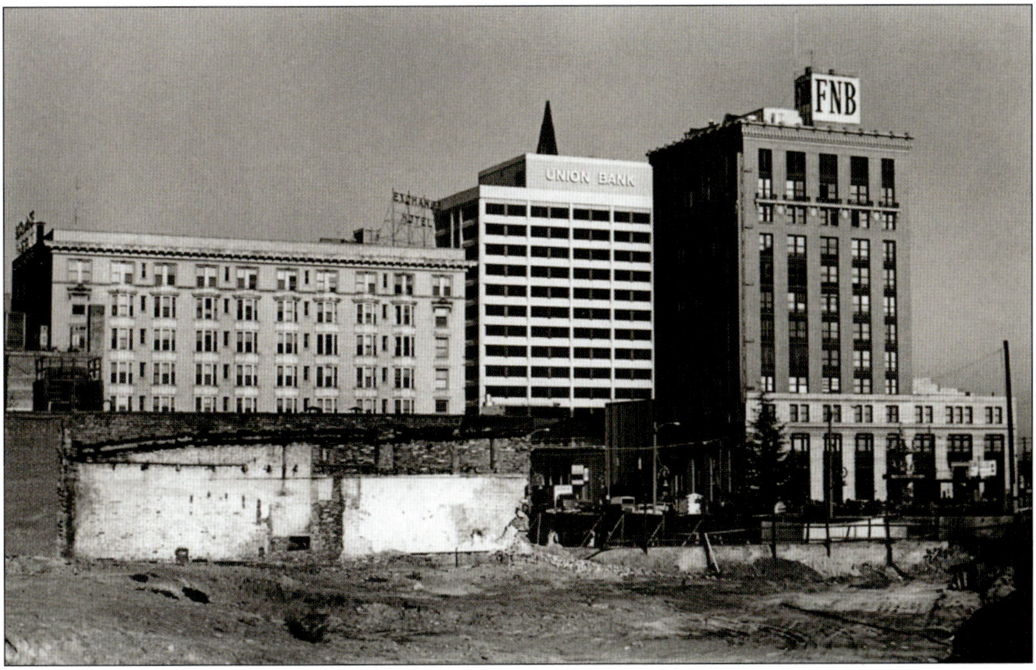

An entire block of 19th-century buildings was demolished behind the Court Square Fountain to make way for the Pizitz Department Store, which opened in 1972. In this photograph, the Exchange Hotel still stands, as does a Christmas tree on top of Union Bank. (Courtesy *Montgomery Advertiser*.)

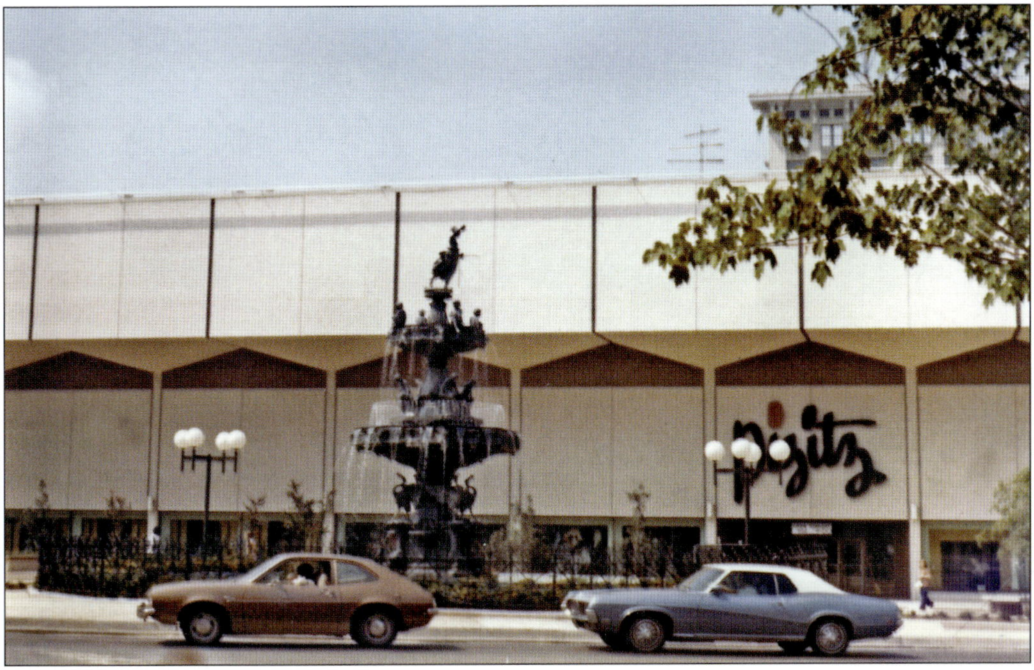

This photograph, dated August 1979, shows the Pizitz Department Store and modern streetlamps behind Hebe and the Court Square Fountain, compliments of urban renewal. (Courtesy Landmarks Foundation.)

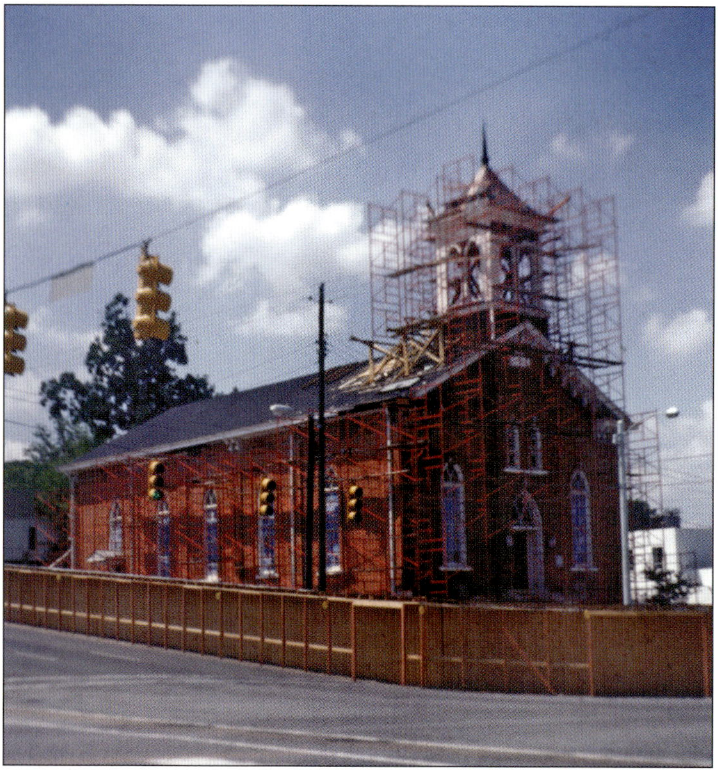

In August 1979, the Dexter Avenue King Memorial Baptist Church had its steeple repaired. Note that the Southern Poverty Law Center building had not yet been constructed behind it. (Courtesy Landmarks Foundation.)

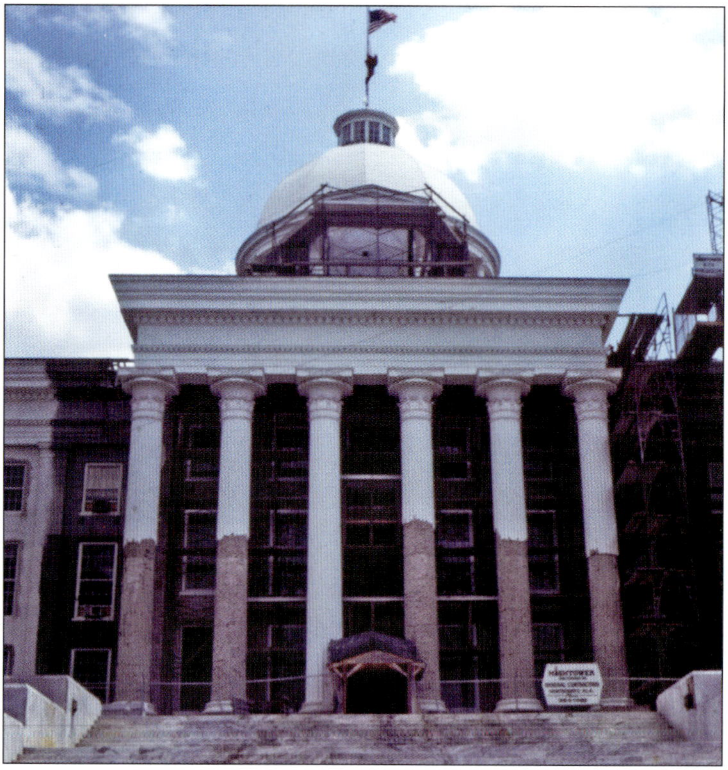

The Alabama State Capitol had some repair work done to its front columns in October 1980. (Courtesy Landmarks Foundation.)

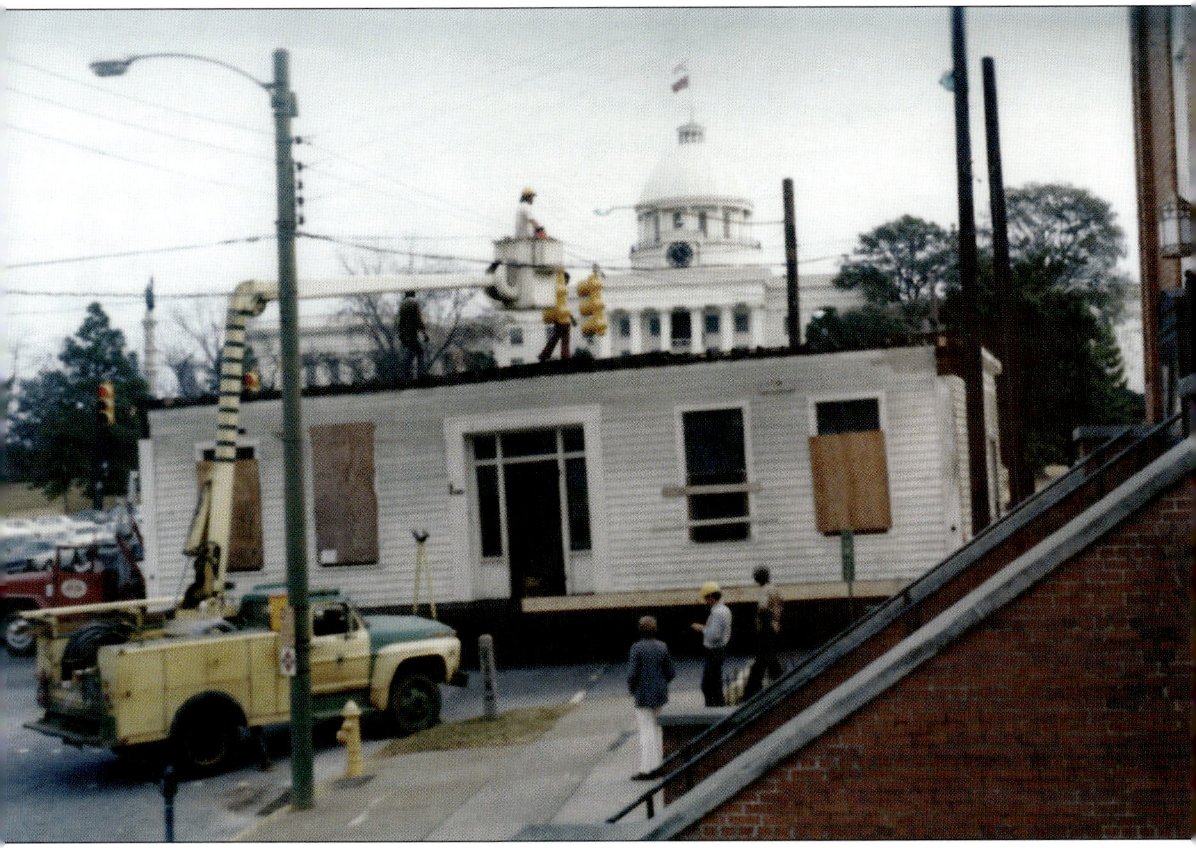

This 1970s photograph shows moving day for the Mayor Reese Cottage. Built in the mid-1850s, the Greek Revival cottage takes its name from Warren Reese, who lived in it while serving two terms as mayor of Montgomery, from 1885 to 1889. The cottage was moved from the southwest corner of Alabama and Decatur Streets to 340 North Hull Street in Old Alabama Town. Beautifully renovated, it serves as office rental property. (Courtesy Landmarks Foundation.)

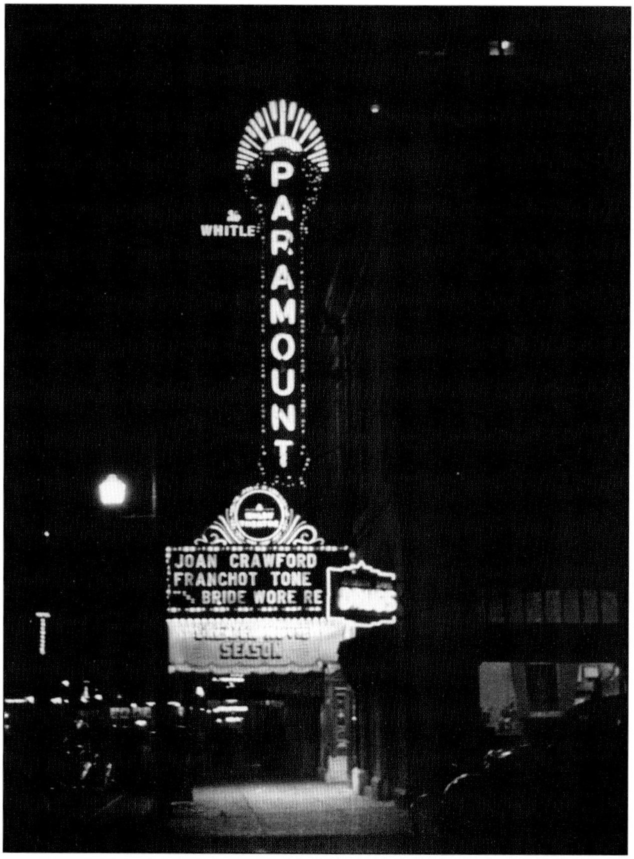

The Paramount Theatre opened on January 25, 1930, and closed in 1976 after showing *Gone with the Wind*. Note the Whitley Hotel sign in the background. (Photograph by Franklin Collier; courtesy Landmarks Foundation.)

This photograph, taken on July 30, 1980, marks Troy University's purchase of the Paramount Theatre. From left to right are Steve Parker, Helen Bern, and D.S. Thomason Jr. The theater was restored to its former glory. On May 21, 1983, a grand opening gala celebrated the venue's reopening as the Davis Theatre for the Performing Arts. (Courtesy *Montgomery Advertiser.*)

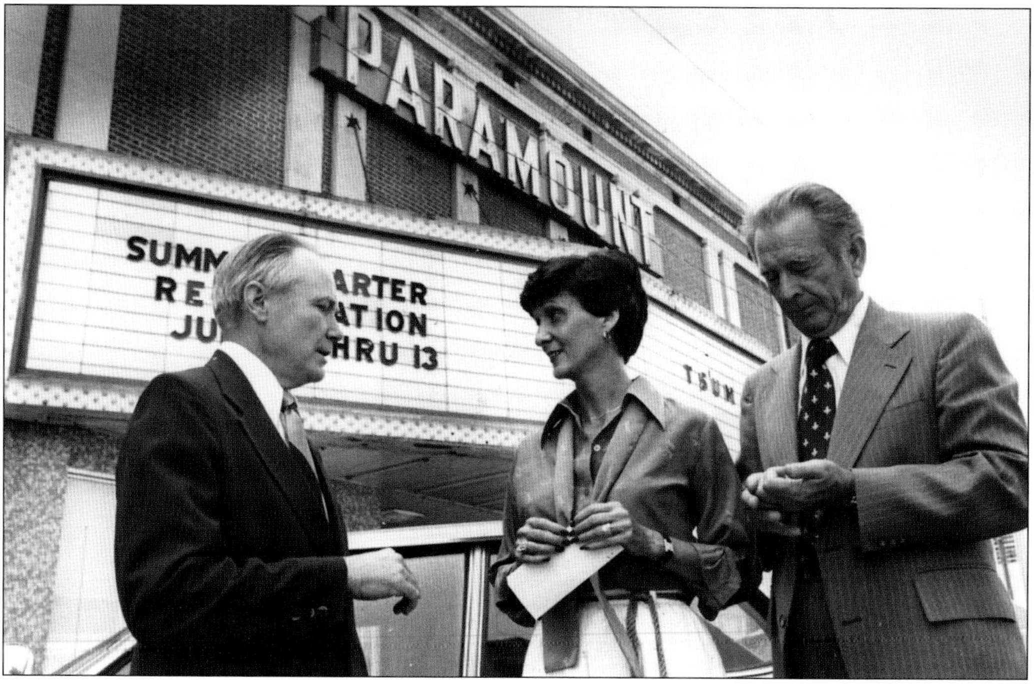

The Empire Theatre, seen here on July 14, 1989, stood across the street from the Paramount Theatre. The Empire was built in 1914 and torn down in 1997. It is designated as the site where Rosa Parks refused to give up her seat on a city bus, thus beginning the Montgomery Bus Boycott. Thus, it is fitting that the location of the former theater is currently that of the Rosa Parks Memorial Library. (Courtesy *Montgomery Advertiser.*)

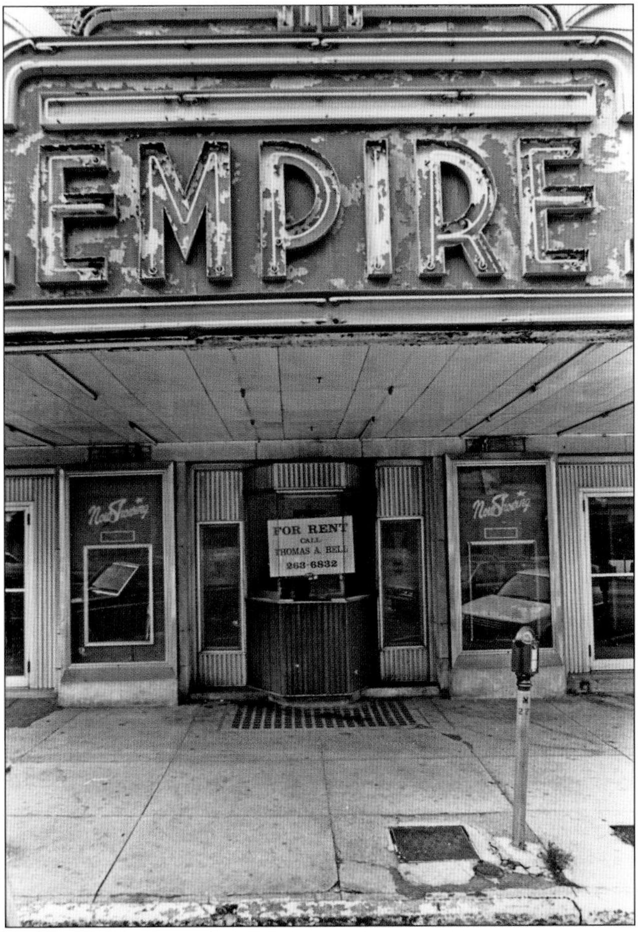

The building of the once popular Candlelight Restaurant and nightspot was razed in 1986. The structure was considered one of three examples of the International style of architecture in Montgomery. The downward life cycle of a building usually follows this sequence: nightclub, antique store, and haunted house, followed by demolition. The lot is currently vacant. (Courtesy *Montgomery Advertiser.*)

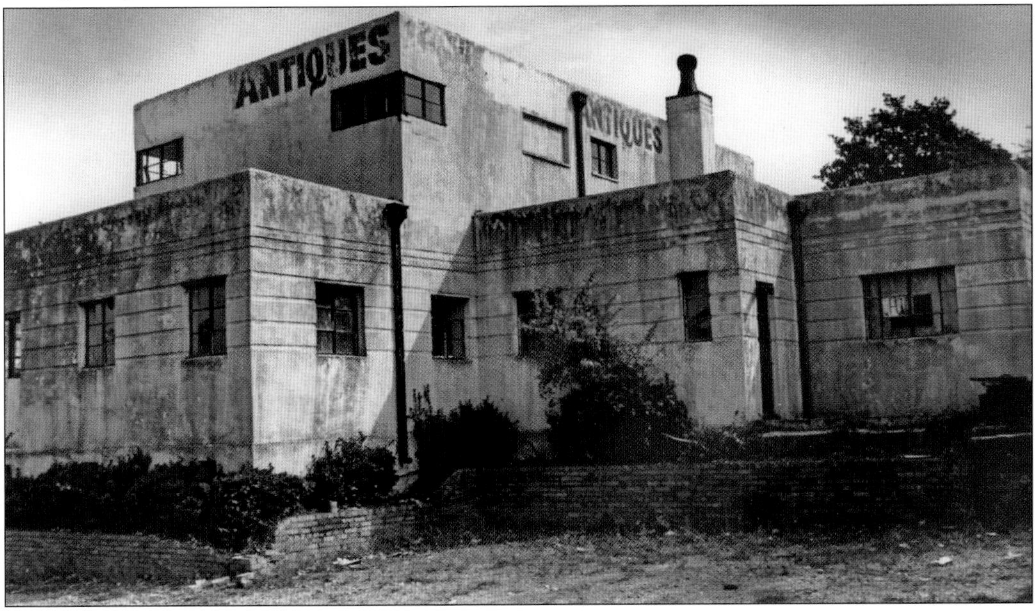

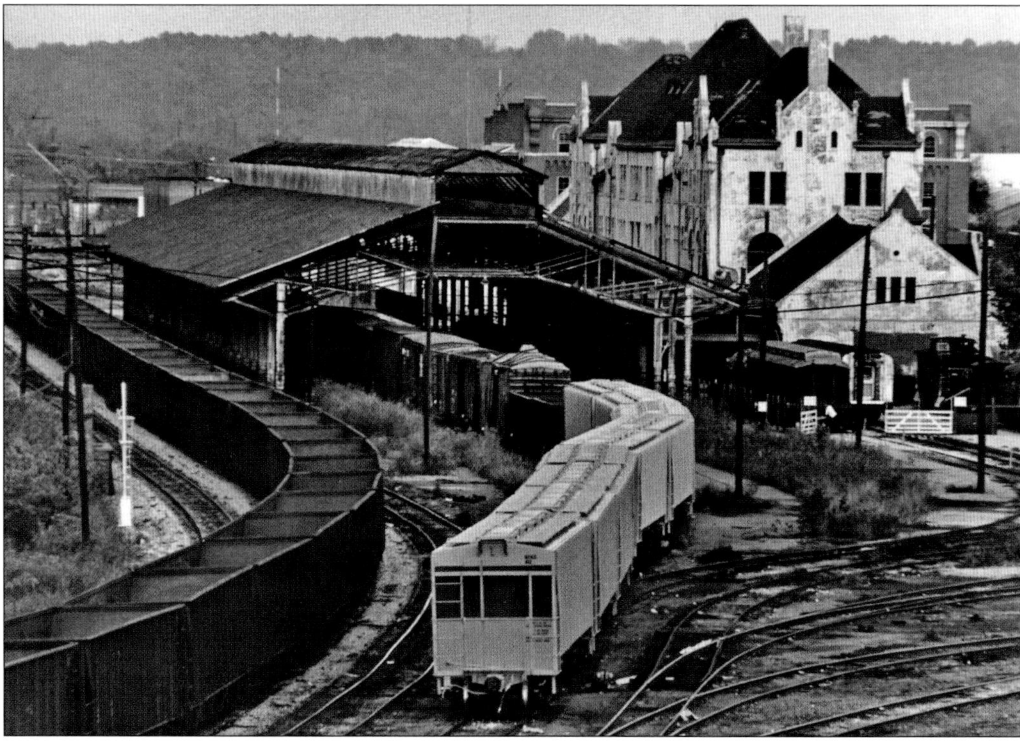

The Louisville & Nashville Railroad (L&N) built Union Station in 1898. Here, a locomotive pulls into the station's train shed in 1980. Although still in commercial use in this photograph, both the station and its train shed are clearly in need of renovation. (Courtesy *Montgomery Advertiser.*)

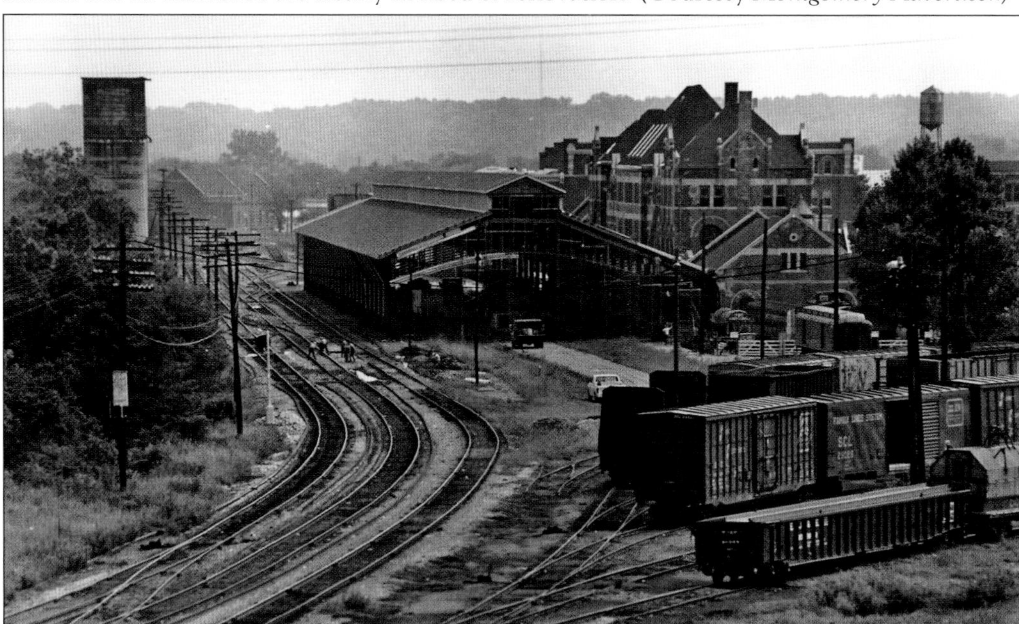

All aspects of Union Station are still functional at the time of this later photograph, taken around 1982. (Courtesy *Montgomery Advertiser.*)

In this photograph from October 1981, the Union Station train shed appears grassy and dormant. (Courtesy Landmarks Foundation.)

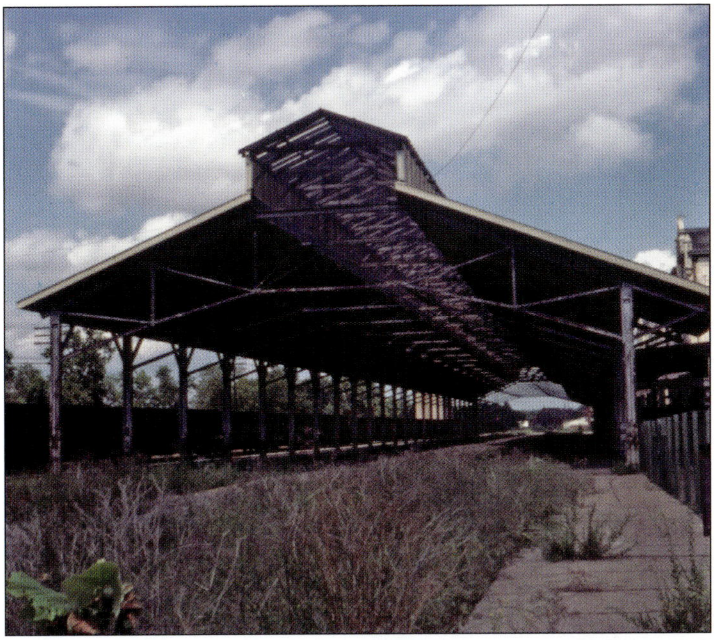

For many years, the beautiful brick facade of Union Station was covered with a rather sickly green paint. (Courtesy Landmarks Foundation.)

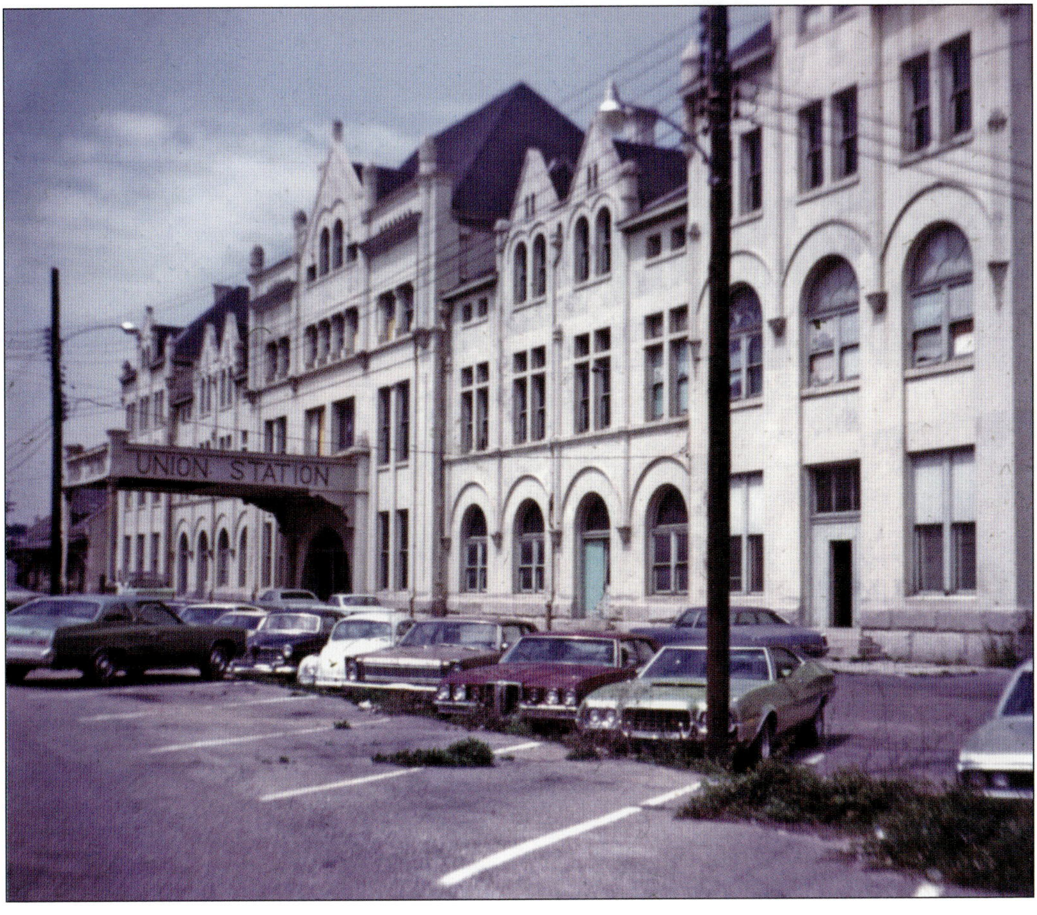

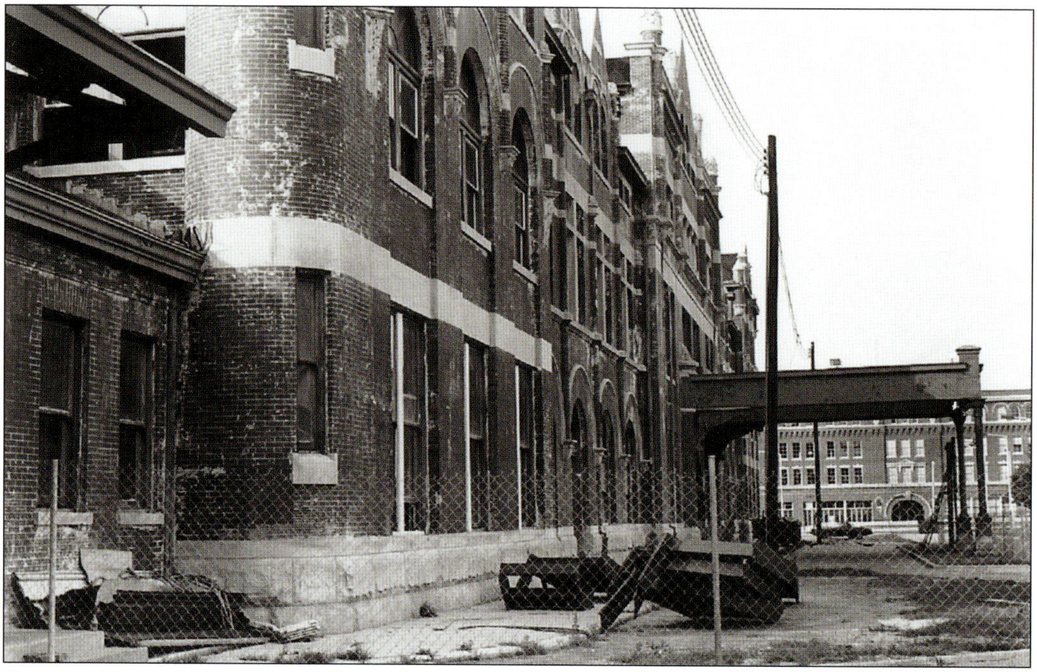

Amtrak discontinued use of Union Station in 1979. This photograph shows the beginning of renovations to the building. Union Station currently houses a restaurant, Railroad Thai, as well as the Montgomery Area Chamber of Commerce and Convention Visitor Bureau and Center. (Courtesy *Montgomery Advertiser.*)

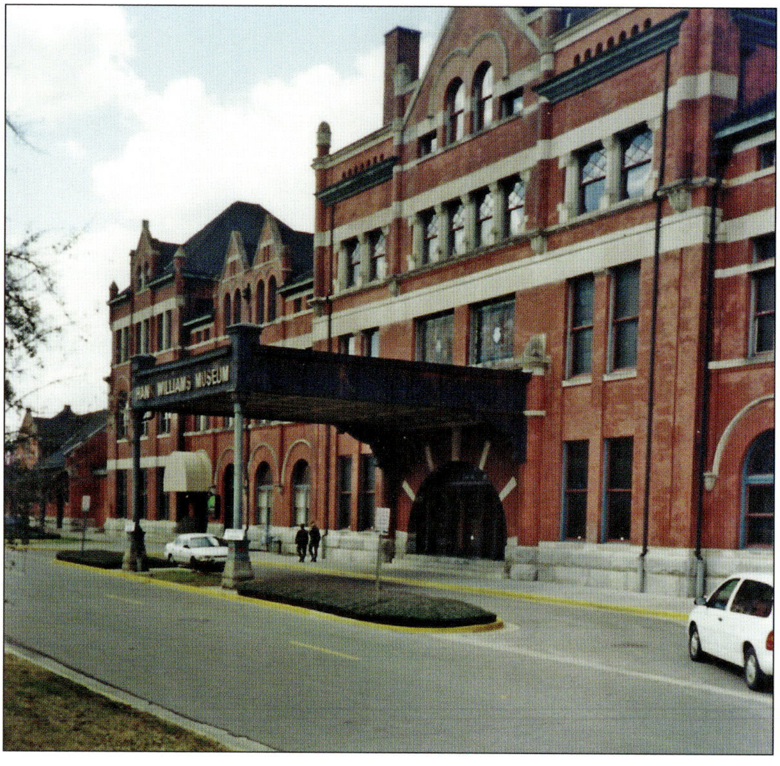

A renovated Union Station is seen here in the 1990s. The visitor center had not yet taken up residence. Instead, the space was home to the Hank Williams Museum. (Courtesy Pell collection.)

Seven

Capital of Dreams

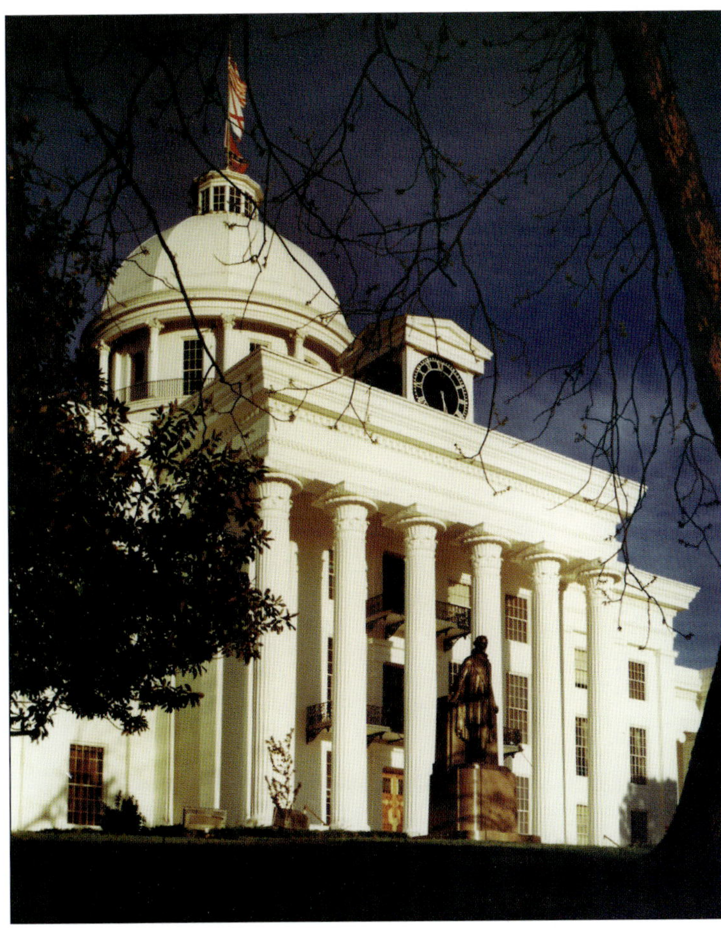

Montgomery is a modern city that honors its past and plans for its future. Here, the Alabama State Capitol stands like a beacon atop Goat Hill. (Courtesy Landmarks Foundation.)

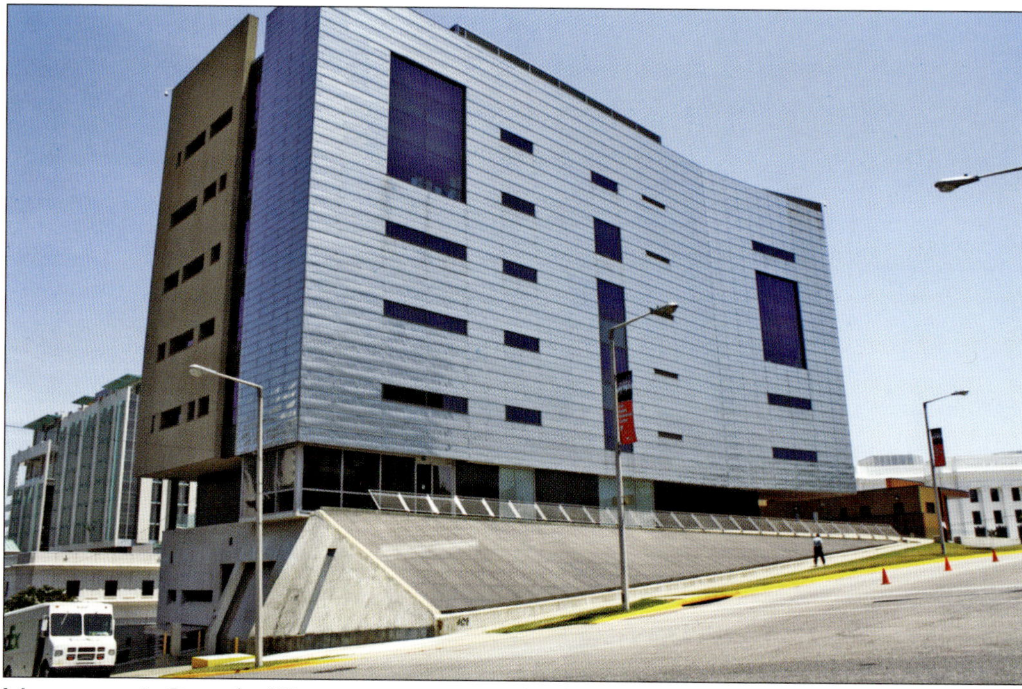

Montgomery's Capital of Dreams campaign is clearly connected to its civil rights legacy. The Southern Poverty Law Center is internationally known for actively continuing that work. (Courtesy Landmarks Foundation.)

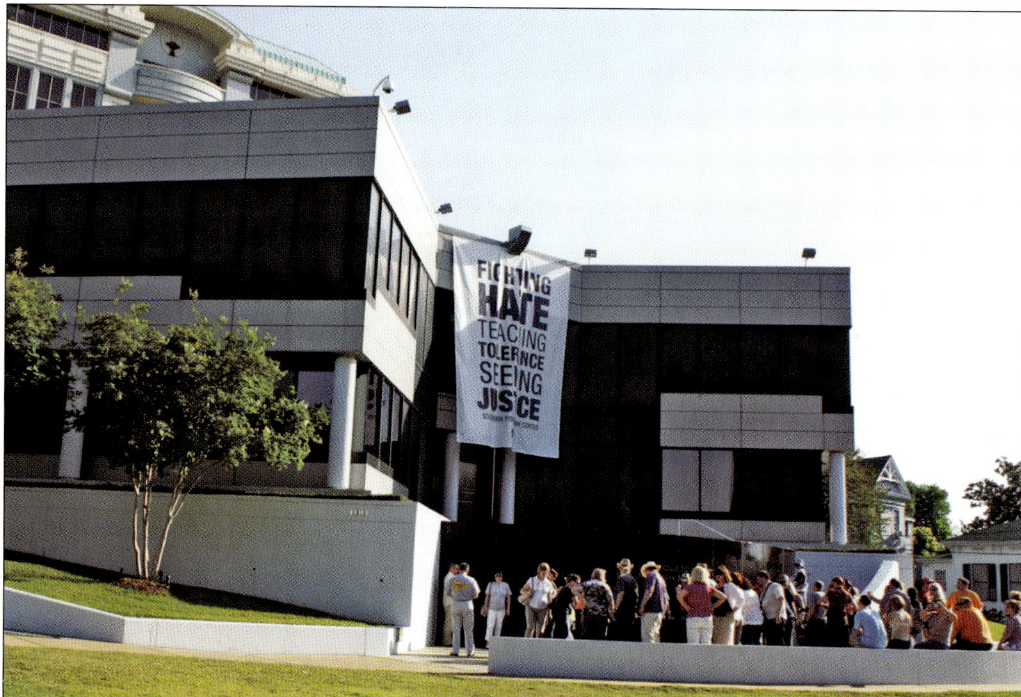

The Civil Rights Memorial is open day and night to those who wish to visit the site and reflect on the sacrifices made by others to achieve a more equal society. (Courtesy Landmarks Foundation.)

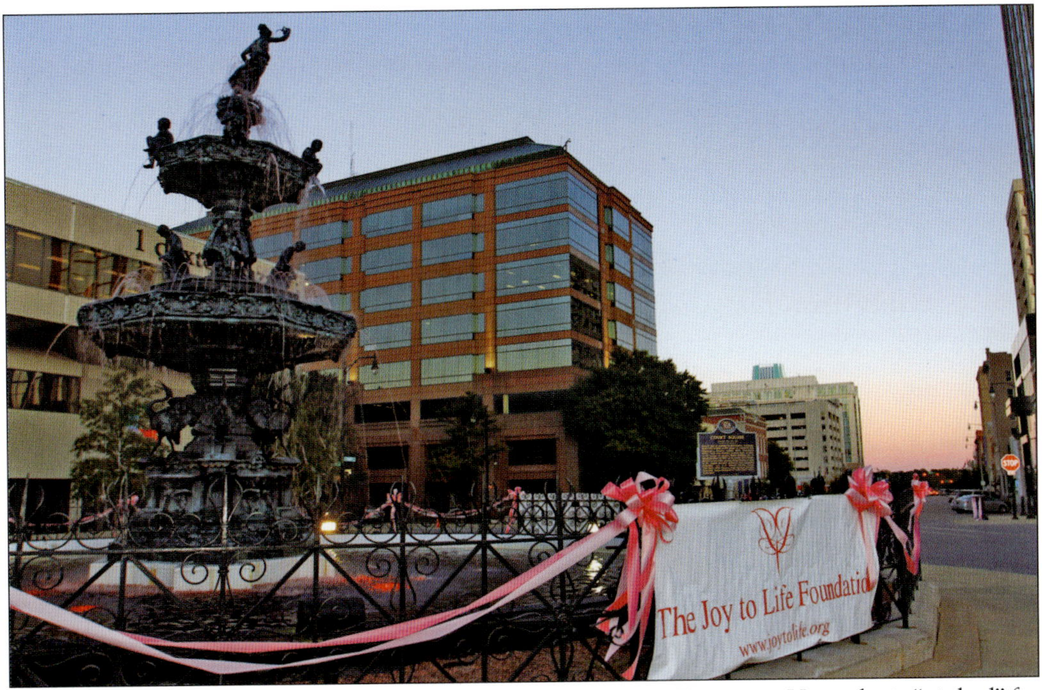

Hebe, cupbearer to the gods, still reigns atop the Court Square Fountain. Here, she is "pinked" for breast cancer awareness, compliments of the Joy to Life Foundation. (Courtesy Dreemz Production and Joy to Life Foundation.)

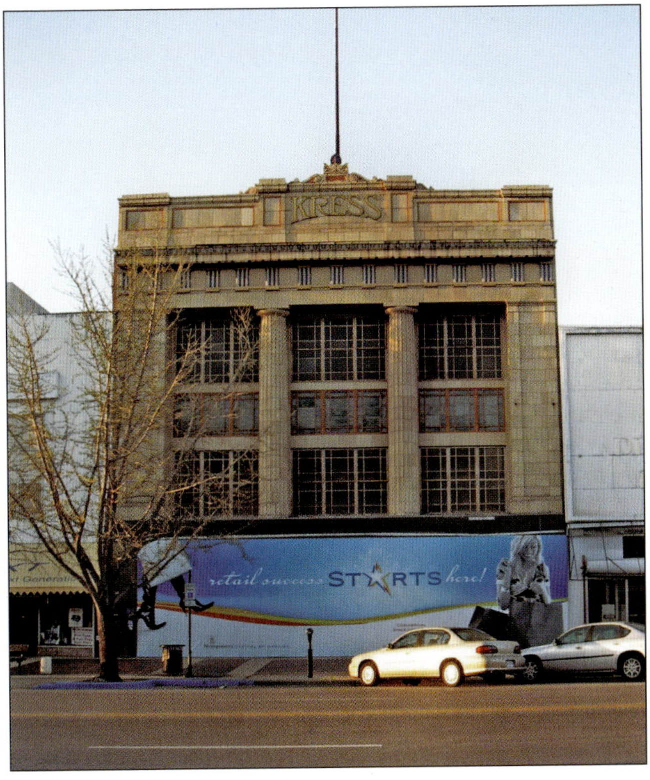

This photograph shows the Kress building on Dexter Avenue in historic downtown Montgomery. It is draped with a banner for the Capital of Dreams campaign. (Courtesy Landmarks Foundation.)

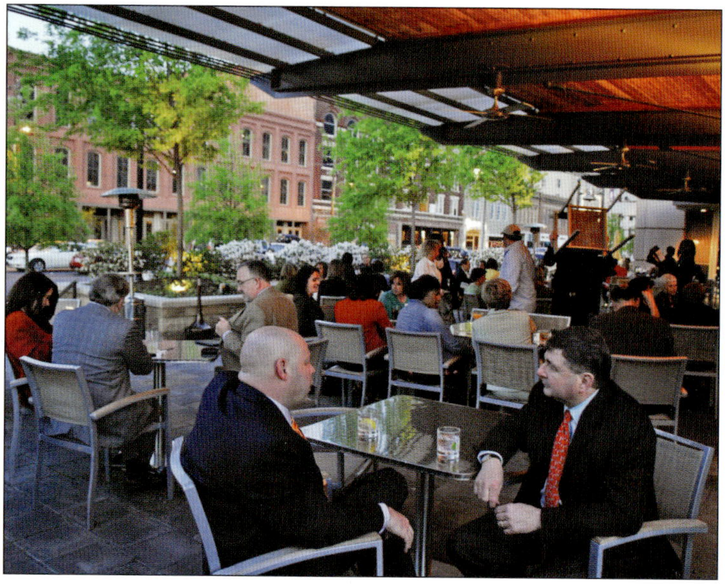

The Renaissance Montgomery Hotel &Spa at the Convention Center is attached to the Montgomery Performing Arts Center. The Renaissance is a four-star hotel with restaurants, as well as indoor and outdoor lounges. Named for the historic hotel, the Exchange Pub (pictured) offers signature cocktails and live entertainment. (Courtesy Montgomery Area Chamber of Commerce Convention and Visitor Bureau.)

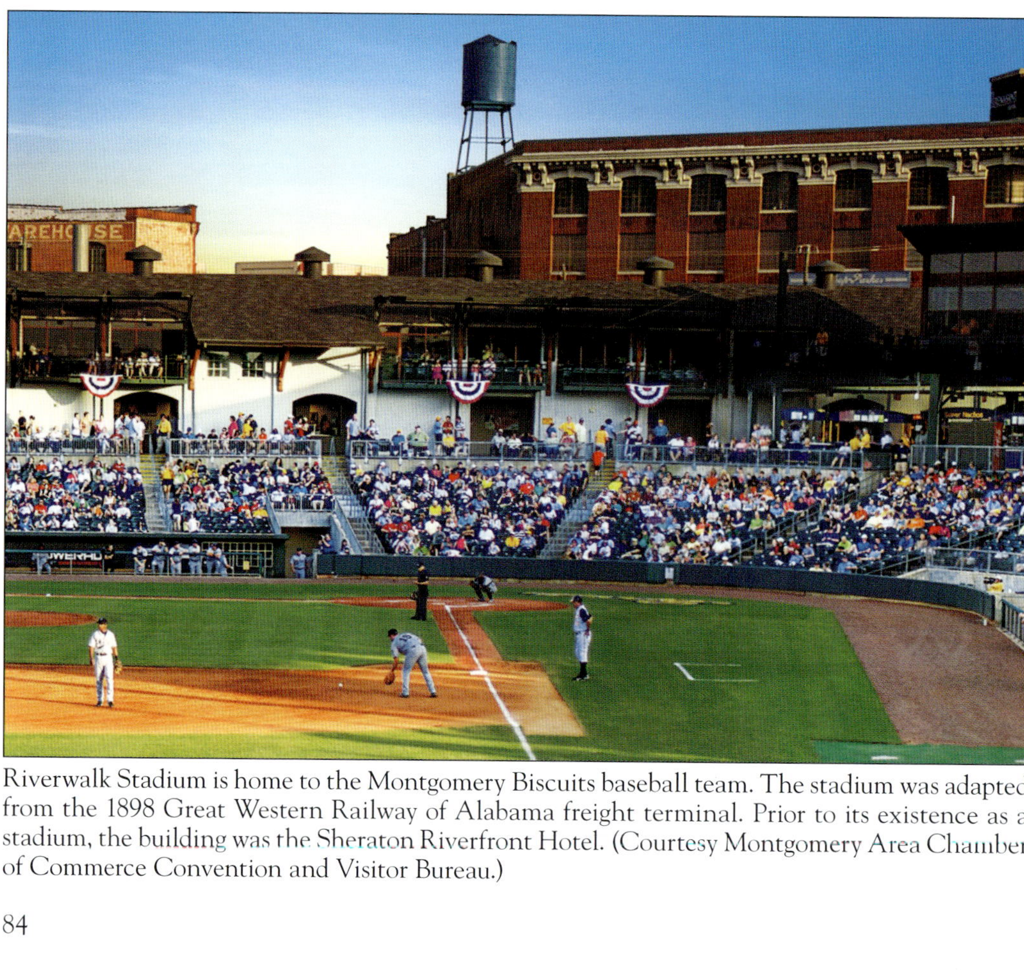

Riverwalk Stadium is home to the Montgomery Biscuits baseball team. The stadium was adapted from the 1898 Great Western Railway of Alabama freight terminal. Prior to its existence as a stadium, the building was the Sheraton Riverfront Hotel. (Courtesy Montgomery Area Chamber of Commerce Convention and Visitor Bureau.)

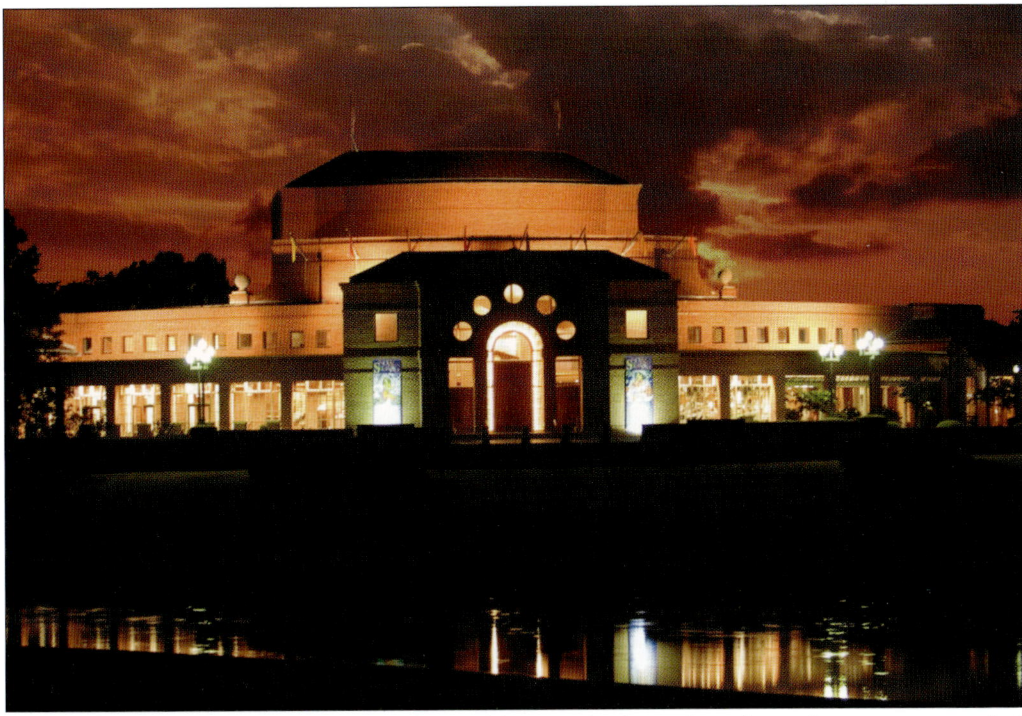

The Alabama Shakespeare Festival is a beautiful venue, both inside and out, that continues to thrill and inspire with productions presented year-round. (Courtesy Alabama Shakespeare Festival.)

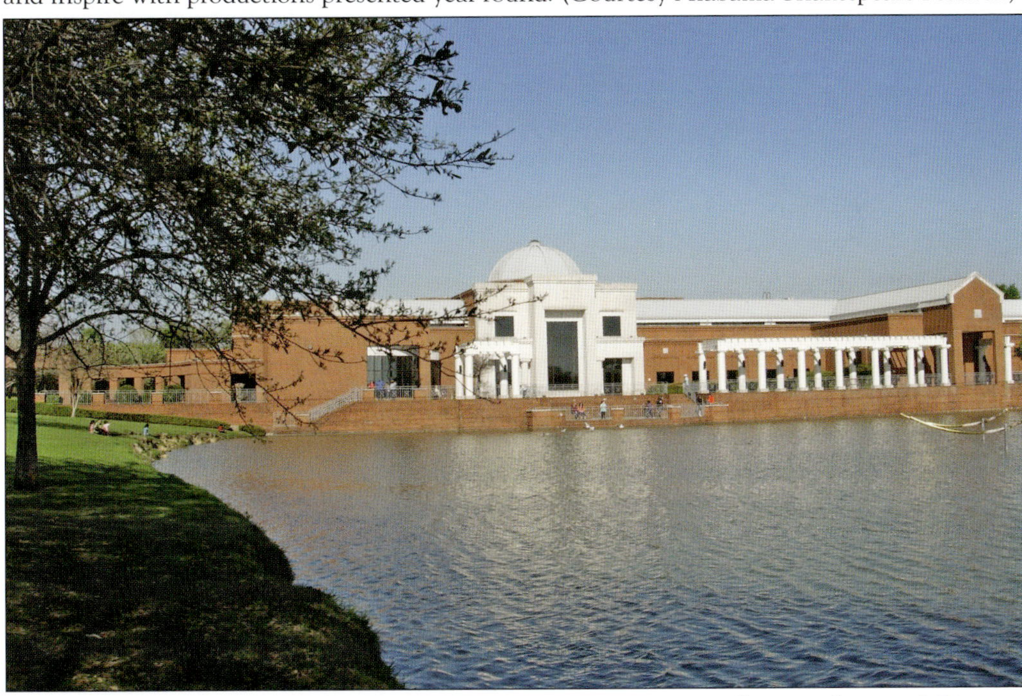

The Montgomery Museum of Fine Arts maintains a permanent collection, hosts exhibits, and offers classes. The institution is always a place to observe and appreciate art and beauty. (Courtesy Tim Henderson.)

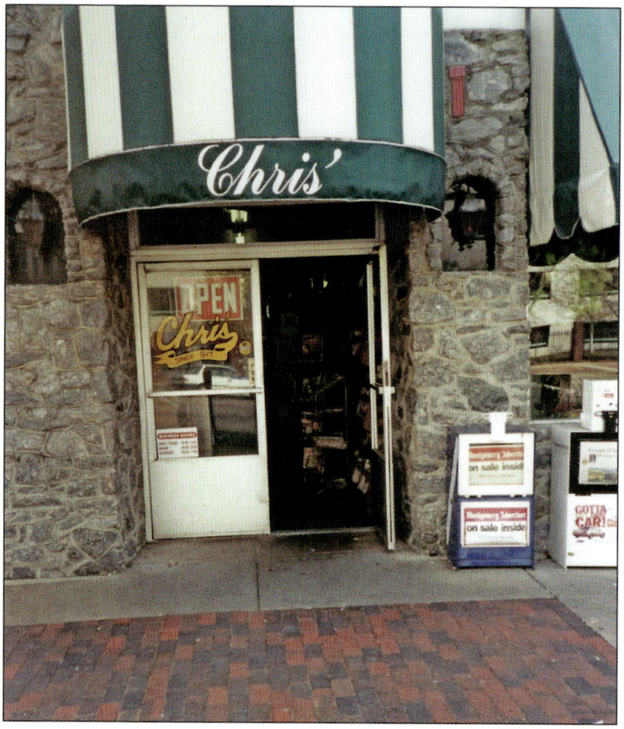

Chris' Hot Dogs is as popular as ever. Once a favorite of Hank Williams, the hot dogs continue to delight customers today. (Courtesy Pell collection.)

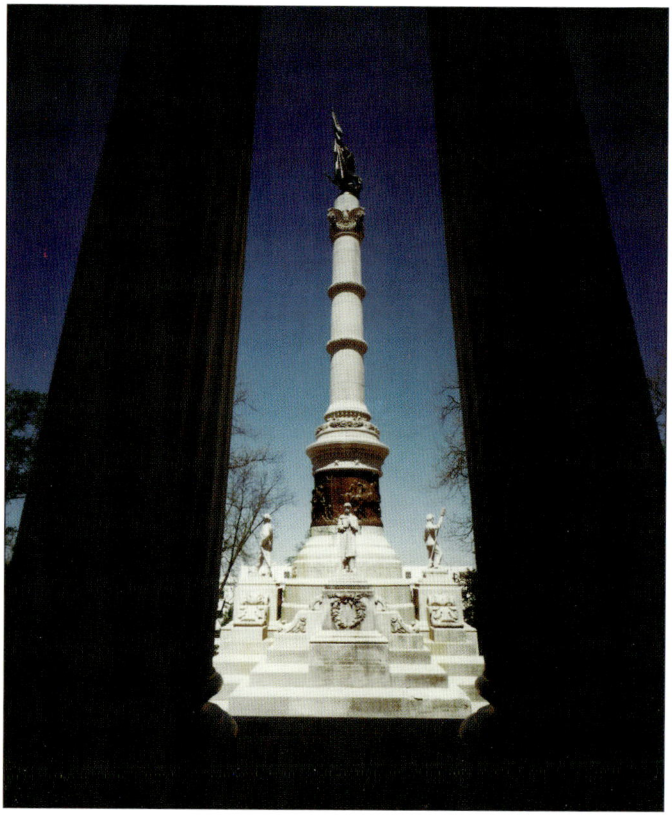

The Confederate Monument, dedicated on the state capitol grounds in 1898, remains an iconic Southern image. (Courtesy Landmarks Foundation.)

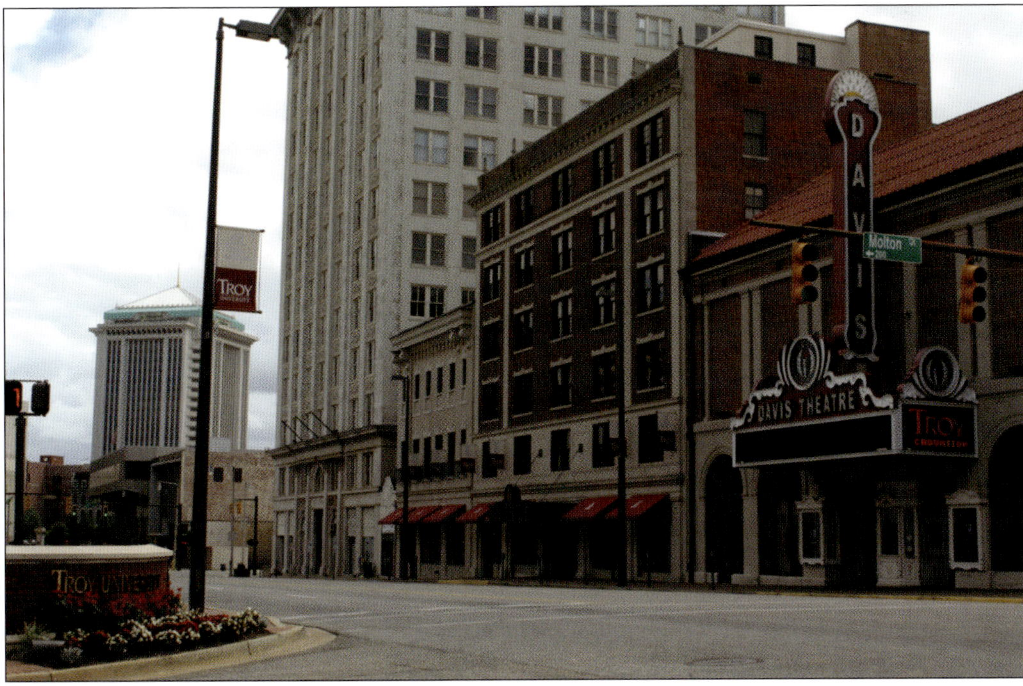

The Davis Theatre for the Performing Arts is the home of the Montgomery Symphony Orchestra. (Courtesy Landmarks Foundation.)

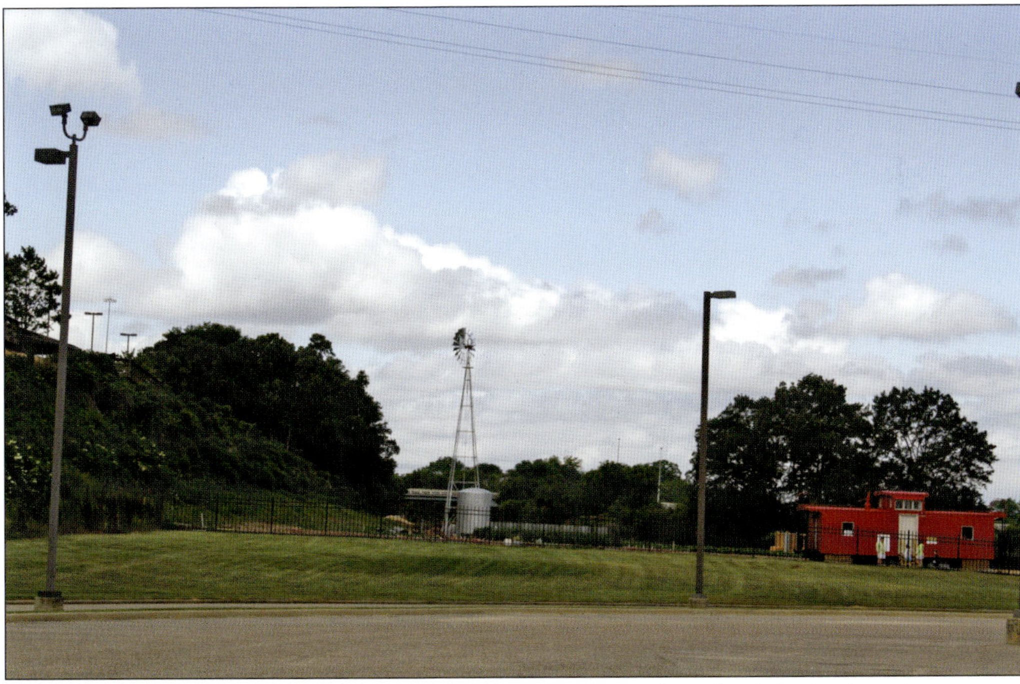

Montgomery's Urban Farm reclaims land, offers education about healthy food production, and provides a fun place to visit. (Courtesy Landmarks Foundation.)

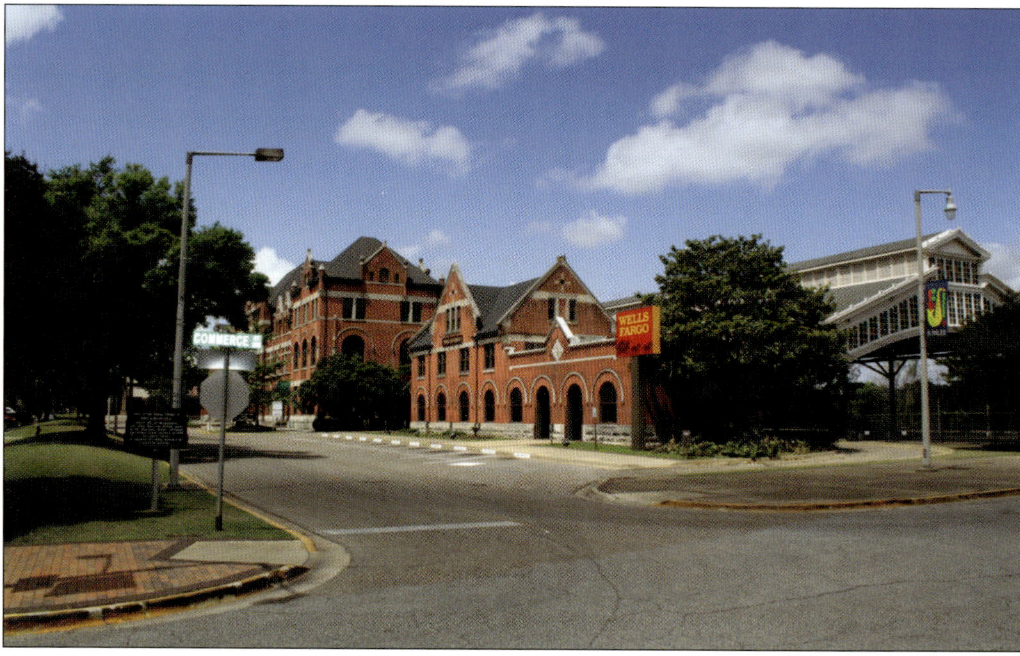

Beautiful Union Station houses the Montgomery Area Chamber of Commerce Convention and Visitor Bureau, as well as the popular restaurant Railroad Thai. The Train Shed event venue is recognized as a National Historic Landmark. And, yes, daily freight trains still run by and toot their whistles. (Courtesy Landmarks Foundation.)

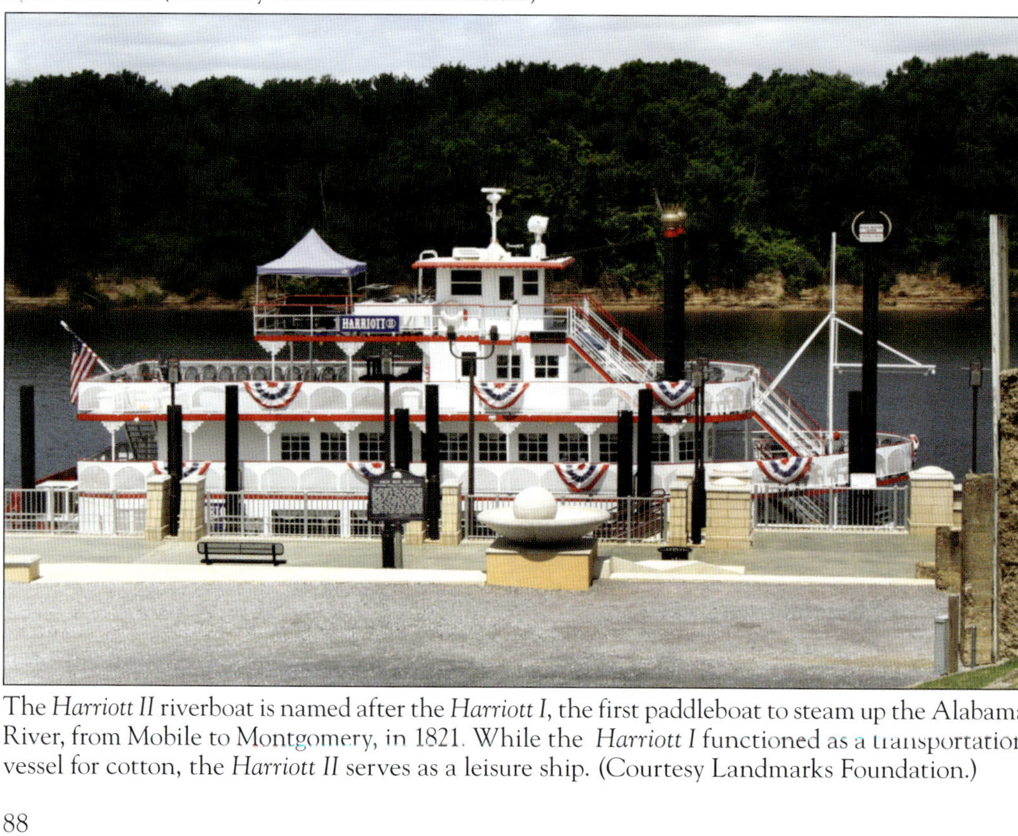

The *Harriott II* riverboat is named after the *Harriott I*, the first paddleboat to steam up the Alabama River, from Mobile to Montgomery, in 1821. While the *Harriott I* functioned as a transportation vessel for cotton, the *Harriott II* serves as a leisure ship. (Courtesy Landmarks Foundation.)

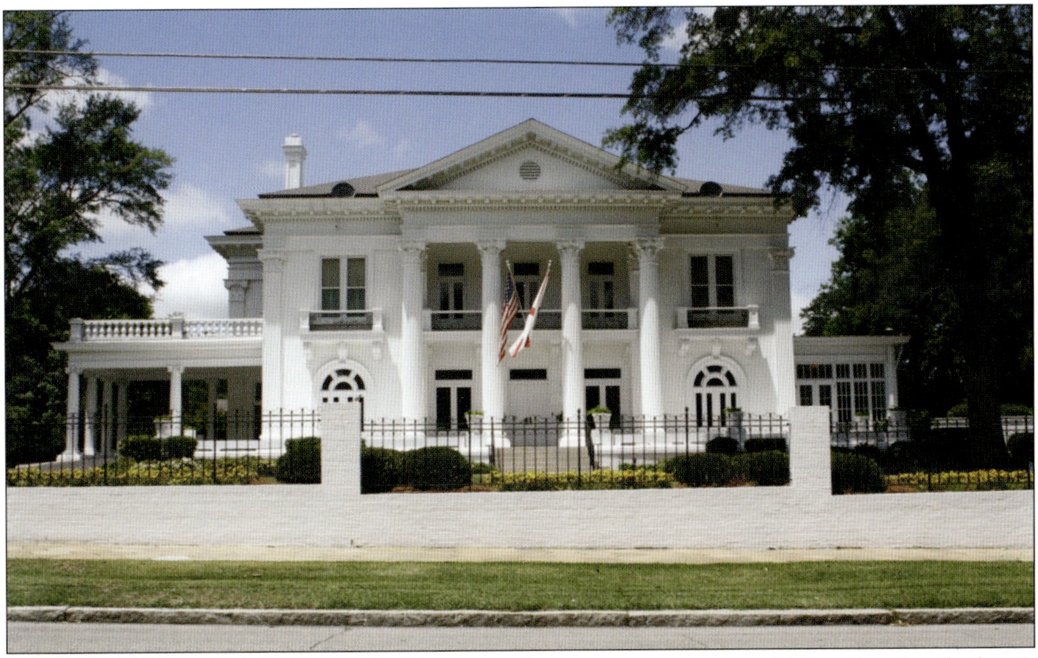

The Alabama Governor's Mansion is home to the sitting governor and his or her family, but it also belongs to the people of Alabama. (Courtesy Landmarks Foundation.)

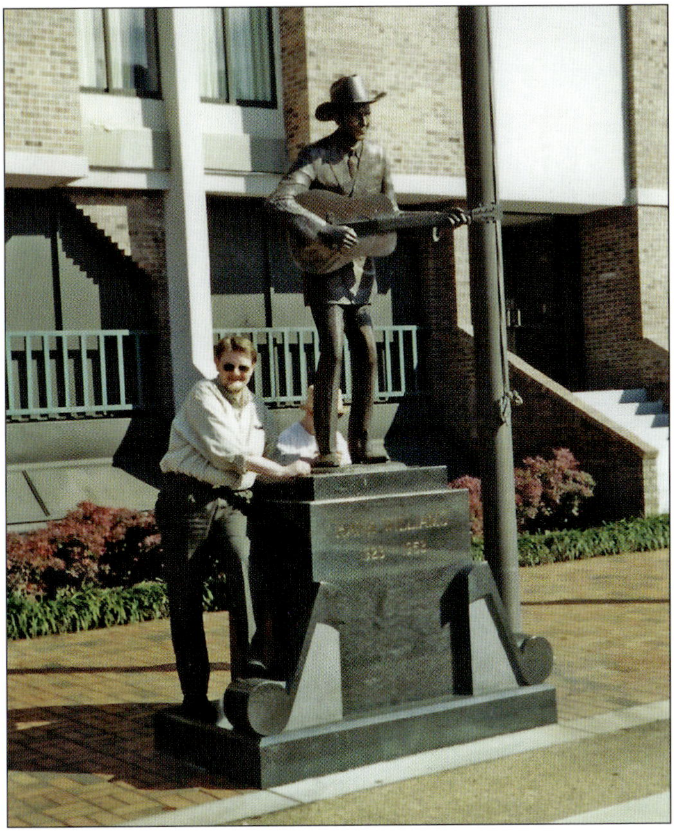

Singer-songwriter Hank Williams is buried in the Oakwood Cemetery Annex. His name, music, and memory live on in Montgomery. His statue stands across from city hall, where his funeral was held. The Hank Williams Museum welcomes visitors at 118 Commerce Street. Here, Danish singer-songwriter Nils Maaetoft visits the statue in honor of the troubadour who is a hero to every singer-songwriter. (Courtesy Pell collection.)

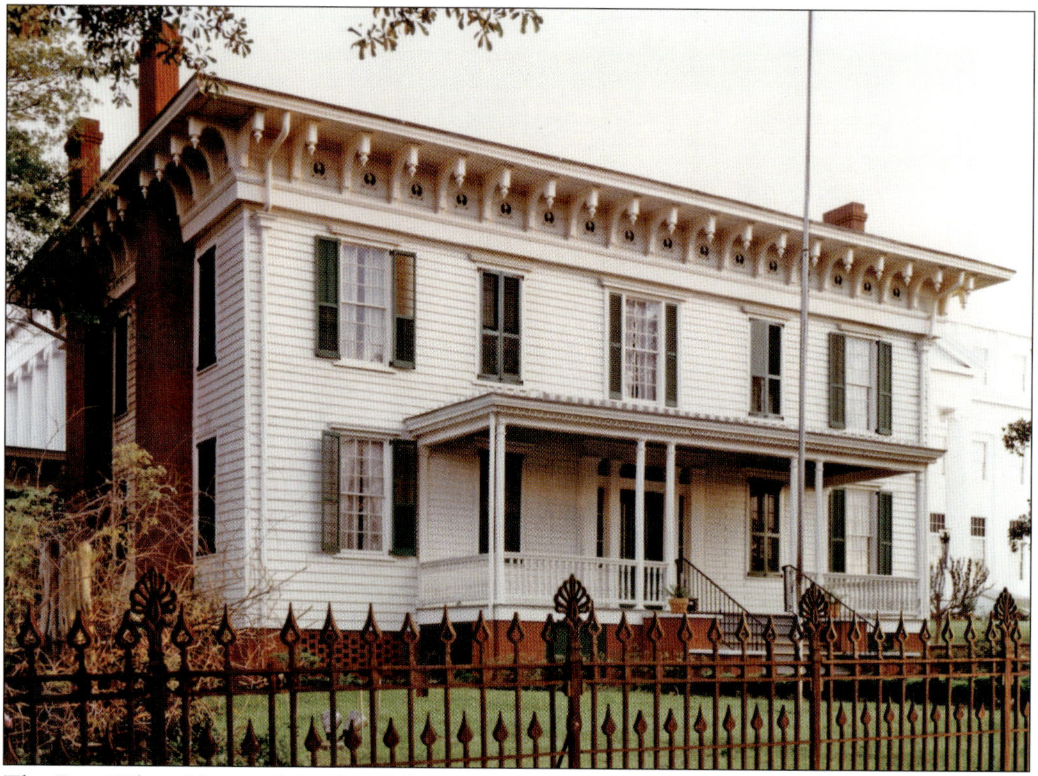

The First White House of the Confederacy was home to Confederate president Jefferson Davis and his wife, Varina, while Montgomery was the capital of the Confederacy. It is now a house museum containing many personal items of the Confederate president and his family. (Courtesy Landmarks Foundation.)

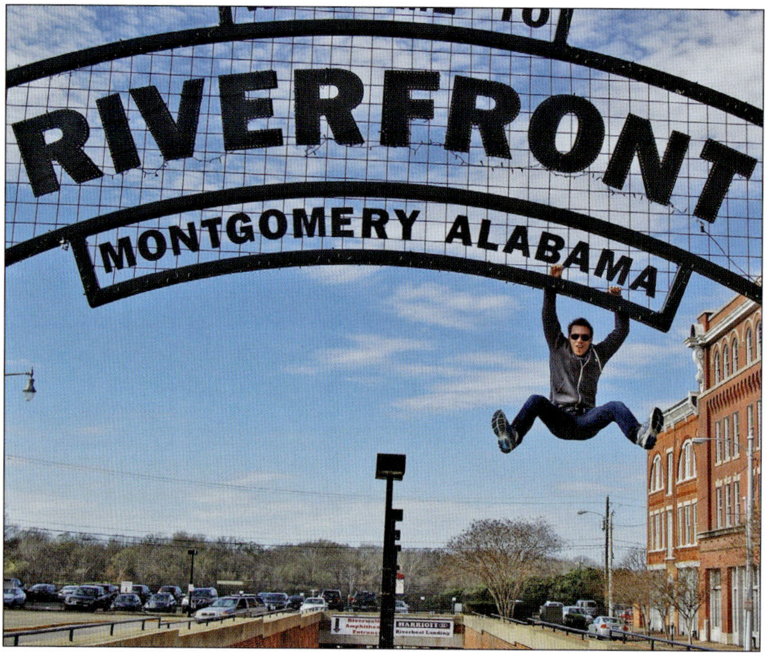

An excited visitor "hangs out" in front of the tunnel that leads to Riverfront Park. (Courtesy Cynthia Jancaterino.)

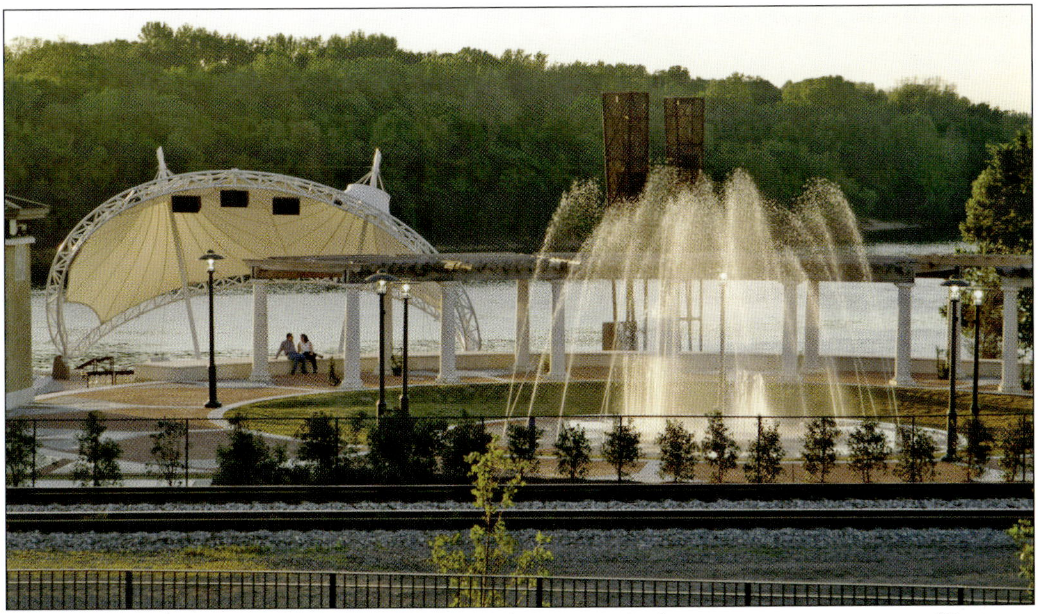

The Riverfront Amphitheater hosts musical productions and other entertainment events. (Courtesy Montgomery Area Chamber of Commerce Convention and Visitor Bureau.)

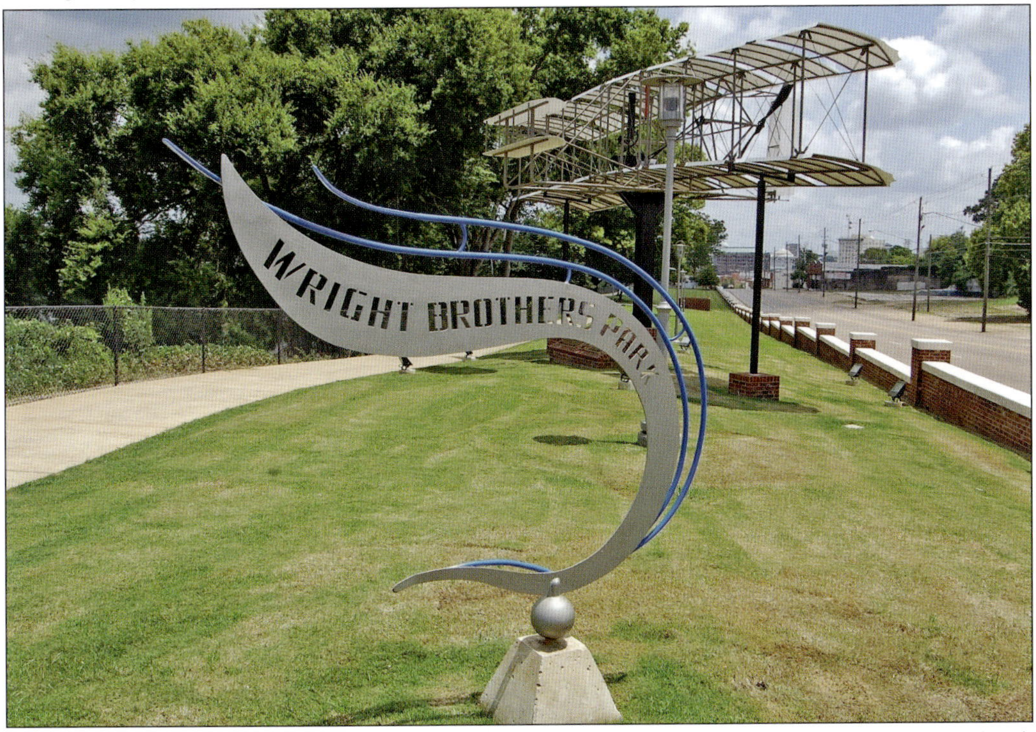

The Wright Brothers Memorial Park honors Orville and Wilbur Wright's first civilian flight school, founded in Montgomery in 1910. The school became the beginnings of Maxwell Air Force Base. The monument is a replica of the Wright brothers' plane. Located between historic downtown and Maxwell Air Force Base, the park overlooks the Alabama River and the cityscape. Picnic tables under a gazebo invite visitors to enjoy both the park and scenery. (Courtesy Cynthia Jancaterino.)

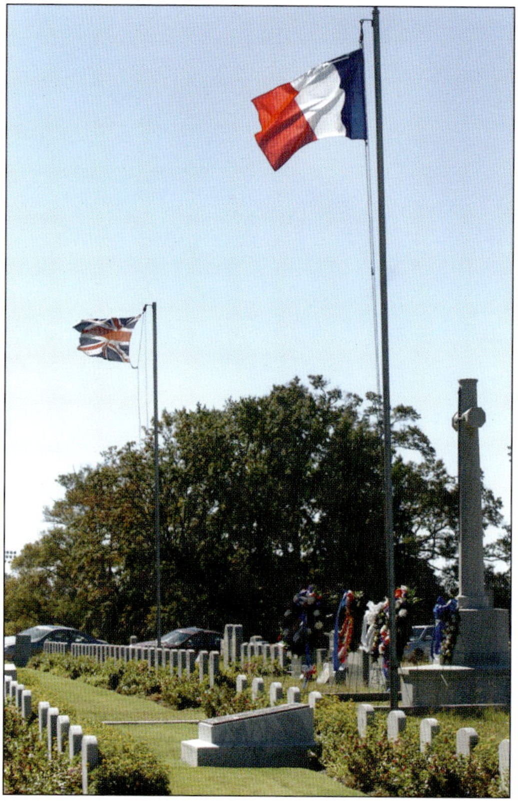

British, Canadian, and French pilots who died while training at Maxwell Air Force Base during World War II are buried in Montgomery's Oakwood Cemetery Annex. The graves are landscaped and tended by local groups. (Courtesy *Montgomery Advertiser*.)

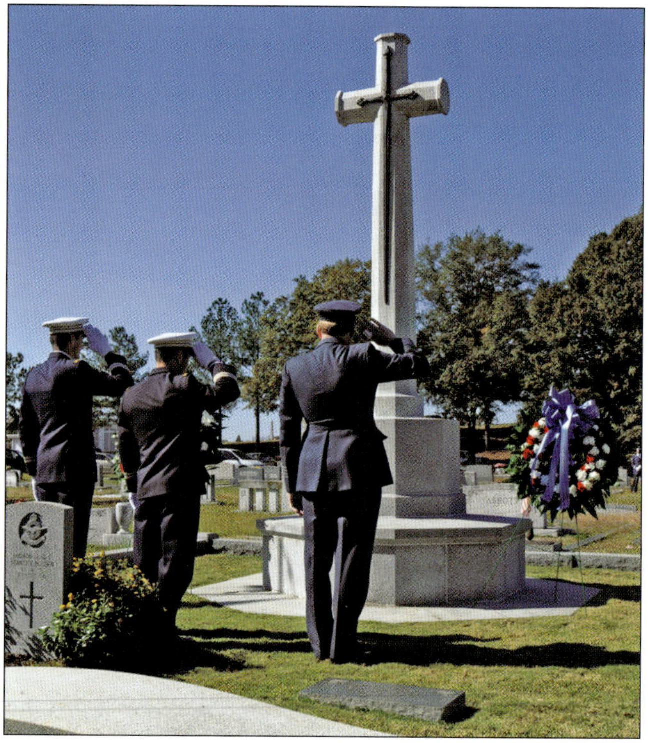

Every year on November 11, Veterans Day, officers from the United States, Great Britain, Canada, and France visit and honor the graves of pilots who died in training accidents at Maxwell Air Force Base during World War II. (Courtesy *Montgomery Advertiser*.)

This impressive fireworks display shows off Montgomery's skyline. Fireworks are not reserved just for the Fourth of July. They are often enjoyed by Montgomery residents after Biscuits baseball games and local events. (Courtesy Montgomery Area Chamber of Commerce Convention and Visitor Bureau.)

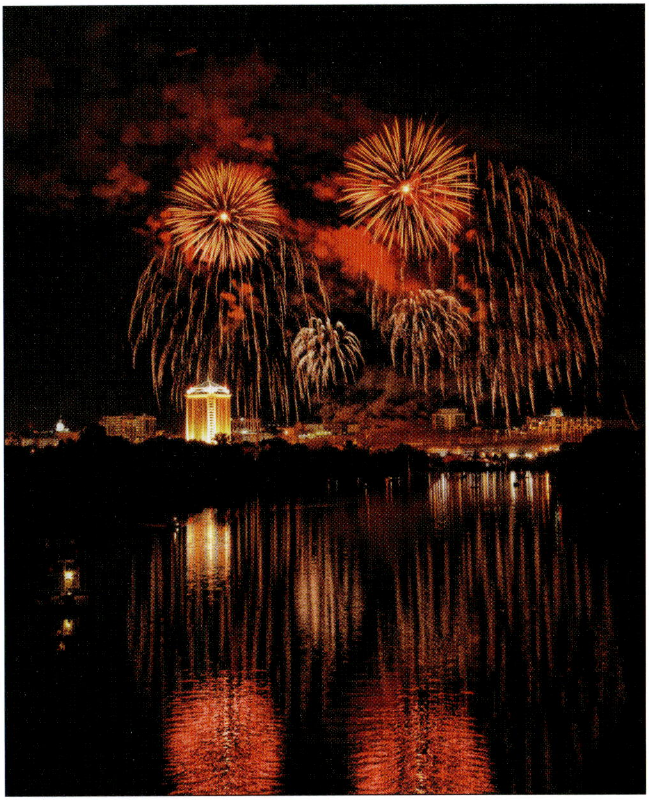

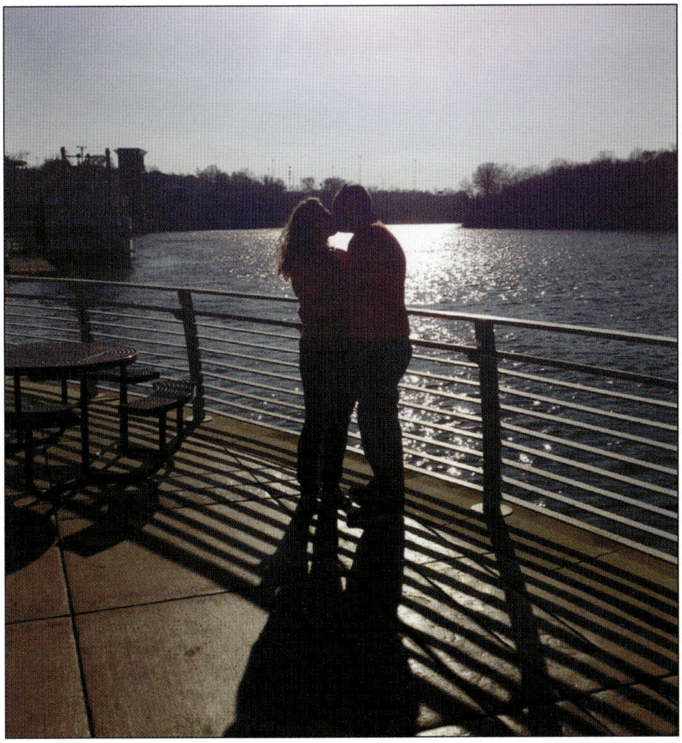

In addition to its historical roots, Montgomery is a romantic city. Here, Meg Lewis and Richard Cash enjoy a romantic stroll along the Riverwalk Overlook. (Courtesy Lewis collection.)

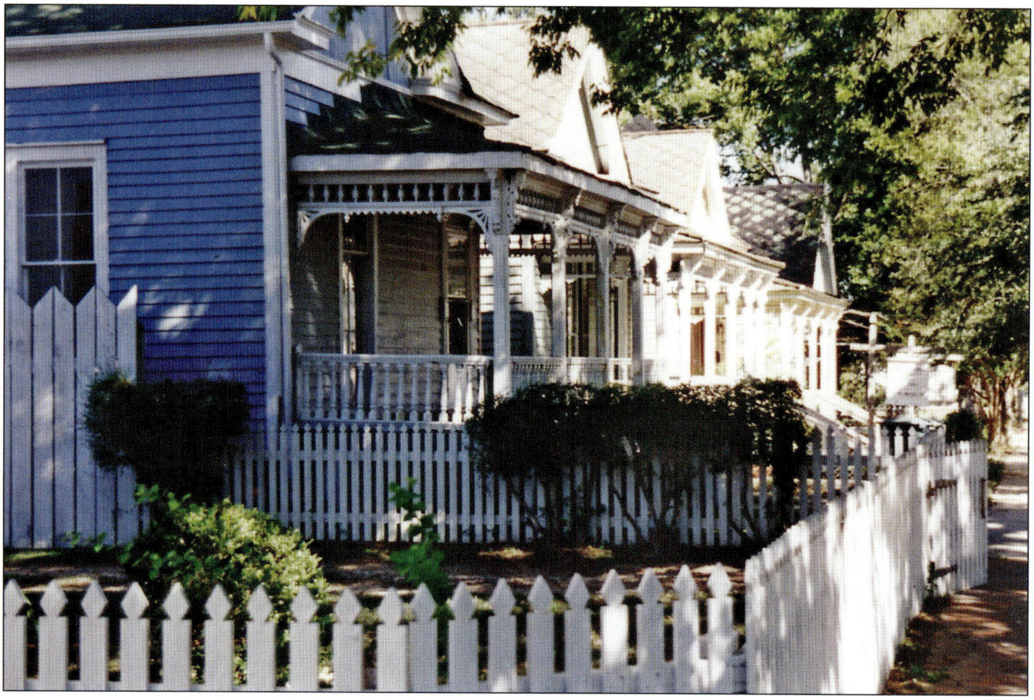

In 1971, the Landmarks Foundation of Montgomery unveiled its initial restoration of the Ordeman House, an urban antebellum house museum complex located at its original downtown site. The Ordeman House became the nucleus around which Old Alabama Town, a six-block, 50-structure museum complex, has grown. (Both, courtesy Landmarks Foundation.)

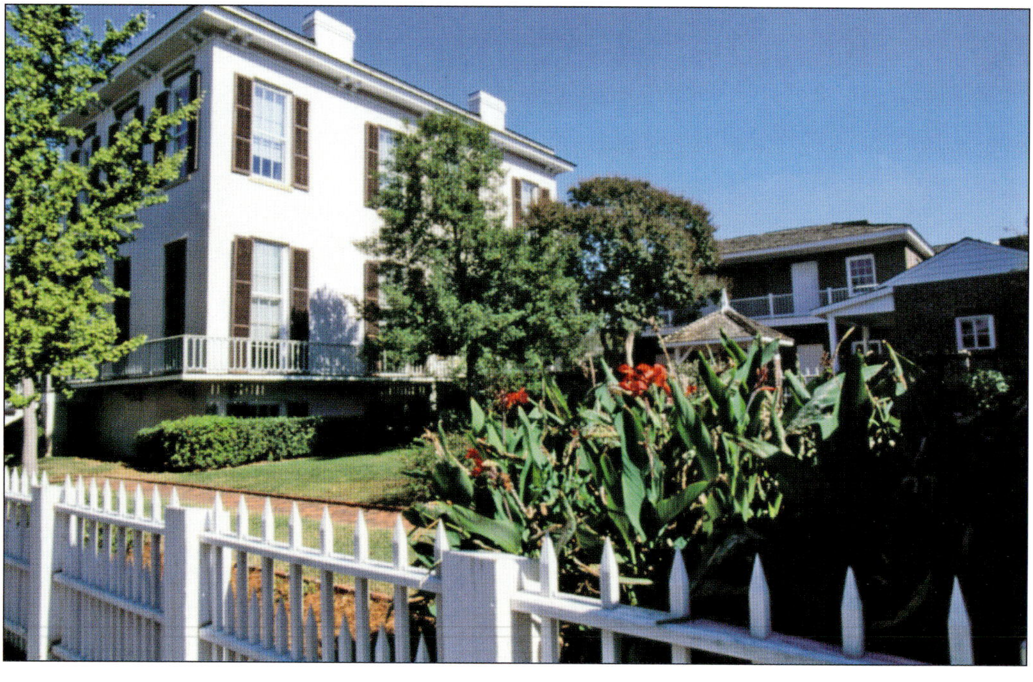

About the Organization

Concerned citizens organized the Landmarks Foundation of Montgomery in 1967, with its purpose being the preservation and interpretation of local history, architecture, and lifestyle. The foundation has encountered many challenges in historic preservation during the past decades and has risen to the occasion as an activist and adviser. It has encouraged commercial restorations in the downtown area and has supported the development of historic residential neighborhoods throughout the city.

Today, the Landmarks Foundation continues its mission to foster, encourage, and lead the historic preservation movement in Montgomery. The Old Alabama Town living history museum conducts educational programs attended by 35,000 Alabama students each year, with a total annual visitation of 60,000. The foundation provides leadership and assistance as a cultural resource and as an important repository of Southern architecture, history, and culture.

The Landmarks Foundation of Montgomery is happy to answer questions about Old Alabama Town and the Landmarks Foundation during regular office hours, from 9:00 a.m. to 4:00 p.m., Monday through Saturday. Please call 334-240-4500 (local) or 1-888-240-1850 (toll-free) for general inquiries, or visit its location downtown at 301 Columbus Street, Montgomery, Alabama, 36104. More information is available at www.oldalabamatown.com.